Batman and the Movies

SB Jeffrey

The role of the book within our culture is changing. The change is brought on by new ways to acquire & use content, the rapid dissemination of information and real-time peer collaboration on a global scale. Despite these changes one thing is clear--"the book" in it's traditional form continues to play an important role in learning and communication. The book you are holding in your hands utilizes the unique characteristics of the Internet -- relying on web infrastructure and collaborative tools to share and use resources in keeping with the characteristics of the medium (user-created, defying control, etc.)--while maintaining all the convenience and utility of a real book.

Contents

Articles

Batman   **1**
- Batman   1
- Bruce Wayne   24

The Franchise   **28**
- Batman franchise media   28
- Batman in film   39

The Batman Serial   **51**
- Batman (serial)   51
- Lewis Wilson   56

Batman and Robin Serial   **57**
- Batman and Robin (serial)   57
- Robert Lowery (actor)   60

Batman with Adam West   **63**
- Batman (1966 film)   63
- Adam West   68

Batman and Batman Returns   **76**
- Batman (1989 film)   76
- Batman Returns   87
- Michael Keaton   99

Batman Forever   **105**
- Batman Forever   105

Val Kilmer	114

Batman & Robin — **123**

Batman & Robin (film)	123
George Clooney	130

Back to the Basics — **144**

Batman Begins	144
The Dark Knight (film)	158
Christian Bale	177

References

Article Sources and Contributors	188
Image Sources, Licenses and Contributors	189

Batman

Batman

Batman	
Promotional art for *Batman* #608 (Oct. 2002, second printing) Pencils by Jim Lee and inks by Scott Williams	
Publication information	
Publisher	DC Comics
First appearance	*Detective Comics* #27 (May 1939)
Created by	Bob Kane (concept) Bill Finger (developer, uncredited)
In-story information	
Alter ego	Bruce Wayne Dick Grayson
Team affiliations	Batman Family Justice League Wayne Enterprises Outsiders
Partnerships	Robin Batgirl Superman
Notable aliases	Matches Malone Sir Hemingford Grey
Abilities	• High human strength and peak conditions • Skilled hand-to-hand combatant • Stealth/Sneaking • Genius-Level Intellect • Proficient with Technology • Exceptional Observational Skills • Excellent detective/crime solver

Batman is a fictional character created by the artist Bob Kane and writer Bill Finger. A comic book superhero, Batman first appeared in *Detective Comics* #27 in May 1939, and since then has appeared in many of DC Comics' publications. Originally referred to as "**the Bat-Man**" and still referred to at times as "**the Batman**", he is additionally known as "**The Caped Crusader**", "**The Dark Knight**", and "**The World's Greatest Detective**".

In the original version of the story and the vast majority of retellings, Batman's secret identity is **Bruce Wayne**, an American millionaire (later billionaire) playboy, industrialist, and philanthropist. Having witnessed the murder of his parents as a child, he swore revenge on crime, an oath tempered with the greater ideal of justice. Wayne trains himself both physically and intellectually and dons a bat-themed costume in order to fight crime. Batman operates in the fictional American Gotham City, assisted by various supporting characters including his crime-fighting partner, Robin, his butler Alfred Pennyworth, the police commissioner Jim Gordon, and occasionally the heroine Batgirl. He fights an assortment of villains such as the Joker, the Penguin, Two-Face, Poison Ivy and Catwoman, influenced by the characters' roots in film and pulp magazines. Unlike most superheroes, he does not possess any superpowers; he makes use of intellect, detective skills, science and technology, wealth, physical prowess, an indomitable will and intimidation in his continuous war on crime.

Batman became a very popular character soon after his introduction and gained his own comic book title, *Batman*, in 1940. As the decades wore on, differing interpretations of the character emerged. The late 1960s *Batman* television series used a camp aesthetic which continued to be associated with the character for years after the show ended. Various creators worked to return the character to his dark roots, culminating in the 1986 miniseries *Batman: The Dark Knight Returns*, by writer-artist Frank Miller, while the successes of director Tim Burton's 1989 film *Batman* and Christopher Nolan's 2005 reboot *Batman Begins* also helped to reignite popular interest in the character. A cultural icon, Batman has been licensed and adapted into a variety of media, from radio to television and film, and appears on a variety of merchandise sold all over the world such as toys and video games.

Publication history

See also: List of Batman comics

Creation

In early 1939, the success of Superman in *Action Comics* prompted editors at the comic book division of National Publications (the future DC Comics) to request more superheroes for its titles. In response, Bob Kane created "the Bat-Man." Collaborator Bill Finger recalled "Kane had an idea for a character called 'Batman', and he'd like me to see the drawings. I went over to Kane's, and he had drawn a character who looked very much like Superman with kind of ... reddish tights, I believe, with boots ... no gloves, no gauntlets ... with a small domino mask, swinging on a rope. He had two stiff wings that were sticking out, looking like bat wings. And under it was a big sign ... BATMAN."

Finger offered such suggestions as giving the character a cowl instead of a simple domino mask, a cape instead of wings, and gloves, and removing the red sections from the original costume. Finger said he devised the name Bruce Wayne for the character's secret identity: "Bruce Wayne's first name came from Robert Bruce, the Scottish patriot. Bruce, being a playboy, was a man of gentry. I searched for a name that would suggest colonialism. I tried Adams, Hancock … then I thought of Mad Anthony Wayne." He later said his suggestions were influenced by Lee Falk's popular *The Phantom*, a syndicated newspaper comic strip character with which Kane was familiar as well.

Various aspects of Batman's personality, character history, visual design, and equipment were inspired by contemporary popular culture of the 1930s, including movies, pulp magazines, comic strips, newspaper headlines, and even aspects of Kane himself. Kane noted especially the influence of the films *The Mark of Zorro* (1920) and *The Bat Whispers* (1930) in the creation of the iconography associated with the character, while Finger drew inspiration from literary characters Doc Savage, The Shadow, and Sherlock Holmes in his depiction of Batman as a master sleuth and scientist.

Kane, in his 1989 autobiography, detailed Finger's contributions to Batman's creation:

> One day I called Bill and said, 'I have a new character called the Bat-Man and I've made some crude, elementary sketches I'd like you to look at'. He came over and I showed him the drawings. At the time, I only had a small domino mask, like the one Robin later wore, on Batman's face. Bill said, 'Why not make him look more like a bat and put a hood on him, and take the eyeballs out and just put slits for eyes to make him look more mysterious?' At this point, the Bat-Man wore a red union suit; the wings, trunks, and mask were black. I thought that red and black would be a good combination. Bill said that the costume was too bright: 'Color it dark gray to make it look more ominous'. The cape looked like two stiff bat wings attached to his arms. As Bill and I talked, we realized that these wings would get cumbersome when Bat-Man was in action, and changed them into a cape, scalloped to look like bat wings when he was fighting or swinging down on a rope. Also, he didn't have any gloves on, and we added them so that he wouldn't leave fingerprints.

Kane signed away ownership in the character in exchange for, among other compensation, a mandatory byline on all Batman comics. This byline did not, originally, say "Batman created by Bob Kane"; his name was simply written on the title page of each story. The name disappeared from the comic book in the mid-1960s, replaced by credits for each story's actual writer and artists. In the late 1970s, when Jerry Siegel and Joe Shuster began receiving a "created by" credit on the Superman titles, along with William Moulton Marston being given the byline for creating Wonder Woman, Batman stories began saying "Created by Bob Kane" in addition to the other credits.

Finger did not receive the same recognition. While he had received credit for other DC work since the 1940s, he began, in the 1960s, to receive limited acknowledgment for his Batman writing; in the letters page of *Batman* #169 (February 1965) for example, editor Julius Schwartz names him as the creator of the Riddler, one of Batman's recurring villains. However, Finger's contract left him only with his writing page rate and no byline. Kane wrote, "Bill was disheartened by the lack of major accomplishments in his career. He felt that he had not used his creative potential to its fullest and that success had passed him by." At the time of Finger's death in 1974, DC had not officially credited Finger as Batman co-creator.

Jerry Robinson, who also worked with Finger and Kane on the strip at this time, has criticized Kane for failing to share the credit. He recalled Finger resenting his position, stating in a 2005 interview with *The Comics Journal*:

> Bob made him more insecure, because while he slaved working on Batman, he wasn't sharing in any of the glory or the money that Bob began to make, which is why... [he was] going to leave [Kane's employ]. ... [Kane] should have credited Bill as co-creator, because I know; I was there. ... That was one thing I would never forgive Bob for, was not to take care of Bill or recognize his vital role in the creation of Batman. As with Siegel and Shuster, it should have been the same, the same co-creator credit in the strip, writer and artist.

Although Kane initially rebutted Finger's claims at having created the character, writing in a 1965 open letter to fans that "it seemed to me that Bill Finger has given out the impression that he and not myself created the "Batman, t' [sic] as well as Robin and all the other leading villains and characters. This statement is fraudulent and entirely untrue." Kane himself also commented on Finger's lack of credit. "The trouble with being a 'ghost' writer or artist is that you must remain rather anonymously without 'credit'. However, if one wants the 'credit', then one has to cease being a 'ghost' or follower and become a leader or innovator."

In 1989, Kane revisited Finger's situation, recalling in an interview,

> In those days it was like, one artist and he had his name over it [the comic strip] — the policy of DC in the comic books was, if you can't write it, obtain other writers, but their names would never appear on the comic book in the finished version. So Bill never asked me for it [the byline] and I never volunteered — I guess my ego at that time. And I felt badly, really, when he [Finger] died.

Early years

The first Batman story, "The Case of the Chemical Syndicate," was published in *Detective Comics* #27 (May 1939). Finger said, "Batman was originally written in the style of the pulps," and this influence was evident with Batman showing little remorse over killing or maiming criminals. Batman proved a hit character, and he received his own solo title in 1940, while continuing to star in *Detective Comics*. By that time, National was the top-selling and most influential publisher in the industry; Batman and the company's other major hero, Superman, were the cornerstones of the company's success. The two characters were featured side-by-side as the stars of *World's Finest Comics*, which was originally titled *World's Best Comics* when it debuted in fall 1940. Creators including Jerry Robinson and Dick Sprang also worked on the strips during this period.

Over the course of the first few Batman strips elements were added to the character and the artistic depiction of Batman evolved. Kane noted that within six issues he drew the character's jawline more pronounced, and lengthened the ears on the costume. "About a year later he was almost the full figure, my mature Batman," Kane said. Batman's characteristic utility belt was introduced in *Detective Comics* #29 (July 1939), followed by the boomerang-like batarang and the first bat-themed vehicle, the Batplane, in #31 (September 1939). The character's origin was revealed in #33 (November 1939), unfolding in a two-page story that establishes the brooding persona of Batman, a character driven by the death of his parents. Written by Finger, it depicts a young Bruce Wayne witnessing his parents' murder at the hands of a mugger. Days later, at their grave, the child vows that "by the spirits of my parents [I will] avenge their deaths by spending the rest of my life warring on all criminals."

The early, pulp-inflected portrayal of Batman started to soften in *Detective Comics* #38 (April 1940) with the introduction of Robin, Batman's kid sidekick. Robin was introduced, based on Finger's suggestion Batman needed a "Watson" with whom Batman could talk. Sales nearly doubled, despite Kane's preference for a solo Batman, and it sparked a proliferation of "kid sidekicks." The first issue of the solo spin-off series *Batman* was notable not only for introducing two of his most persistent antagonists, the Joker and Catwoman, but for a story in which Batman shoots some monstrous giants to death. That story prompted editor Whitney Ellsworth to decree that the character could no longer kill or use a gun.

By 1942, the writers and artists behind the Batman comics had established most of the basic elements of the Batman mythos. In the years following World War II, DC Comics "adopted a postwar editorial direction that increasingly de-emphasized social commentary in favor of lighthearted juvenile fantasy." The impact of this editorial approach was evident in *Batman* comics of the postwar period; removed from the "bleak and menacing world" of the strips of the early 1940s, Batman was instead portrayed as a respectable citizen and paternal figure that inhabited a "bright and colorful" environment.

The 1950s and early 1960s

Batman was one of the few superhero characters to be continuously published as interest in the genre waned during the 1950s. In the story "The Mightiest Team in the World" in *Superman* #76 (June 1952), Batman teams up with Superman for the first time and the pair discovers each other's secret identity. Following the success of this story, *World's Finest Comics* was revamped so it featured stories starring both heroes together, instead of the separate Batman and Superman features that had been running before. The team-up of the characters was "a financial success in an era when those were few and far between"; this series of stories ran until the book's cancellation in 1986.

Batman comics were among those criticized when the comic book industry came under scrutiny with the publication of psychologist Fredric Wertham's book *Seduction of the Innocent* in 1954. Wertham's thesis was that children imitated crimes committed in comic books, and that these works corrupt the morals of the youth. Wertham criticized Batman comics for their supposed homosexual overtones and argued that Batman and Robin were portrayed as lovers. Wertham's criticisms raised a public outcry during the 1950s, eventually leading to the establishment of the Comics Code Authority. The tendency towards a "sunnier Batman" in the postwar years intensified after the introduction of the Comics Code. It has also been suggested by scholars that the characters of Batwoman (in 1956) and the pre-Barbara Gordon Bat-Girl (in 1961) were introduced in part to refute the allegation that Batman and Robin were gay, and the stories took on a campier, lighter feel.

In the late 1950s, Batman stories gradually became more science fiction-oriented, an attempt at mimicking the success of other DC characters that had dabbled in the genre. New characters such as Batwoman, Ace the Bat-Hound, and Bat-Mite were introduced. Batman's adventures often involved odd transformations or bizarre space aliens. In 1960, Batman debuted as a member of the Justice League of America in *The Brave and the Bold* #28 (February 1960), and went on to appear in several Justice League comic series starting later that same year.

"New Look" Batman and camp

By 1964, sales on Batman titles had fallen drastically. Bob Kane noted that, as a result, DC was "planning to kill Batman off altogether." In response to this, editor Julius Schwartz was assigned to the Batman titles. He presided over drastic changes, beginning with 1964's *Detective Comics* #327 (May 1964), which was cover-billed as the "New Look". Schwartz introduced changes designed to make Batman more contemporary, and to return him to more detective-oriented stories. He brought in artist Carmine Infantino to help overhaul the character. The Batmobile was redesigned, and Batman's costume was modified to incorporate a yellow ellipse behind the bat-insignia. The space aliens and characters of the 1950s such as Batwoman, Ace, and Bat-Mite were retired. Batman's butler Alfred was killed off (though his death was quickly reversed due to fan response) while a new female relative for the Wayne family, Aunt Harriet, came to live with Bruce Wayne and Dick Grayson.

The debut of the *Batman* television series in 1966 had a profound influence on the character. The success of the series increased sales throughout the comic book industry, and *Batman* reached a circulation of close to 900,000 copies. Elements such as the character of Batgirl and the show's campy nature were introduced into the comics; the series also initiated the return of Alfred. Although both the comics and TV show were successful for a time, the camp approach eventually wore thin and the show was canceled in 1968. In the aftermath, the Batman comics themselves lost popularity once again. As Julius Schwartz noted, "When the television show was a success, I was asked to be campy, and of course when the show faded, so did the comic books."

Starting in 1969, writer Dennis O'Neil and artist Neal Adams made a deliberate effort to distance Batman from the campy portrayal of the 1960s TV series and to return the character to his roots as a "grim avenger of the night." O'Neil said his idea was "simply to take it back to where it started. I went to the DC library and read some of the early stories. I tried to get a sense of what Kane and Finger were after."

O'Neil and Adams first collaborated on the story "The Secret of the Waiting Graves" (*Detective Comics* #395, January 1970). Few stories were true collaborations between O'Neil, Adams, Schwartz, and inker Dick Giordano, and in actuality these men were mixed and matched with various other creators during the 1970s; nevertheless the influence of their work was "tremendous." Giordano said: "We went back to a grimmer, darker Batman, and I think that's why these stories did so well... Even today we're still using Neal's Batman with the long flowing cape and the pointy ears." While the work of O'Neil and Adams was popular with fans, the acclaim did little to help declining sales; the same held true with a similarly acclaimed run by writer Steve Englehart and penciler Marshall Rogers in *Detective Comics* #471-476 (August 1977 - April 1978), which went on to influence the 1989 movie *Batman* and be adapted for *Batman: The Animated Series*, which debuted in 1992. Regardless, circulation continued to drop through the 1970s and 1980s, hitting an all-time low in 1985.

The Dark Knight Returns and later

Frank Miller's limited series *Batman: The Dark Knight Returns* (Feb.-June 1986), which tells the story of a 50-year old Batman coming out of retirement in a possible future, reinvigorated the character. *The Dark Knight Returns* was a financial success and has since become one of the medium's most noted touchstones. The series also sparked a major resurgence in the character's popularity.

That year Dennis O'Neil took over as editor of the Batman titles and set the template for the portrayal of Batman following DC's status quo-altering miniseries *Crisis on Infinite Earths*. O'Neil operated under the assumption that he was hired to revamp the character and as a result tried to instill a different tone in the books than had gone before. One outcome of this new approach was the "Year One" storyline in *Batman* #404-407 (Feb.-May 1987), in which Frank Miller and artist David Mazzucchelli redefined the character's origins. Writer Alan Moore and artist Brian Bolland continued this dark trend with 1988's 48-page one-shot *Batman: The Killing Joke*, in which the Joker, attempting to drive Commissioner Gordon insane, cripples Gordon's daughter Barbara, and then kidnaps and tortures the commissioner, physically and psychologically.

The Batman comics garnered major attention in 1988 when DC Comics created a 900 number for readers to call to vote on whether Jason Todd, the second Robin, lived or died. Voters decided in favor of Jason's death by a narrow margin of 28 votes (see *Batman: A Death in the Family*). The following year saw the release of Tim Burton's *Batman* feature film, which firmly brought the character back to the public's attention, grossing millions of dollars at the box office, and millions more in merchandising. However, the three sequels, Tim Burton's *Batman Returns* and director Joel Schumacher's *Batman Forever* and *Batman & Robin*, did not perform as well at the box office. The *Batman* movie franchise was rebooted with director and co-writer Christopher Nolan's *Batman Begins* in 2005 and *The Dark Knight* in 2008. In 1989, the first issue of *Legends of the Dark Knight*, the first new solo Batman title in nearly fifty years, sold close to a million copies.

The 1993 "Knightfall" story arc introduced a new villain, Bane, who critically injures Bruce Wayne. Jean-Paul Valley, known as Azrael, is called upon to wear the Batsuit during Wayne's convalescence. Writers Doug Moench, Chuck Dixon, and Alan Grant worked on the Batman titles during "Knightfall," and would also contribute to other Batman crossovers throughout the 1990s. 1998's "Cataclysm" storyline served as the precursor to 1999's "No Man's Land", a year-long storyline that ran through all the Batman-related titles dealing with the effects of an earthquake-ravaged Gotham City. At the conclusion of "No Man's Land", O'Neil stepped down as editor and was replaced by Bob Schreck.

Another writer who rose to prominence on the Batman comic series, was Jeph Loeb. Along with longtime collaborator Tim Sale, they wrote two miniseries ("The Long Halloween" and "Dark Victory") that pit an early in his career version of Batman against his entire rogue's gallery (most notably Two-Face, whose origin was re-envisioned by Loeb) while dealing with various mysteries involving serial killers Holiday and the Hangman, of which the former was the subject of intense debate and speculation amongst Batman fans. In 2003, Loeb teamed with artist Jim Lee to work on another mystery arc: "Batman: Hush" for the main Batman book. The twelve issue storyline saw Batman and Catwoman running the gauntlet against Batman's entire rogue's gallery, including an apparently resurrected Jason Todd, while seeking to find the identity of the mysterious supervillain Hush. While the character of Hush failed to catch on with readers, the arc was a sales success for DC. As the storyline was Jim Lee's first regular comic book work in nearly a decade, the series became #1 on the Diamond Comic Distributors sales chart for the first time since *Batman* #500 (October 1993) and Jason Todd's appearance laid the groundwork for writer Judd Winick's subsequent run as writer on *Batman*, with another multi-issue epic, "Under the Hood," which ran from *Batman* #637-650.

In 2005, DC launched *All-Star Batman and Robin*, a stand-alone comic series set outside the existing DC Universe. Written by Frank Miller and drawn by Jim Lee, the series was a commercial success for DC Comics though widely panned by critics for its writing.

Starting in 2006, the regular writers on *Batman* and *Detective Comics* were Grant Morrison and Paul Dini, with Grant Morrison reincorporating controversial elements of Batman lore (most notably, the science fiction themed storylines of the 1950s Batman comics, which Morrison revised as hallucinations Batman suffered under the influence of various mind-bending gases and extensive sensory deprivation training) into the character. Morrison's run climaxed with "Batman R.I.P.", which brought Batman up against the villainous "Black Glove" organization, which sought to drive Batman into madness. "Batman R.I.P." segued into *Final Crisis* (also written by Morrison), which saw the apparent death of Batman at the hands of Darkseid. In the 2009 miniseries *Batman: Battle for the Cowl*, Wayne's former protégé Dick Grayson becomes the new Batman, and Wayne's son Damian becomes the new Robin. In June 2009, Judd Winick returned to writing *Batman*, while Grant Morrison was given his own series, titled *Batman and Robin*.

Another Batman tale once more starring Bruce as Batman titled Batman: Unseen deals with Bruce Wayne's early career and him fighting the invisible man.

Fictional character biography

Batman's history has undergone various revisions, both minor and major. Few elements of the character's history have remained constant. Scholars William Uricchio and Roberta E. Pearson noted in the early 1990s, "Unlike some fictional characters, the Batman has no primary urtext set in a specific period, but has rather existed in a plethora of equally valid texts constantly appearing over more than five decades."

The central fixed event in the Batman stories is the character's origin story. As a little boy, Bruce Wayne is horrified and traumatized to see his parents, the physician Dr. Thomas Wayne and his wife Martha, being murdered by a mugger in front of his very eyes. This drives him to fight crime in Gotham City as Batman. Pearson and Uricchio also noted beyond the origin story and such events as the introduction of Robin, "Until recently, the fixed and accruing and hence, canonized, events have been few in number," a situation altered by an increased effort by later Batman editors such as Dennis O'Neil to ensure consistency and continuity between stories.

Golden Age

In Batman's first appearance in *Detective Comics* #27, he is already operating as a crime fighter. Batman's origin is first presented in *Detective Comics* #33 (Nov. 1939), and is later fleshed out in *Batman* #47. As these comics state, Bruce Wayne is born to Dr. Thomas Wayne and his wife Martha, two very wealthy and charitable Gotham City socialites. Bruce is brought up in Wayne Manor, with its wealthy splendor, and leads a happy and privileged existence until the age of eight, when his parents are killed by a small-time criminal named Joe Chill while on their way home from a movie theater. Bruce Wayne swears an oath to rid the city of the evil that had taken his parents' lives. He engages in intense intellectual and physical training; however, he realizes that these skills alone would not be enough. "Criminals are a superstitious cowardly lot," Wayne remarks, "so my disguise must be able to strike terror into their hearts. I must be a creature of the night, black, terrible..." As if responding to his desires, a bat suddenly flies through the window, inspiring Bruce to take on the persona of Batman.

In early strips, Batman's career as a vigilante earns him the ire of the police. During this period Wayne has a fiancée named Julie Madison. Wayne takes in an orphaned circus acrobat, Dick Grayson, who becomes his sidekick, Robin. Batman also becomes a founding member of the Justice Society of America, although he, like Superman, is an honorary member, and thus only participates occasionally. Batman's relationship with the law thaws quickly, and he is made an honorary member of Gotham City's police department. During this time, butler Alfred Pennyworth arrives at Wayne Manor, and after deducing the Dynamic Duo's secret identities joins their service.

Silver Age

See also: Batman (Earth-Two)

The Silver Age of Comic Books in DC Comics is sometimes held to have begun in 1956 when the publisher introduced Barry Allen as a new, updated version of The Flash. Batman is not significantly changed by the late 1950s for the continuity which would be later referred to as Earth-One. The lighter tone Batman had taken in the period between the Golden and Silver Ages led to the stories of the late 1950s and early 1960s that often feature a large number of science-fiction elements, and Batman is not significantly updated in the manner of other characters until *Detective Comics* #327 (May 1964), in which Batman reverts to his detective roots, with most science-fiction elements jettisoned from the series.

After the introduction of DC Comics' multiverse in the 1960s, DC established that stories from the Golden Age star the Earth-Two Batman, a character from a parallel world. This version of Batman partners with and marries the reformed Earth-Two Catwoman, Selina Kyle (as shown in *Superman Family* #211) and fathers Helena Wayne, who, as the Huntress, becomes (along with Dick Grayson, the Earth-Two Robin) Gotham's protector once Wayne retires from the position to become police commissioner, a position he occupies until he is killed during one final adventure as Batman. Batman titles however often ignored that a distinction had been made between the pre-revamp and post-revamp Batmen (since unlike The Flash or Green Lantern, Batman comics had been published without interruption through the 1950s) and would on occasion make reference to stories from the Golden Age. Nevertheless, details of Batman's history were altered or expanded upon through the decades. Additions include meetings with a future Superman during his youth, his upbringing by his uncle Philip Wayne (introduced in *Batman* #208, January/February 1969) after his parents' death, and appearances of his father and himself as prototypical versions of Batman and Robin, respectively. In 1980 then-editor Paul Levitz commissioned the *Untold Legend of the Batman* limited series to thoroughly chronicle Batman's origin and history.

Batman meets and regularly works with other heroes during the Silver Age, most notably Superman, whom he began regularly working alongside in a series of team-ups in *World's Finest Comics*, starting in 1954 and continuing through the series' cancellation in 1986. Batman and Superman are usually depicted as close friends. Batman becomes a founding member of the Justice League of America, appearing in its first story in 1960s *Brave and the Bold* #28. In the 1970s and 1980s, *Brave and the Bold* became a Batman title, in which Batman teams up with a different DC Universe superhero each month.

In 1969, Dick Grayson attends college as part of DC Comics' effort to revise the Batman comics. Additionally, Batman also moves from his mansion, Wayne Manor into a penthouse apartment atop the Wayne Foundation building in downtown Gotham City, in order to be closer to Gotham City's crime. Batman spends the 1970s and early 1980s mainly working solo, with occasional team-ups with Robin and/or Batgirl. Batman's adventures also become somewhat darker and more grim during this period, depicting increasingly violent crimes, including the first appearance (since the early Golden Age) of the Joker as a homicidal psychopath, and the arrival of Ra's al Ghul, a centuries-old terrorist who knows Batman's secret identity. In the 1980s, Dick Grayson becomes Nightwing.

In the final issue of *Brave and the Bold* in 1983, Batman quits the Justice League and forms a new group called the Outsiders. He serves as the team's leader until *Batman and the Outsiders* #32 (1986) and the comic subsequently changed its title.

Modern Batman

After the 12-issue limited series *Crisis on Infinite Earths*, DC Comics retconned the histories of some major characters in an attempt at updating them for contemporary audiences. Frank Miller retold Batman's origin in the storyline "Year One" from *Batman* #404-407, which emphasizes a grittier tone in the character. Though the Earth-Two Batman is erased from history, many stories of Batman's Silver Age/Earth-One career (along with an amount of Golden Age ones) remain canonical in the post-Crisis universe, with his origins remaining the same in essence, despite alteration. For example, Gotham's police are mostly corrupt, setting up further need for Batman's existence. While Dick Grayson's past remains much the same, the history of Jason Todd, the second Robin, is altered, turning the boy into the orphan son of a petty crook, who tries to steal the tires from the Batmobile. Also removed is the guardian Phillip Wayne leaving young Bruce to be raised by Alfred Pennyworth. Additionally, Batman is no longer a founding member of the Justice League of America, although he becomes leader for a short time of a new incarnation of the team launched in 1987. To help fill in the revised backstory for Batman following *Crisis*, DC launched a new Batman title called *Legends of the Dark Knight* in 1989 and has published various miniseries and one-shot stories since then that largely take place during the "Year One" period. Various stories from Jeph Loeb and Matt Wagner also touch upon this era.

In 1988's "Batman: A Death in the Family" storyline from *Batman* #426-429 Jason Todd, the second Robin, is killed by the Joker. Subsequently Batman begins exhibiting an excessive, reckless approach to his crime-fighting, a result of the pain of losing Jason Todd. Batman works solo until the decade's close, when Tim Drake becomes the new Robin. In 2005, writers resurrected the Jason Todd character and have pitted him against his former mentor.

Many of the major Batman storylines since the 1990s have been inter-title crossovers that run for a number of issues. In 1993, DC published both the "Death of Superman" storyline and "Knightfall" . In the Knightfall storyline's first phase, the new villain Bane paralyzes Batman, leading Wayne to ask Azrael to take on the role. After the end of "Knightfall," the storylines split in two directions, following both the Azrael-Batman's adventures, and Bruce Wayne's quest to become Batman once more. The story arcs realign in "KnightsEnd," as Azrael becomes increasingly violent and is defeated by a healed Bruce Wayne. Wayne hands the Batman mantle to Dick Grayson (then Nightwing) for an interim period, while Wayne trains to return to the role.

The 1994 company-wide crossover *Zero Hour* changes aspects of DC continuity again, including those of Batman. Noteworthy among these changes is that the general populace and the criminal element now considers Batman an urban legend rather than a known force. Similarly, the Waynes' killer is never caught or identified, effectively removing Joe Chill from the new continuity, rendering stories such as "Year Two" non-canon.

Batman once again becomes a member of the Justice League during Grant Morrison's 1996 relaunch of the series, titled *JLA*. While Batman contributes greatly to many of the team's successes, the Justice League is largely uninvolved as Batman and Gotham City face catastrophe in the decade's closing crossover arc. In 1998's "Cataclysm" storyline, Gotham City is devastated by an earthquake and ultimately cut off from the United States Government afterwards. Deprived of many of his technological resources, Batman fights to reclaim the city from legions of gangs during 1999's "No Man's Land".

Meanwhile, Batman's relationship with the Gotham City Police Department changed for the worse with the events of "Batman: Officer Down" and "Batman: War Games/War Crimes"; Batman's long-time law enforcement allies Commissioner Gordon and Harvey Bullock are forced out of the police department in "Officer Down", while "War Games" and "War Crimes" saw Batman become a wanted fugitive after a contingency plan of his to neutralize Gotham City's criminal underworld is accidentally triggered, resulting in a massive gang war that ends with the sadistic Black Mask the undisputed ruler of the city's criminal gangs. Other troubles come for Batman in the form of Lex Luthor (secretly behind the events of "No Man's Land"), who seeks revenge for Bruce Wayne cancelling all of his company's government contracts upon Luthor being elected President of the United States. Luthor arranges for the murder of Batman's on-again, off-again love interest Vesper (introduced in the mid-1990s) during the "Bruce Wayne: Murderer?" and "Bruce Wayne: Fugitive" story arcs. Though Batman is able to clear his name, he loses another ally in the form of his new bodyguard Sasha, who is recruited into the organization known as "Checkmate" while stuck in prison due to her refusal to turn states evidence against her employer. While he was unable to prove that Luthor was behind the murder of Vesper, Batman does get his revenge with help from Talia al Ghul in *Superman/Batman* #1-6: not only does he bring down Lex Luthor's Presidency but also engages in a hostile take-over of Luthor's corporate holdings, bankrupting the villain in the process.

DC's 2005 limited series *Identity Crisis* reveals that JLA member Zatanna had edited Batman's memories to prevent him from stopping the League from lobotomizing Dr. Light after he raped Sue Dibny. This served as a retcon for Batman's complete distrust for his fellow superheroes, which, under writers such as Mark Waid in the "Tower of Babel" arc in JLA, manifested itself in the form of Batman keeping extensive files on how to kill his fellow superheroes. Batman later creates the Brother I satellite surveillance system to watch over and if necessary, kill the other heroes. It is eventually co-opted by Maxwell Lord, who then kills superhero Blue Beetle to keep him from alerting the Justice League of the existence of Batman's murderous creation. The revelation of Batman's creation and his tacit responsibility for Blue Beetle's death becomes a driving force in the lead-up to the *Infinite Crisis* miniseries, which again restructures DC continuity. In *Infinite Crisis* #7, Alexander Luthor, Jr. mentions that in the newly rewritten history of the "New Earth", created in the previous issue, the murderer of Martha and Thomas Wayne — again, Joe Chill — was captured, thus undoing the retcon created after *Zero Hour*. Batman and a team of superheroes destroy Brother Eye and the OMACs, though at the very end Batman reaches his apparent breaking point when Alexander Luthor Jr. seriously wounds Nightwing. Picking up a gun, Batman nearly shoots Luthor in order to avenge his former sidekick, until Wonder Woman convinces him to not pull the trigger.

Following *Infinite Crisis*, Bruce Wayne, Dick Grayson (having recovered from his wounds), and Tim Drake retrace the steps Bruce had taken when he originally left Gotham City, to "rebuild Batman." In the *Face the Face* storyline, Batman and Robin return to Gotham City after their year-long absence. Part of this absence is captured during Week 30 of the *52* series, which shows Batman fighting his inner demons. Later on in *52*, Batman is shown undergoing an intense meditation ritual in Nanda Parbat. This becomes an important part of the regular *Batman* title, which reveals that Batman is reborn as a more effective crime fighter while undergoing this ritual, having "hunted down and ate" the last traces of fear in his mind.

At the end of the "Face the Face" story arc, Bruce officially adopts Tim (who had lost both of his parents at various points in the character's history) as his son. The follow-up story arc in *Batman*, *Batman & Son*, introduces Damian Wayne, who is Batman's son with Talia al Ghul. Batman, along with Superman and Wonder Woman, reforms the Justice League in the new *Justice League of America* series, and is leading the newest incarnation of the Outsiders.

Grant Morrison's 2008 storyline, *Batman R.I.P.*, featuring Batman being physically and mentally broken by the enigmatic "Black Glove," garnered much news coverage in advance of its highly-promoted conclusion, which would supposedly feature the death of Bruce Wayne. The original intention was, in fact, not for Batman to die in the pages of "R.I.P.," but for the story to continue with the current DC event *Final Crisis* and have the death occur there. As such, a two-issue bridge arc was designed called "Last Rites" that showed Batman survive his helicopter crash into the Gotham City River and return to the Batcave, only to be summoned to the Hall of Justice by the JLA to help investigate Orion's death. This in turn led into the events of "Final Crisis" (which began publication during the conclusion of "Batman RIP"), where Batman is kidnapped by Granny Goodness. "Last Rites" told the tale of Batman being mentally probed by Darkseid's minions Mokkari and Simyon, in an attempt to cull the personality traits that make Batman the successful superhero that he is in order to transplant them into cloned bodies. The plan fails due to the clones, imparted with Batman's sense of justice, choosing to kill themselves rather than serve Darkseid. The two-parter concludes with a major "Final Crisis" plot point, as it is revealed that Batman kept the bullet used to kill Orion in his utility belt.

The Batman's apparent death occurs in *Final Crisis* #6 when he confronts Darkseid. Batman announces that he will break his "no gun" rule while facing the villain. Wielding a sidearm made by Apokolips, Batman shoots Darkseid in the chest with a bullet made of Radion (the same bullet used to kill Orion), just as Darkseid unleashes his Omega Sanction, or the "death that is life", upon Batman. However, the Omega Sanction does not actually *kill* its target, but sends its consciousness into parallel worlds. Although the presence of Batman's corpse would suggest that he is dead, at the conclusion of *Final Crisis* it is revealed that Batman has been sent to the distant past where he is able to watch the passing of Anthro.

The three-issue *Battle for the Cowl* miniseries, ('cowl' referring to Batman's mask) sees those closest to Wayne compete for the "right" to assume the role of Batman. Eventually, Grayson reluctantly assumes the role. Tim Drake takes on the identity of Red Robin, questing around the world searching for Bruce Wayne, who he believes is still alive.

In *Blackest Night*, the villain Black Hand is seen digging up Bruce Wayne's body, stealing his skull, and recruiting it into the Black Lantern Corps. Deadman, whose body has also become a Black Lantern, rushes to aid the new Batman and Robin, along with Red Robin against the Gotham villains who have been reanimated as Black Lanterns, as well as their own family members. The skull was briefly reanimated as a Black Lantern, reconstructing a body in the process by Black Hand's lord, Nekron, to move against the Justice League and the Titans. After the Black Lantern Batman created several black power rings to attach to and kill the majority of the Justice League, the skull was returned to normal after Nekron explained it served its purpose as an emotional tether. Nekron also referred to the skull as "Bruce Wayne", knowing that the body was not authentic.

In *Batman and Robin*'s third storyline, "Blackest Knight," it is revealed that the body left behind at the end of *Final Crisis* #6 was actually a clone created from a failed attempt by Darkseid to amass an army of "Batmen". Because of this, the skull that was used by the Black Lantern Corps and reanimated by Nekron was a fake. Dick Grayson, thinking it was Bruce Wayne's real body, attempted to resurrect it in a Lazarus Pit only to be met with a fierce, mindless combatant. He then realized the truth about the body.

Morrison's storyline continues with the miniseries *Batman: The Return of Bruce Wayne*. In the miniseries, Bruce travels through time from the prehistoric era back to present-day Gotham.

Characterization

Batman's primary character traits can be summarized as "wealth; physical prowess; deductive abilities and obsession." The details and tone of Batman comic books have varied over the years due to different creative teams. Dennis O'Neil noted that character consistency was not a major concern during early editorial regimes: "Julie Schwartz did a Batman in *Batman* and *Detective* and Murray Boltinoff did a Batman in the *Brave and the Bold* and apart from the costume they bore very little resemblance to each other. Julie and Murray did not coordinate their efforts, did not pretend to, did not want to, were not asked to. Continuity was not important in those days."

The driving force behind Batman's character is from his childhood. Bob Kane and Bill Finger discussed Batman's background and decided that "there's nothing more traumatic than having your parents murdered before your eyes." Despite his trauma, he is driven to train to become a brilliant scientist and train his body into absolute physical perfection to fight crime in Gotham City as Batman, an inspired idea from Wayne's insight into the criminal mind. Another of Batman's characterizations is a vigilante; in order to stop evil that started with the death of his parents, he must sometimes break laws himself. Although manifested differently by being re-told by different artists, it is nevertheless that the details and the prime components of Batman's origin have never varied at all in the comic books, the "reiteration of the basic origin events holds together otherwise divergent expressions". The origin is the source of the character's traits and attributes, which play out in many of the character's adventures.

Batman is often treated as a vigilante by other characters in his stories. Frank Miller views the character as "a dionysian figure, a force for anarchy that imposes an individual order." Dressed as a bat, Batman deliberately cultivates a frightening persona in order to aid him in crime-fighting, a fear that originates from the criminals' own guilty conscience.

Bruce Wayne

Main article: Bruce Wayne

In his secret identity, Batman is Bruce Wayne, a wealthy businessman who lives in Gotham City. To the world at large, Bruce Wayne is often seen as an irresponsible, superficial playboy who lives off his family's personal fortune (amassed when his family invested in Gotham real estate before the city was a bustling metropolis) and the profits of Wayne Enterprises, a major private technology firm that he inherits. However, Wayne is also known for his contributions to charity, notably through his Wayne Foundation. Bruce creates the playboy public persona to aid in throwing off suspicion of his secret identity, often acting dim-witted and self-absorbed to further the act. Among the more noted measures he uses to maintain the facade is pretending he is a heavy drinker by claiming his glasses of ginger ale are strong beverages; Bruce is actually a strict teetotaler to maintain his physical fitness and mental acuity.

Writers of both Batman and Superman stories have often compared the two within the context of various stories, to varying conclusions. Like Superman, the prominent persona of Batman's dual identities varies with time. Modern age comics have tended to portray "Bruce Wayne" as the facade, with "Batman" as the truer representation of his personality (in counterpoint to the post-Crisis Superman, whose "Clark Kent" persona is the 'real' personality, and "Superman" is the 'mask'). In *Batman Unmasked*, a television documentary about the psychology of the character, Associate Professor of Social Psychology at the University of California, Los Angeles, and an adjunct behavioral scientist at the Rand Corporation Benjamin Karney, notes that Batman's personality is driven by Bruce Wayne's inherent humanity; that "Batman, for all its benefits and for all of the time Bruce Wayne devotes to it, is ultimately a tool for Bruce Wayne's efforts to make the world better".

As noted in the Will Brooker book, *Batman Unmasked*, "the confirmation of Batman's identity lies with the young audience...he doesn't have to be Bruce Wayne; he just needs the suit and gadgets, the abilities, and most importantly the morality, the humanity. There's just a sense about him: 'they trust him... and they're never wrong."

Dick Grayson

Main article: Dick Grayson

While Wayne travels through time to get back to the present, Dick Grayson has become the new Batman. This is the second time he has taken on the mantle in Bruce Wayne's absence, albeit the first time (when Wayne was recovering from his broken back) reluctantly. After Wayne's "death", Dick stated that he has no problem becoming Batman, but Wayne had left a prerecorded message telling him not to take up the mantle and to continue fighting crime as Nightwing with Robin at his side. Realizing that Gotham still needed the Dark Knight, Dick retired his Nightwing mantle to become the new Batman.

In an interview with IGN, Morrison details that having Grayson as Batman and Damian Wayne as Robin will be a "reverse" of the normal dynamic between Batman and Robin, with, "a more light-hearted and spontaneous Batman and a scowling, badass Robin." Morrison explains his intentions for the new characterization of Batman: "Dick Grayson is kind of this consummate superhero. The guy has been Batman's partner since he was a kid, he's led the Teen Titans, and he's trained with everybody in the DC Universe. So he's a very different kind of Batman. He's a lot easier; He's a lot looser and more relaxed."

Skills, abilities, and resources

There are a plethora of superheroes without superpowers but of them all the Batman character relies on "his own scientific knowledge, detective skills, and athletic prowess." In the stories Batman is regarded as one of the world's greatest detectives. In Grant Morrison's first storyline in *JLA*, Superman describes Batman as "the most dangerous man on Earth," able to defeat a team of superpowered aliens all by himself in order to rescue his imprisoned teammates. He is a master of disguise, often gathering information under the identity of Matches Malone, a notorious gangster. Additionally, the Batman has been repeatedly described as one of the greatest martial artists in the DC Universe, having either trained with or fought against the very best of them including such notables as Lady Shiva, Bronze Tiger, and Richard Dragon.

Costume

Main article: Batsuit

Batman's costume incorporates the imagery of a bat in order to frighten criminals. The details of the Batman costume change repeatedly through various stories and media, but the most distinctive elements remain consistent: a scallop-hem cape, a cowl covering most of the face featuring a pair of batlike ears, and a stylized bat emblem on the chest, and the ever-present utility belt. The costumes' colors are traditionally blue and grey, although this colorization arose due to the way comic book art is colored. Finger and Kane conceptualized Batman as having a black cape and cowl and grey suit, but conventions in coloring called for black to be highlighted with blue. This coloring has been claimed by Larry Ford, in *Place, Power, Situation, and Spectacle: A Geography of Film*, to be a reversion of conventional color-coding symbolism, which sees "bad guys" wearing dark colors. Batman's gloves typically feature three scallops that protrude from long, gauntlet-like cuffs, although in his earliest appearances he wore short, plain gloves without the scallops. A yellow ellipse around the bat logo on the character's chest was added in 1964, and became the hero's trademark symbol, akin to the red and yellow "S" symbol of Superman. The overall look of the character, particularly the length of the cowl's ears and of the cape, varies greatly depending on the artist. Dennis O'Neil said, "We now say that Batman has two hundred suits hanging in the Batcave so they don't have to look the same . . . Everybody loves to draw Batman, and everybody wants to put their own spin on it."

Equipment

See also: Batman's utility belt

Batman uses a large arsenal of specialized gadgets in his war against crime, the designs of which usually share a bat motif. Batman historian Les Daniels credits Gardner Fox with creating the concept of Batman's arsenal with the introduction of the utility belt in *Detective Comics* #29 (July 1939) and the first bat-themed weapons the batarang and the "Batgyro" in *Detective Comics* #31 and #32 (September; October, 1939). Batman's primary vehicle is the Batmobile, which is usually depicted as an imposing black car with large tailfins that suggest a bat's wings. Batman's other vehicles include the Batplane (aka the Batwing), Batboat, Bat-Sub, and Batcycle.

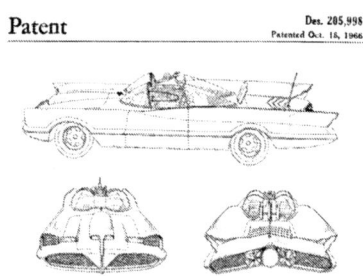

The 1966 television Batmobile was built by George Barris from a Lincoln Futura concept car.

In proper practice, the "bat" prefix (as in batmobile or batarang) is rarely used by Batman himself when referring to his equipment, particularly after some portrayals (primarily the 1960s *Batman* live-action television show and the *Super Friends* animated series) stretched the practice to campy proportions.

The 1960s television series Batman has an arsenal that includes such "bat-" names as the bat-computer, bat-scanner, bat-radar, bat-cuffs, bat-pontoons, bat-drinking water dispenser, bat-camera with polarized bat-filter, bat-shark repellent bat-spray, and bat-rope. The storyline "A Death in the Family" suggests that given Batman's grim nature, he is unlikely to have adopted the "bat" prefix on his own.

Batman keeps most of his field equipment in a utility belt. Over the years it is shown to contain a virtually limitless variety of crime- fighting tools. Different versions of the belt have these items stored in either pouches or hard cylinders attached evenly around it. A typical major exception to the range of Batman's equipment are conventional firearms, which he refuses to use on principle considering that weapon class was the instrument of his parents' murder. Modern depictions of Batman have him compromise for practicality by arming his vehicles mainly for the purpose of removing obstacles or disabling enemy vehicles.

Bat-Signal

Main article: Bat-Signal

When Batman is needed, the Gotham City police activate a searchlight with a bat-shaped insignia over the lens called the Bat-Signal which shines into the night sky, creating a bat-symbol on a passing cloud which can be seen from any point in Gotham. The origin of the signal varies, depending on the continuity and medium.

In various incarnations, most notably the 1960s *Batman* TV series, Commissioner Gordon also has a dedicated phone line, dubbed the Bat-Phone, connected to a bright red telephone (in the TV series) which sits on a wooden base and has a transparent cake cover on top. The line connects directly to Batman's residence, Wayne Manor, specifically both to a similar phone sitting on the desk in Bruce Wayne's study and the extension phone in the Batcave.

Batcave

Main article: Batcave

The Batcave is Batman's secret headquarters, consisting of a series of subterranean caves beneath his mansion, Wayne Manor. It serves as his command center for both local and global surveillance, as well as housing his vehicles and equipment for his war on crime. It also is a storeroom for Batman's memorabilia. In both the comic *Batman: Shadow of the Bat* (issue #45) and the 2005 film *Batman Begins*, the cave is said to have been part of the Underground Railroad. Of the heroes and villains who see the Batcave, few know where it is located.

Supporting characters

Main article: List of Batman supporting characters

Batman's interactions with the characters around him, both heroes and villains, help to define the character. Commissioner James "Jim" Gordon, Batman's ally in the Gotham City police, debuted along with Batman in *Detective Comics* #27 and has been a consistent presence since then. Later on, Batman gained Alfred as his butler and Lucius Fox as his business manager and apparently unwitting armorer. However, the most important supporting role in the Batman mythos is filled by the hero's young sidekick Robin. The first Robin, Dick Grayson, eventually leaves his mentor and becomes the hero Nightwing, though he and Batman would still continue to work together. The second Robin, Jason Todd, is badly beaten and then killed in an explosion set by the Joker, but later returns as an adversary. Tim Drake, the third Robin, first appeared in 1989 and went on to star in his own comic series. Alfred, Bruce Wayne's loyal butler, father figure, and one of the few to know his secret identity, "[lends] a homey touch to Batman's environs and [is] ever ready to provide a steadying and reassuring hand" to the hero and his sidekick.

Batman is at times a member of superhero teams such as the Justice League of America and the Outsiders. Batman has often been paired in adventure with his Justice League teammate Superman, notably as the co-stars of *World's Finest* and *Superman/Batman* series. In pre-Crisis continuity, the two are depicted as close friends; however, in current continuity, they have a mutually respectful but uneasy relationship, with an emphasis on their differing views on crime-fighting and justice. In *Superman/Batman* #3 (December 2003), Superman observes, "Sometimes, I admit, I think of Bruce as a man in a costume. Then, with some gadget from his utility belt, he reminds me that he has an extraordinarily inventive mind. And how lucky I am to be able to call on him."

Batman is involved romantically with many women throughout his various incarnations. These range from society women such as Julie Madison, Vicki Vale, and Silver St. Cloud, to allies like Wonder Woman and Sasha Bordeaux, to even villainesses such as Catwoman and Talia al Ghul, with the latter of whom he sired a son, Damian, and with the former of whom sired a daughter, Helena (on Earth-Two). While these relationships tend to be short, Batman's attraction to Catwoman is present in nearly every version and medium in which the characters appear. Authors have gone back and forth over the years as to how Batman manages the 'playboy' aspect of Bruce Wayne's personality; at different times he embraces or flees from the women interested in attracting "Gotham's most eligible bachelor."

Other supporting characters in Batman's world include former Batgirl Barbara Gordon, Commissioner Gordon's daughter who, now using a wheelchair due to a gunshot wound inflicted by the Joker, serves the superhero community at large as the computer hacker Oracle; Azrael, a would-be assassin who replaces Bruce Wayne as Batman for a time; Cassandra Cain, an assassin's daughter who became the new Batgirl, Huntress, the sole surviving member of a mob family turned Gotham vigilante who has worked with Batman on occasion, Stephanie Brown, the daughter of a criminal who operated as the

Spoiler and temporarily as Robin, Ace the Bat-Hound, Batman's Canine partner; and Bat-Mite, an extra-dimensional imp who idolizes Batman.

Enemies

Main article: List of Batman enemies

Batman faces a variety of foes ranging from common criminals to outlandish supervillains. The list is one of the most recognizable in popular culture, many of them mirror aspects of the Batman's character and development, often having tragic origin stories that lead them to a life of crime. Batman's "most implacable foe" is the Joker, a psychopathic, clown-like criminal who, as a "personification of the irrational", represents "everything Batman [opposes]." Other long time recurring antagonists include Catwoman, the Scarecrow, the Penguin, Two-Face, the Riddler, Mr. Freeze, Poison Ivy, and Ra's al Ghul, among many others.

Cultural impact

See also: List of Batman related topics

Batman has become a pop culture icon, recognized around the world. The character's presence has extended beyond his comic book origins; events such as the release of the 1989 *Batman* film and its accompanying merchandising "brought the Batman to the forefront of public consciousness." In an article commemorating the sixtieth anniversary of the character, *The Guardian* wrote, "Batman is a figure blurred by the endless reinvention that is modern mass culture. He is at once an icon and a commodity: the perfect cultural artefact for the 21st century." In addition, media outlets have often used the character in trivial and comprehensive surveys — *Forbes* magazine estimated Bruce Wayne to be the 9th-richest fictional character with his $5.8 billion fortune, several places after Iron Man, who is at 6. *BusinessWeek* listed the character as one of the ten most intelligent superheroes appearing in American comics. Entertainment Weekly named Batman as one of *The 20 All Time Coolest Heroes in Pop Culture*. He also was placed on *AFI's 100 Years...100 Heroes and Villains* from the 1989 feature film by the American Film Institute.

In other media

Main article: Batman franchise media

The character of Batman has appeared in various media aside from comic books. The character has been developed as a vehicle for newspaper syndicated comic strips, books, radio dramas, television, and several theatrical feature films. The first adaptation of Batman was as a daily newspaper comic strip which premiered on October 25, 1943. That same year the character was adapted in the 15-part serial *Batman*, with Lewis Wilson becoming the first actor to portray Batman on screen. While Batman never had a radio series of his own, the character made occasional guest appearance in *The Adventures of Superman* starting in 1945 on occasions when Superman voice actor Bud Collyer needed time off. A second movie serial, *Batman and Robin*, followed in 1949, with Robert Lowery taking over the role of Batman. The exposure provided by these adaptations during the 1940s "helped make [Batman] a household name for millions who never bought a comic book.".

In the 1964 publication of Donald Barthelme's collection of short stories "Come Back, Dr. Caligari", Barthelme wrote "The Joker's Greatest Triumph." Batman is portrayed for purposes of spoof as a pretentious French-speaking rich man.

The *Batman* television series, starring Adam West, premiered in January 1966 on the ABC television network. Inflected with a camp sense of humor, the show became a pop culture phenomenon. In his memoir, *Back to the Batcave*, West notes his dislike for the term 'camp' as it was applied to the 1960s series, opining that the show was instead a farce or lampoon, and a deliberate one, at that. The series ran for 120 episodes, ending in 1968. In between the first and second season of the *Batman* television series the cast and crew made the theatrical release *Batman* (1966). The popularity of the *Batman* TV series also resulted in the first animated adaptation of Batman in the series *The Batman/Superman Hour*; the Batman segments of the series were repackaged as *Batman with Robin the Boy Wonder* which produced thirty-three episodes between 1968 and 1977. From 1973 until 1986, Batman had a starring role in ABC's *Super Friends* series, which was animated by Hanna-Barbera. Olan Soule was the voice of Batman in all these series, but was eventually replaced during *Super Friends* by Adam West, who voiced the character in Filmation's 1977 series *The New Adventures of Batman*.

In 1989, Batman returned to movie theaters in director Tim Burton's *Batman* starring Michael Keaton as the title character. The film was a huge success; not only was it the top-grossing film of the year, but at the time was the fifth highest-grossing film in history. The film spawned three sequels: *Batman Returns* (1992), *Batman Forever* (1995), and *Batman & Robin* (1997), the last two of which were directed by Joel Schumacher instead of Burton, and replaced Keaton as Batman with Val Kilmer and George Clooney, respectively. The second Schumacher film was a critical and commercial failure, causing Warner Bros. to cancel the planned fifth film, *Batman Triumphant*, and place the film series on hiatus.

In 1992, Batman returned to television in *Batman: The Animated Series*, which was produced by Warner Bros. and broadcast on the Fox television network. Author Les Daniels described the series as "[coming] as close as any artistic statement has to defining the look of Batman for the 1990s." The success of *Batman: The Animated Series* led to the animated spin-off film *Batman: Mask of the Phantasm* (1993), as well as various other animated series set in the same continuity, including *The New Batman Adventures*, *Batman Beyond*, and *Justice League*. As with *Batman: The Animated Series*, each of these productions featured Kevin Conroy as the voice of Batman. In 2004, a new animated series titled *The Batman* made its debut with Rino Romano as the title character. In 2008, this show was replaced by another animated series, *Batman: The Brave and the Bold*, with Diedrich Bader as Batman.

In 2005, *Batman Begins*, a reboot of the film series, was released, directed by Christopher Nolan and starring Christian Bale as Batman. Its sequel, *The Dark Knight* (2008), set the record for the highest grossing opening weekend of all time in the U.S., earning approximately $158 million, and became the fastest film to reach the $400 million mark in the history of American cinema (eighteenth day of release). These record breaking attendances saw *The Dark Knight* listed as the third-highest domestic grossing film of all time with $533 million, bested only by *Titanic* and *Avatar*. An animated anthology feature set between the Nolan films, *Batman: Gotham Knight*, was also released in 2008.

Homosexual interpretations

Further information: Homosexuality in the Batman franchise

Controversy has arisen over various sexual interpretations made regarding the content of Batman comics in the early decades. Homosexual interpretations have been part of the academic study of Batman since psychologist Fredric Wertham asserted in his *Seduction of the Innocent* in 1954 that "Batman stories are psychologically homosexual." He claimed, "The Batman type of story may stimulate children to homosexual fantasies, of the nature of which they may be unconscious." Wertham wrote, "Only someone ignorant of the fundamentals of psychiatry and of the psychopathology of sex can fail to realize a subtle atmosphere of homoeroticism which pervades the adventures of the mature 'Batman' and his young friend 'Robin.'"

Andy Medhurst wrote in his 1991 essay "Batman, Deviance, and Camp" that Batman is interesting to gay audiences because "he was one of the first fictional characters to be attacked on the grounds of his presumed homosexuality," "the 1960s TV series remains a touchstone of camp," and "[he] merits analysis as a notably successful construction of masculinity."

Creators associated with the character have expressed their own opinions. Writer Alan Grant has stated, "The Batman I wrote for 13 years isn't gay. Denny O'Neil's Batman, Marv Wolfman's Batman, everybody's Batman all the way back to Bob Kane... none of them wrote him as a gay character. Only Joel Schumacher might have had an opposing view." Writer Devin Grayson has commented, "It depends who you ask, doesn't it? Since you're asking me, I'll say no, I don't think he is ... I certainly understand the gay readings, though." While Frank Miller has described the relationship between Batman and the Joker as a "homophobic nightmare," he views the character as sublimating his sexual urges into crime-fighting, concluding, "He'd be *much* healthier if he were gay." Burt Ward, who portrayed Robin in the 1960s television show, has also remarked upon this interpretation in his autobiography *Boy Wonder: My Life in Tights*; He writes that the relationship could be interpreted as a sexual one, with the show's double entendres and lavish camp also possibly offering ambiguous interpretation.

Such homosexual interpretations continue to attract attention. One notable example occurred in 2000, when DC Comics refused to allow permission for the reprinting of four panels (from *Batman* #79, 92, 105 and 139) to illustrate Christopher York's paper *All in the Family: Homophobia and Batman Comics in the 1950s*. Another happened in the summer of 2005, when painter Mark Chamberlain displayed a number of watercolors depicting both Batman and Robin in suggestive and sexually explicit poses. DC threatened both artist and the Kathleen Cullen Fine Arts gallery with legal action if they did not cease selling the works and demanded all remaining art, as well as any profits derived from them.

References

- Beatty, Scott; *et al.* (2005). The Batman Handbook: The Ultimate Training Manual.. Quirk Books. ISBN 1-59474-023-2.
- Daniels, Les. *Batman: The Complete History*. Chronicle Books, 1999. ISBN 0-8118-4232-0
- Daniels, Les. *DC Comics: Sixty Years of the World's Favorite Comic Book Heroes*. Bulfinch, 1995. ISBN 0-8212-2076-4
- Jones, Gerard. *Men of Tomorrow: Geeks, Gangsters, and the Birth of the Comic Book*. Basic Books, 1995. ISBN 0-465-03657-0
- Pearson, Roberta E.; Uricchio, William (editors). *The Many Lives of the Batman: Critical Approaches to a Superhero and His Media*. Routledge: London, 1991. ISBN 0-85170-276-7
- Wright, Bradford W. *Comic Book Nation: The Transformation of Youth Culture in America*. Johns Hopkins, 2001. ISBN 0-8018-7450-5

External links

- Official website [1]
- Earth-1 Batman Index [2]
- Earth-2 Batman Index [3]
- Post-Crisis Batman Index [4]
- Batman Bio at the Unofficial Guide to the DC Universe [5]
- Batman [6] at the DC Database Project
- The Batman Wiki [7]
- Another Earth-1 Batman Index [8]
- ComicsInventory.com | Batman [9]
- Batman [10] at the Open Directory Project

pnb:باتمان

Bruce Wayne

Bruce Wayne	
Publication information	
Publisher	DC Comics
First appearance	*Detective Comics* #27 (May 1939)
Created by	Bob Kane (concept) Bill Finger (developer, uncredited)
In-story information	
Alter ego	Batman
Team affiliations	Batman Family Justice League Wayne Enterprises Outsiders
Partnerships	Robin Batgirl Superman Nightwing
Notable aliases	Matches Malone Sir Hemingford Grey

Bruce Wayne is a fictional character created by Bob Kane and Bill Finger as the civilian secret identity of the DC Comics superhero Batman. He first appeared in *Detective Comics* #27, May 1939.

Concept and creation

Finger came up with the name "Bruce Wayne" for the superhero's secret identity. In Jim Steranko's History of the Comics, vol. 1, Bill Finger reveals, "Bruce Wayne's first name came from Robert Bruce, the Scottish patriot. Wayne, being a playboy, was a man of gentry. I searched for a name that would suggest colonialism. I tried Adams, Hancock...then I thought of Mad Anthony Wayne."

To the world at large, Bruce Wayne is seen as an irresponsible, superficial playboy who lives off his family's personal fortune and the major private technology firm that he inherits. Bruce creates the public persona to aid in throwing off suspicion of his secret identity, often acting dim-witted and self-absorbed to further the act. Batman makes it clear that he considers keeping his secret identity a top priority; on various occasions, he often risks death rather than exposing his skills in public as Bruce Wayne. However, Wayne is also known for his contributions to charity, notably through the Wayne Foundation, a charity devoted to helping the victims of crime and preventing people from becoming criminals.

Publication History

The *Batman* series started in Spring 1940 and has been in publication ever since. In September 2010 it reached issue #703. His debut series, Detective Comics, has reached almost nine hundred issues. He has also spawned numerous spin-off titles including: *Robin, Nightwing, Batgirl, Batman: Streets of Gotham, Batman Confidential, Batman & Robin, Gotham City Sirens, Superman/Batman, Azrael, Birds of Prey*, and *Red Robin*.

Fictional character biography

Bruce Wayne is a billionaire industrialist and philanthropist, and the son of Thomas and Martha Wayne. When Bruce Wayne was a child his parents were murdered by Joe Chill, a low level thug in the Black Glove organization, who then was arrested the same night he murdered them, which made Bruce determined to rid Gotham City of crime. He traveled the world for many years and he returned to Gotham when he was around 25 years old and claimed the mantle of Batman after a bat crashed through the window of his study. He spent his first year of crime fighting battling the corrupt police force and gaining trust from future police commissioner James Gordon, and the help of his first ally, future District Attorney Harvey Dent. He also began to rid the city of Carmine Falcone's mafia. During that period he also had his first encounter with Hugo Strange. He also dealt with Joe Chill. He stalked Chill every night for a month, and on the last day of the month he confronted Chill. After Batman confronted Chill, he realized that he was the one to create Batman (by murdering Batman's parents) and he killed himself. Over the next few years of his career criminals like the Joker and the Riddler started to appear in Gotham. Gordon was also made Commissioner of Police at this point and then they lost Harvey as both a friend and ally when he became Two-Face.

Around the fourth year of his career as Batman he witnessed the murder of acrobat Dick Grayson's parents by the mob, who were extorting money from the circus in which they worked in. Bruce adopts Dick and later Dick becomes Robin, Batman's new partner in the war on crime. During this time Batman also finally destroys the remnants of the Falcone mafia. During the following years Bruce joined the Justice League with other heroes like Superman and Wonder Woman. Eventually Barbara Gordon joined the "dynamic duo" and became the first Batgirl. After serving as Batgirl for a few years, she began to feel useless because of her lack of super-powers. In this time Batman encountered Ra's al Ghul for the first time and Dick Grayson moved on from being Robin and became Nightwing.

Batman then adopted orphan Jason Todd and he became the second Robin. After retiring from crime fighting for good, Barbara was shot and paralyzed by the Joker. As per Gordon's request, Batman brought the Joker in by the book and did not seek retribution. Even though she lost the use of her legs, she still helped Batman by becoming Oracle. After the Joker escaped from his most recent stay at Arkham Asylum (a result of his capture after shooting Barbara), he killed Jason Todd and was almost killed by Batman before disappearing for some time. After Jason's death Bruce became increasingly more violent and dark. Batman remained Robin-less for a while until Tim Drake discovered that Bruce was Batman and Dick was Robin and tried to re-unite the dynamic duo. Dick suggested that Tim become Robin and after some hesitation from Bruce, he did become the new Robin.

Soon after a new villain would appear, Bane. Bane came to Gotham and after releasing the inmates of Arkham, he broke Bruce Wayne's back. Jean-Paul Valley, who had been training with Tim, became the temporary Batman while Bruce recovered. Eventually Bruce fully healed and had to reclaim the mantle of Batman by force, as Jean-Paul had become insane due to being brainwashed from an early age. After dealing with Jean-Paul, Bruce asked Dick to fill in for Bruce as Batman while he prepared himself again. Soon after Gotham was hit by a plague created by Ra's al Ghul to destroy Gotham City. Very soon after that, Gotham City was hit by a massive earthquake and the city was abandoned by the United States government and Bruce went to Washington, D.C. for three months to try and get help from the government, but since he was seen as a "playboy" he was ignored. While he was gone Helena Bertinelli became the new Batgirl to keep the bat family present in Gotham. When Bruce returned to Gotham, he let her keep the identity. Gordon had lost faith in Batman during has absence, and to try and regain his trust Batman offered to show Gordon that he was Bruce Wayne, but Gordon refused the offer. Eventually the city was rebuilt and law was re-established. Bruce fired Helena Bertinelli as Batgirl after she failed him during this crisis, and Cassandra Cain became the next Batgirl.

Later on after the earthquake, Bruce Wayne's childhood friend, Tommy Elliot returned to Gotham as the villain Hush and tried to destroy Batman and failed. Soon after Jason Todd as the Red Hood was resurrected and returned to Gotham, and tried to kill the Joker and take revenge for his death. Tim Drake's dad finds out that Tim is Robin and so he is forced to give it up for a while, so he gives the mantle to Stephanie Brown. He later returns to being Robin after she is apparently killed. It was later revealed that her death was faked. Cassandra Cain later retired from being Batgirl and passed the mantle on to Stephanie. Afterwords, Talia al Ghul revealed to Bruce that they had a son, Damian Wayne. A little while later, the Black Glove organization started to act on their plan to kill Bruce Wayne and nearly succeeded numerous times. Eventually Bruce seemingly defeated the Black Glove (and their leader Dr. Hurt), but was presumed dead. After re-appearing, Bruce helped the Justice League defeat Darkseid but in the process was sent back in time, although he was presumed dead again. He is currently jumping through time towards the present, unaware that he is now a doomsday weapon. The Justice League knows this however, and is trying to stop him.

In other media

Animation

Bruce Wayne has appeared in many animated series, including *The Batman/Superman Hour*, *The New Adventures of Batman*, *The Super Powers Team: Galactic Guardians*, *Batman: The Animated Series*, *The New Batman Adventures*, *Batman Beyond*, *Justice League*, *Justice League Unlimited*, *The Batman*, and *Batman: The Brave and the Bold*.

Live-action film

Batman and *Batman Returns*

Michael Keaton portrayed Bruce Wayne in Tim Burton's *Batman* and *Batman Returns*.

Batman Forever

In *Batman Forever*, Bruce Wayne is played by Val Kilmer, and is the boss of Wayne Enterprises.

Batman & Robin

George Clooney portrays him as an engaged socialite in *Batman & Robin*.

Batman Begins and *The Dark Knight*

Batman Begins was the first live action film to fully explore the character behind the mask of Batman, rather than depict Batman as more of an enigma. In this film, he was portrayed by English actor Christian Bale, who stated that the previous films had overplayed the villains and didn't focus on Batman enough. Bale returned as Batman in the sequel *The Dark Knight* and is set to reprise the role in the upcoming 2012 sequel.

Critical interpretations

In his book *Unleashing the Superhero in Us All*, T. James Musler explores the extent to which money is important in Bruce Wayne's life.

The Franchise

Batman franchise media

Adaptations of Batman in other media	
Created by	Bob Kane Bill Finger
Original source	Comics published by DC Comics
First appearance	*Detective Comics* #27 (May 1939)
Print publications	
Novel(s)	*Batman: Dead White* (2006)
Reference book(s)	*Batman: The Complete History* *The Batman Handbook: The Ultimate Training Manual*
Films and television	
Film(s)	*Batman* (1943) *Batman* (1966) *Batman* (1989) *Batman: Mask of the Phantasm* (1993) *Batman Begins* (2005)
Television show(s)	*Batman* (1966) *The Batman/Superman Hour* (1968) *Batman: The Animated Series* (1992) *The Batman* (2004) *Batman: The Brave and the Bold* (2008)
Theatrical presentations	
Musical(s)	*Batman: The Musical* (2002, never produced)
Audio presentations	
Radio show(s)	*The Adventures of Superman* (1940) Batman: The Lazarus Syndrome *Batman: Knightfall* (1994)
Games	
Board game(s)	HeroClix (2002)

Video game(s)	*Batman* (1986) *Batman* (1990) *Batman: The Animated Series* (1993) *Batman: Rise of Sin Tzu* (2003) *Lego Batman: The Video Game* (2008)

Since his first appearance in 1939, Batman has appeared in several adaptations as radio programs, animated series, and movies, as well as numerous merchandising items.

Theatrical movies

Main article: Batman in film

A number of Batman theatrical films have been made. There have also been several attempted projects during the hiatus between *Batman & Robin* and *Batman Begins*.

- 1943: *Batman*, 15-chapter serial starring Lewis Wilson as Batman and Douglas Croft as Robin.
- 1949: *Batman and Robin*, 15-chapter serial starring Robert Lowery as Batman and Johnny Duncan as Robin.
- 1966: *Batman*, feature film based on the contemporaneous *Batman* television series; starring Adam West as Batman, Burt Ward as Robin, Cesar Romero as the Joker, Burgess Meredith as the Penguin, Frank Gorshin as the Riddler, and Lee Meriweather as Catwoman.
- 1989: *Batman*, directed by Tim Burton; starring Michael Keaton as Batman, Jack Nicholson as the Joker, and Kim Basinger as Vicki Vale.
- 1992: *Batman Returns*, directed by Tim Burton; starring Michael Keaton as Batman, Michelle Pfeiffer as Catwoman, Danny DeVito as the Penguin, and Christopher Walken as Max Shreck.
- 1993: *Batman: Mask of the Phantasm*, an animated feature based on *Batman: The Animated Series*; starring Kevin Conroy as Batman, Mark Hamill as the Joker, and Dana Delany as Andrea Beaumont/The Phantasm.
- 1995: *Batman Forever*, directed by Joel Schumacher; starring Val Kilmer as Batman, Chris O'Donnell as Robin, Nicole Kidman as Chase Meridian, Tommy Lee Jones as Two-Face, and Jim Carrey as the Riddler.
- 1997: *Batman & Robin*, directed by Joel Schumacher; starring George Clooney as Batman, Chris O'Donnell as Robin, Alicia Silverstone as Batgirl, Arnold Schwarzenegger as Mr. Freeze, Uma Thurman as Poison Ivy and Robert Swenson as Bane.
- 2005: *Batman Begins*, directed by Christopher Nolan; starring Christian Bale as Batman, Michael Caine as Alfred Pennyworth, Gary Oldman as James Gordon, Katie Holmes as Rachel Dawes, Liam Neeson as Ra's al Ghul, Cillian Murphy as the Scarecrow, and Morgan Freeman as Lucius Fox.
- 2008: *The Dark Knight*, directed by Christopher Nolan; starring Christian Bale as Batman, Michael Caine as Alfred Pennyworth, Gary Oldman as James Gordon, Maggie Gyllenhaal as Rachel Dawes, Aaron Eckhart as Harvey Dent/Two-Face, Heath Ledger as the Joker, and Morgan Freeman as

Lucius Fox.

Direct-to-video

- 1998: *Batman & Mr. Freeze: SubZero*, based on *Batman: The Animated Series*.
- 2000: *Batman Beyond: Return of the Joker*, based on *Batman Beyond*.
- 2003: *Batman: Mystery of the Batwoman*, based on *The New Batman Adventures*.
- 2005: *The Batman vs. Dracula*, based on *The Batman*.
- 2008: *Justice League: The New Frontier*
- 2008: *Batman: Gotham Knight*
- 2009: *Superman/Batman: Public Enemies*
- 2010: *Justice League: Crisis on Two Earths*
- 2010: *Batman: Under the Red Hood*
- 2010: *Superman/Batman: Apocalypse*

Television

Live action

- 1966 - 1968: *Batman* starring Adam West and Burt Ward as Batman and Robin.
- 1972: "Equal pay" Public Service Announcement featuring Dick Gautier as Batman, Burt Ward as Robin, and Yvonne Craig as Batgirl.
- 1979: *Legends of the Superheroes* by Hanna Barbera, featuring West and Ward as Batman and Robin.
- 2001: "OnStar" commercials featuring Bruce Thomas as Batman and Michael Gough as Alfred, and followed the visual style of the 1989-1997 film series.
- 2002: *Birds of Prey*, TV series that featured Batman in the first episode, Bruce Thomas reprises his role as Batman.

Bruce Wayne

In 1999, Tim McCanlies wrote a pilot script and series bible for a planned series called *Bruce Wayne*. Taking place in his teenage years, the series would cover his passage into young adulthood, training, and development into becoming Batman. Other characters would include Alfred, Sergeant Jim Gordon, law school student Harvey Dent, and a seductive young Selina Kyle. Planned to run for five to six seasons, it would show how he acquired his martial arts skills, his equipment, and detective abilities he would use in his war on crime. It would also focus on corruption within the board of Wayne Enterprises (an element which found its way into the movie *Batman Begins*, to some extent), police affiliation with the mafia, etc. *Bruce Wayne* was nearing pre-production when Warner Bros. movie division felt it would conflict with the planned *Year One* movie and scrapped it. The result was *Batman*

Begins.

Animated

- 1968 - 1969: *The Batman/Superman Hour* produced by Filmation; featured Batman in *Batman with Robin the Boy Wonder*. In this cartoon, Batman is voiced by Olan Soule.
- 1972: *The New Scooby-Doo Movies* produced by Hanna-Barbera; Batman and Robin appeared in episodes "The Dynamic Scooby-Doo Affair" (9/16/72) and "The Caped Crusader Caper" (12/16/72), where Olan Soule first reprises his role as the Caped Crusader.
- 1973 - 1986: Various *Super Friends* series produced by Hanna-Barbera; Olan Soule again reprises his role as Batman in all but the last two *Super Friends* series, where he is replaced by Adam West
  - 1973 - 1974: *Super Friends*
  - 1977 - 1978: *The All-New Super Friends Hour*
  - 1978 - 1979: *Challenge of the SuperFriends*
  - 1979 - 1980: *The World's Greatest Super Friends*
  - 1980 - 1983: *Super Friends*
  - 1984 - 1985: *Super Friends: The Legendary Super Powers Show*
  - 1985 - 1986: *The Super Powers Team: Galactic Guardians*
- 1977 - 1978: *The New Adventures of Batman* produced by Filmation; while the H-B produced *Super Friends* ran on ABC, Adam West and Burt Ward (Robin) voiced their previously live-action roles for this CBS cartoon series; later rerun as part of *The Batman/Tarzan Adventure Hour* (the Tarzan segments had also been previously seen as their own series)
- 1992 - 2006: The DC Animated Universe produced by Warner Bros. Animation. Batman is voiced by Kevin Conroy in all appearances;
  - 1992 - 1995: *Batman: The Animated Series*; the first series of the DCAU.
  - 1997, 1998, 1999: *Superman: The Animated Series*; Batman guest stars in multiple episodes.
  - 1997 - 1999: *The New Batman Adventures*; a continuation of *Batman: The Animated Series*.
  - 1999 - 2001: *Batman Beyond*; an aged Bruce Wayne passes the mantle of Batman onto Terry McGinnis (voiced by Will Friedle).
  - 2001: *The Zeta Project*; the future Batman guest stars in one episode.
  - 2001 - 2004: *Justice League*; the original Batman becomes one of the founding members of the League.
  - 2002, 2003, 2004: *Static Shock*; Batman guest stars in multiple episodes.
  - 2004 - 2006 *Justice League Unlimited*; a continuation of *Justice League*.
- 1997: He appeared in the *Animaniacs* episode "Boo Wonder". Adam West reprises his role as the Caped Crusader.
- 2004: *Teen Titans*; Batman appeared in silhouette in the episode "Haunted", in a flashback sequence. He is not voiced by anybody.

- 2004 - 2008: *The Batman*; in this series, Bruce Wayne is a young crime fighter just three years into his career as Batman. He is voiced by Rino Romano.
- 2005 - 2006: In *Krypto the Superdog*, Batman himself makes no appearances, but his pet dog Ace the Bat-Hound does, although Ace prefers to refer to himself as "Batman's partner," rather than his pet.
- 2008–present: *Batman: The Brave and the Bold*; based in part on the comic book series of the same name, the series has Batman (voiced by Diedrich Bader) team-up with several other DC Comics heroes.
- 2010: *Young Justice*; the animated series of Young Justice will feature Justice League members as well as Batman voiced by Bruce Greenwood, who played the role in the animated film *Batman: Under the Red Hood*.

Newspaper

Main article: Batman (comic strip)

From 1943 to 1946, Batman and Robin appeared in a syndicated daily newspaper comic strip produced by the McClure Syndicate. Other versions appeared in 1953, 1966, and 1989. The original run is collected in the book *Batman: The Dailies*. One more comic strip series ran briefly after the success of the 1989 film.

Books

Batman appears in a novel by cyberpunk/horror novelist John Shirley, entitled *Batman: Dead White* from Del Rey. Many other novels and short story collections featuring Batman have been published over the years, including novelizations of each of the recent movies and several of the more popular comic book arcs. There are also several more scholarly works, aimed at either Batman's history or art, such as Les Daniels' *Batman: The Complete History* and compilations such as *Batman: Cover to Cover : The Greatest Comic Book Covers of the Dark Knight*. In 2004, *The Batman Handbook: The Ultimate Training Manual*, written by Scott Beatty was published by Quirk Books (ISBN 1-59474-023-2). Written in the same style as *The Worst-Case Scenario Survival Handbook* series, the book explained the basics on how to be Batman. Amongst the skills included in the book are "How to Train a Sidekick", "How to Execute a Backflip", "How to Throw a Grappling Hook", and "How to Survive a Poison Gas Attack". Finally, there are of course countless *sticker, coloring, activity, and other children's books* featuring the Dark Knight.

Foreign comics

- *Batman: Child of Dreams* by Kia Asamiya - Manga
- *Batman: Dark Mask* - Manga
- *Bat-Manga!: The Secret History of Batman in Japan* by Jiro Kuwata - Manga
- *Batman trong Hốtử Thần* by Nguyễn Th - Vietnamese comics
- *Batman: God of Africa* - Manhua

Radio

Beginning in March 1945, Batman and Robin made regular appearances on the radio drama "The Adventures of Superman" on the Mutual Broadcasting System. Efforts were made to launch a Batman radio series in 1943 and again in 1950, but neither came to fruition.

In 1989 an original radio drama, *Batman: The Lazarus Syndrome*, was produced by Dirk Maggs for BBC Radio 4.

A second Maggs production aired on BBC Radio 1 in 1994, this time adapting the comic book storyline *Batman: Knightfall*. It was adapted, produced and directed by Maggs - with music composed by Mark Russell - who had also recently made *Superman: Doomsday & Beyond* on BBC Radio 5. This show, however was not commissioned of its own, but rather to be three minute episodes on the Mark Goodier Show. This meant it was written with a sense of immediacy; having to make an instant effect and each three minute segment contains a major plot development or sound effect stunt and end on a cliffhanger. DC acknowledged the effort in an issue *Shadow of The Bat* by having villains jump past a sign reading "Dirk Maggs Radio". Michael Gough reprised the role of Alfred Pennyworth from the Burton/Schumacher film series.

Novelty singles

Several musical singles featuring cast members of the television show singing in-character were released in 1966: Burgess Meredith as the Penguin in "The Capture" and "The Escape", Frank Gorshin as the Riddler in "The Riddler", and Adam West as Batman in "Miranda". In 1976 West performed a pair of novelty songs, "The Story of Batman" and "Batman and Robin", for Target Records. All six of these recordings (sans the b-sides to Gorshin and West's singles) were later included on the 1997 compilation, *Batmania: Songs Inspired by Batman TV Series*.

In 1966, Burt Ward also recorded a limited "disc jokey only" release with Frank Zappa called "Boy Wonder, I Love You".

Audio drama

Following the popularity of the Adam West television series, a pair of LPs were released in 1966 on MGM's "Leo the Lion" label. Each contained three dramatizations, including stories adapted from Batman comic books:

- The Official Adventures Of Batman And Robin:
  - The Legend of Batman and Robin
  - The Penguin's Plunder
  - The Joker's Revenge
- More Official Adventures of Batman & Robin:
  - The Marriage of Batman and Batwoman
  - The Fake Boy Wonder
  - When Batman Became a Coward

Throughout the 1970s Batman was the subject of a number of Power Records Book-and-record sets, as well as records unaccompanied by books:

45 rpm book and record sets:

- Batman: Stacked Cards
- Batman: Robin Meets Man-Bat

7" 33 1/3rpm records no comic:

- Batman: If Music be the Food of Death
- Batman: The Scarecrow's Mirages
- Batman: Catwoman's Revenge

33 1/3 rpm 12 book and record sets:

- Batman: Gorilla City & Mystery of the Scarecrow Corpse
- Batman (Collects Stacked Cards, The Scarecrow's Mirage, Challenge of the Catwoman, If Music Be the Food of Death)
- Batman (Collects Robin Meets Man Bat, Gorilla City, Mystery of the Scarecrow Corpse, The Catwoman's Revenge)
- A Super Hero Christmas (segment Batman: Christmas Carol Caper)

The 1980 mini-series, *The Untold Legend of the Batman* was available in a special "MPI Audio Edition." Each of the three issues were accompanied by an audio cassette containing a performance of the text of the issue, with musical cues.

As part of its DC Superheroes collection, in 1982 Fisher-Price released *Batman: The Case of the Laughing Sphinx*, an audio cassette accompanied by a hard back illustrated book.

In 2007, the audiobook publisher GraphicAudio licensed DC Comics properties to adapt as audiodramas. They have produced three adaptations of Batman novels: *Batman: Dead White* by John

Shirley, *Batman: Inferno* by Alex Irvine, and Alan Grant's *Batman: The Stone King*. Batman also appears as a supporting cast member in the GraphicAudio's adaptations of *Crisis on Infinite Earths*, *Infinite Crisis* and *JLA: Exterminators*.

Musical theatre

While a parody of a *Batman* musical was featured in one of the most recent series' comics, in 2002, Jim Steinman, David Ives, and Tim Burton had worked on a theatre production called *Batman: The Musical* although it was ultimately cancelled. Steinman has recently revealed five songs from the musical. The first is the opening theme for "Gotham City" and the entry of Batman with his tortured solo "The Graveyard Shift"; followed by "The Joker's Song (Where Does He Get All Those Wonderful Toys?)", "The Catwoman's Song (I Need All The Love I Can Get)", "We're Still The Children We Once Were" (the climactic sequence) and "In The Land Of The Pig The Butcher Is King", sung by the corrupt blood-suckers ruling Gotham, recently covered on the Meat Loaf album *Bat Out of Hell III: The Monster Is Loose*. These songs can be heard at the *Batman: The Musical* memorial site, *Dark Knight of the Soul*[1]

A Batman musical is also parodied in the animated series *Batman Beyond*. The episode "Out of the Past", (first aired October 21, 2000) opens with Bruce Wayne and Terry McGinnis attending a performance of (a fictional) *Batman: The Musical*, featuring caricatures of prominent members of the Rogues Gallery (the Joker, the Penguin, Two-Face, Catwoman, Poison Ivy, and Harley Quinn). Series creator Paul Dini, who wrote the episode in question, also wrote a song for the fictitious musical entitled *Superstitious and Cowardly Lot*.

An episode of the sketch comedy show *MADtv* also featured a *Batman: The Musical* parody called *Batman V: Out of the Cave* which starred Tommy Tune as Batman, and Ben Vereen as Robin.

Video games

Main article: List of Batman video games

Several Batman video games were created:

- *Batman* (1986) for the ZX Spectrum, MSX and Amstrad PCW. Now known as *Batman 3D*.
- *Batman: The Caped Crusader* (1988) for various 8-bit and 16-bit platforms.
- *Batman* (1989) for Mega Drive/Sega Genesis, Nintendo Entertainment System (NES), Atari Lynx, Commodore Amiga, Sinclair ZX Spectrum and other platforms. (In October 1989, the Amiga 500 was bundled with this game as part of the *Batman Pack*, which was sold in the United Kingdom and was a phenomenal success).
- *Batman: Return of the Joker* (1991) for Nintendo Entertainment System (NES) and Game Boy.
- *Batman Returns* (1993) for Nintendo Entertainment System (NES), Super NES, Mega Drive/Sega Genesis, Sega CD, Sega Game Gear, and Atari Lynx.

- *Batman: The Animated Series* (1993) for Game Boy.
- *Batman & Robin: The Animated Series* (1993) for Game Gear.
- *The Adventures of Batman & Robin* (1994) for Super NES, Mega Drive/Sega Genesis, Sega CD, and Sega Game Gear.
- *Batman Forever* (1996) for Super Nintendo (Super NES), Game Boy, Mega Drive/Sega Genesis, and Sega Game Gear.
- *Batman Forever: The Arcade Game* (1996) for Arcade, PlayStation and Sega Saturn.
- *Batman & Robin* (1997) for the Tiger Game.com and the PlayStation.
- *Batman Beyond: Return of the Joker* (2000) for the Nintendo 64 and the PlayStation.
- *Batman: Chaos in Gotham* (2001) for Game Boy Color.
- *Batman: Gotham City Racer* (2001) A racing game for the PlayStation.
- *Batman Vengeance* (2001) for the Nintendo GameCube, PlayStation 2, PC, Game Boy Advance and Xbox.
- *Batman: Dark Tomorrow* (2003) for Xbox and Nintendo GameCube
- *Batman: Rise of Sin Tzu* (2004) for the PlayStation 2, PC, Xbox, the Nintendo GameCube and Game Boy Advance.
- *Batman Begins* (2005) for the PlayStation 2, Xbox, Nintendo GameCube and Game Boy Advance (2005).
- *Lego Batman: The Video Game* (2008) A video game in the style of *Lego Star Wars* based on the LEGO Batman toyline. (vocals by Steven Blum.)
- *The Dark Knight* (cancelled) Planned video game based on the 2008 box office smash, to be released in 2009. Was cancelled after the bankruptcy of the Pandemic studio working on it.
- *Batman: Arkham Asylum* (2009) for the Xbox 360, PlayStation 3, and Windows PC.
- *Batman: The Brave and the Bold – The Videogame* (2010) for the Wii and Nintendo DS.
- *Batman: Arkham City* (2011) The sequel to *Batman: Arkham Asylum*. For the Xbox 360, PlayStation 3, and Windows PC.

Batman appears in the *Justice League Task Force* Super Nintendo fighting game, a couple of *Justice League* games for Game Boy Advance, and an arcade game based on Tim Burton's original movie. Also, the 16-bit Sega game *The Revenge of Shinobi* features a (non-authorized) Batman as a boss. The 8-bit Nintendo Entertainment System game *Final Fantasy* features "Badman", a character with strong resemblances to Batman, as one of the enemies of the final area. He appears in the *Justice League Heroes* game for PS2, Xbox, and PSP and has appeared in the crossover game *Mortal Kombat vs. DC Universe*. In the trailer for the story of the game, Batman sees the merging of the two Earths and faces off against Sub-Zero (his counterpart from Mortal Kombat Universe) in the Batcave. Batman's Brutality is where he throws a Batarang at the opponent which begins emitting sonic shouts, attracting a swarm of bats that begin antagonizing the opponent, causing them to fall over and try and fight them off.

Games, action figures, and other toys

Main article: Batman action figures

Batman is one of the few fictional characters that can be defined by his toys and merchandising. The first boom started in 1966 during the hit television series, and since then, along with every major movie or cartoon series has come a wave of toys, collectibles, and just about any other merchandise imaginable. Over the years, hundreds of Batman action figures, die-cast models, and other miscellaneous items have reserved the store shelves. Of the many companies that have acquired the rights to make Batman merchandise, some of the most well known include:

- Ideal - Captain Action
- Mego - Action figures and dolls
- Corgi - Die-cast metal vehicles
- Remco - Playsets and roleplaying toys
- Toy Biz - Action figures
- Ertl - Die-cast figures & vehicles and model kits
- Applause - PVC figures and dolls
- Hasbro - Action figures
- Monogram - Bobble heads
- Mattel - Action figures and jigsaw puzzles
- Lego - Building bricks and minifigures

Batman has appeared as a HeroClix figure along with other Batman characters in the following HeroClix sets:

- Hypertime
- Cosmic Justice
- Unleashed
- Legacy
- Icons

For April 2006, Lego introduced a Batman line which also includes characters such as the Joker and Two-Face, at American International Toy Fair.

Theme park attractions

Main article: Batman amusement rides and stunt shows

Several Six Flags theme parks, formerly owned by Warner Bros., opened live-action "Batman Stunt Shows" as the movies increased in popularity. The now closed Six Flags Astroworld in Houston, Texas was home to a standing roller coaster known as Batman: The Escape. Six Flags Over Texas in Arlington, Texas is home to two roller coasters called Mr. Freeze (Six Flags Over Texas), and Batman: The Ride. Six Flags México in Mexico City, Mexico has also a looping, suspended roller coaster named Batman: The Ride (Six Flags St. Louis has the same ride, as does Six Flags Great America in Gurnee, Illinois) as well as twin roller coasters named Batman and Robin: The Chiller. On the latter attraction, riders may ride on either the Batman or Robin versions of the coaster. But unfortunately in the 2007 off-season, the ride was removed after a long history of technical difficulties and occasionally breaking down. Six Flags Over Georgia contains a Gotham City area that contains the same Batman: The Ride and also features a looping coaster called The Mindbender that was adapted to fit the color tone of the Riddler after *Batman Forever* came out to fit the Gotham City section of the park it shares with Batman: The Ride. Six Flags Magic Mountain in Valencia, California has two Batman-themed coasters, the suspended coaster Batman: The Ride, and The Riddler's Revenge, a stand-up type roller coaster. This Six Flags park also features an entire themed area called "Gotham City" complete with architecture to match that of the fictional Gotham City. Warner Bros. Movie World in the Gold Coast, Australia, also has two Batman-themed rides. Batman Adventure - The Ride, revamped in 2001, is a motion simulator style simulator ride while Batwing Spaceshot is a vertical free-fall ride.

In 2008, The Dark Knight Coaster opened in Six Flags Great Adventure and Six Flags Great America. Based on *The Dark Knight* film, they are Wild Mouse roller coasters, indoors, heavily themed, and give riders a feeling that they are being stalked by the Joker. Six Flags New England was originally going to receive this roller coaster; however, due to problems with building permits, the park scratched the project.

See also
- List of Batman related topics
- Robin in other media
- Barbara Gordon in other media

External links
- Warner Bros. official Batman.com [2]
- Warner Bros. official Batman Shop [3]
- *Batman Begins* official site [4]
- The New Batman Adventures [5] — Official Warner Bros. site
- *Batman: The Animated Series* [6] — Official site
- *Batman Beyond* [7] — Official site
- *Dark Knight of the Soul (Batman: The Musical Memorial)* [1] — Collects all known information about this canceled project, as well as Steinman's demo recordings
- Batman Films and TV series [8] at the Internet Movie Database
- Encyclopedia of Television [9]

Batman in film

The fictional character Batman, a comic book superhero featured in DC Comics publications, has appeared in various films since his inception. The character first starred in two serial films in the 1940s, *Batman* and *Batman and Robin*. The character also appeared in the 1966 film *Batman*, which was a feature film adaptation of the campy 1960s *Batman* TV series starring Adam West, who also starred in the film.

Toward the end of the 1980s, the Warner Bros. studio began producing a series of feature films starring Batman, beginning with the 1989 film *Batman*, directed by Tim Burton with Batman played by Michael Keaton. Burton and Keaton reprised their roles for the 1992 film *Batman Returns*, and in 1995, Joel Schumacher directed *Batman Forever* with Val Kilmer as Batman. Schumacher also directed the 1997 film *Batman & Robin*, which starred George Clooney. *Batman & Robin* was poorly received by both the critics and the fans, and after a long hiatus in which multiple possible Batman scripts were developed, Warner Bros. rebooted the film franchise in 2005 with *Batman Begins*, directed by Christopher Nolan and starring Christian Bale. Nolan also directed the 2008 sequel *The Dark Knight* with Bale reprising his role. A third installment is in pre-production and will be released in Summer 2012.

Batman has also appeared in multiple animated films, both as a starring character and as an ensemble character. While most animated films were released direct-to-video, the 1993 animated feature *Batman: Mask of the Phantasm* was released theatrically.

1940s film serials

Batman (1943 serial)

Main article: Batman (serial)

Batman was a 15-chapter serial film released in 1943 by Columbia Pictures. The serial starred Lewis Wilson as Batman and Douglas Croft as Robin. J. Carrol Naish played the villain, an original character named Dr. Daka. Rounding out the cast were Shirley Patterson as Linda Page (Bruce Wayne's love interest), and William Austin as Alfred. The plot is based on Batman, a US government agent, attempting to defeat the Japanese agent Dr. Daka, at the height of World War II.

The film is notable for being the first filmed appearance of Batman and for providing two core elements of the Batman mythos. The film introduced "The Bat's Cave" and the Grandfather clock entrance. The name was altered to the Batcave in the comic. William Austin, who played Alfred, had a trim physique and sported a thin mustache, while the contemporary comic book version of Alfred was overweight and clean-shaven prior to the serial's release. The comics version of Alfred was altered to match that of Austin's, and has stayed that way.

Batman and Robin (1949 serial)

Main article: Batman and Robin (serial)

Batman and Robin was another 15-chapter serial film released in 1949 by Columbia Pictures. Robert Lowery played Batman, while Johnny Duncan played Robin. Supporting players included Jane Adams as Vicki Vale and veteran character actor Lyle Talbot as Commissioner Gordon. The plot dealt with the Dynamic Duo facing off against the Wizard, a hooded villain whose identity remains a mystery throughout the serial until the end.

1960s theatrical film

Batman (1966)

Main article: Batman (1966 film)

Batman (also known as *Batman: The Movie*) is a 1966 film adaptation of the popular *Batman* television series, and was the first full-length theatrical adaptation of the DC Comics character. The 20th Century Fox release starred Adam West as Batman and Burt Ward as Robin. As well as Cesar Romero as the Joker, Burgess Meredith as the Penguin, Lee Meriwether as Catwoman, and Frank Gorshin as the Riddler.

The film was directed by Leslie H. Martinson, who also directed a pair of *Batman* episodes; "The Penguin Goes Straight" and "Not Yet, He Ain't," both from season one.

Warner Bros. live-action productions

Development

In the late 1970s, Batman's popularity was waning. CBS was interested in producing a *Batman in Outer Space* film. Producers Michael Uslan and Benjamin Melniker purchased the film rights of Batman from DC Comics in April 1979. It was Uslan's wish "to make the definitive, dark, serious version of Batman, the way Bob Kane and Bill Finger had envisioned him in 1939. A creature of the night; stalking criminals in the shadows." Richard Maibaum was approached to write a script with Guy Hamilton to direct, but the two turned down the offer. Uslan was unsuccessful with pitching *Batman* to various movie studios because they wanted the film to be similar to the campy 1960s TV series. Columbia Pictures and United Artists were among those to turn down the film.

A disappointed Uslan then wrote a script titled *Return of the Batman* to give the film industry a better idea of his vision for the film. Uslan later compared its dark tone to that of *The Dark Knight Returns*, which his script pre-dated by six years. In November 1979, producers Jon Peters and Peter Guber joined the project. The four producers felt it was best to pattern the film's development after that of *Superman* (1978). Uslan, Melniker and Guber pitched *Batman* to Universal Pictures, but the studio turned it down. Though no movie studios were yet involved, in late 1981 the project was publicly announced with a budget of $15 million. Warner Bros. decided to accept *Batman*.

Tom Mankiewicz completed a script titled *The Batman* in June 1983, focusing on Batman and Dick Grayson's origins, with the Joker and Rupert Thorne as villains, and Silver St. Cloud as the romantic interest. Mankiewicz took inspiration from the limited series *Batman: Strange Apparitions* (ISBN 1-56389-500-5), written by Steve Englehart. Comic book artist Marshall Rogers, who worked with Englehart on *Strange Apparitions*, was hired for concept art. *The Batman* was then announced in late 1983 for a mid-1985 release date on a budget of $20 million. Originally, Uslan had wanted an unknown actor for Batman, William Holden for James Gordon, and David Niven as Alfred Pennyworth. Holden died in 1981 and Niven in 1983, so this would never come to pass. A number of filmmakers were attached to Mankiewicz' script, including Ivan Reitman and Joe Dante. Nine rewrites were performed by nine separate writers. Most of them were based on *Strange Apparitions*. However it was Mankiewicz' script that was still being used to guide the project.

Batman (1989)

Main article: Batman (1989 film)

Tim Burton took over as director in 1986. Steve Englehart and Julie Hickson wrote film treatments before Sam Hamm wrote the first screenplay. Numerous A-list actors were considered for the role of Batman before Michael Keaton was cast. Keaton's casting caused a controversy since, by 1988, Keaton had become typecast as a comedic actor and many observers doubted he could portray a serious role. Jack Nicholson accepted the role of the Joker under strict conditions that dictated a high salary, a portion of the box office profits and his shooting schedule. Nicholson's final salary is reported to be as high as $50 million. Principal photography took place at Pinewood Studios from October 1988 to January 1989. The budget escalated from $30 million to $48 million, while the 1988 Writers Guild of America strike forced Hamm to drop out. Uncredited rewrites were performed by Warren Skaaren, Charles McKeown and Jonathan Gems. *Batman* received positive reviews, broke numerous box office records, and won the Academy Award for Best Art Direction. The film grossed over $400 million, and left a legacy over the modern perception of the superhero film genre.

Batman Returns (1992)

Main article: Batman Returns

Burton originally did not want to direct a sequel because of his mixed emotions of the previous film. Sam Hamm's first script had Penguin and Catwoman searching for hidden treasure. Daniel Waters delivered a script that satisfied Burton, which convinced him to reprise his duties as director. Wesley Strick did an uncredited rewrite, deleting characterizations of Harvey Dent and Robin and rewriting the climax. Various A-list actresses lobbied hard for the role of Catwoman before Michelle Pfeiffer was cast, while Danny DeVito signed on to portray the Penguin. Filming started at Warner Bros. in

Burbank, California in June 1991. *Batman Returns* was released with financial success, but Warner Bros. was disappointed with the film's box office run because it earned less than its predecessor. However, *Batman Returns* was released with generally positive reviews, but a "parental backlash" criticized the film with violence and sexual innuendos that were unsuitable for children. McDonald's shut down their Happy Meal tie-in for *Batman Returns*. The film's legacy is also notable for leaving behind what would become the critically-panned *Catwoman* spin-off.

Batman Forever (1995)

Main article: Batman Forever

Although *Batman Returns* was a financial success, Warner Bros. felt the film should have made more money. The studio decided to change the direction of the *Batman* film series to be more mainstream. Joel Schumacher replaced Tim Burton as director, while Burton decided to stay on as producer. However, Michael Keaton did not like the new direction the film series was heading in, and was replaced by Val Kilmer. Chris O'Donnell was introduced as Robin, Jim Carrey starred as The Riddler, while Tommy Lee Jones starred as Two-Face. Filming started in September 1994, and Schumacher encountered problems communicating with Kilmer and Jones. *Batman Forever* was released on June 16, 1995 with financial success, earning over $350 million worldwide and three Academy Award nominations, but the film was met with mixed reviews from critics.

Batman & Robin (1997)

Main article: Batman & Robin (film)

Development for *Batman & Robin* started immediately after *Batman Forever*, and Warner Bros. commissioned the film on fast track for an adamant June 1997 release. Val Kilmer did not return, because of scheduling conflicts with *The Saint*, and was replaced by George Clooney. Arnold Schwarzenegger starred as Mr. Freeze, while Uma Thurman starred as Poison Ivy. Chris O'Donnell reprised his role as Robin. Principal photography began in September 1996 and finished in January 1997, two weeks ahead of the shooting schedule. *Batman & Robin* was released on June 20, 1997, and was critically panned. Observers criticized the film for its toyetic and campy approach, and for homosexual innuendos added by Schumacher. Still, the film was a financial success, but remains to be the least commercially successful live-action Batman film ever. *Batman & Robin* received numerous nominations at the Razzie Awards and ranks among the worst superhero films of all time.

Proposals for fifth film

Batman Triumphant

During the filming of *Batman & Robin*, Warner Bros. was impressed with the dailies. This prompted them to immediately hire Joel Schumacher to return as director for a sequel, but writer Akiva Goldsman, who worked on *Batman Forever* and *Batman & Robin* with Schumacher, turned down the chance to write the script. In late 1996, Warner Bros. and Schumacher hired Mark Protosevich to write the script for a fifth *Batman* film. A projected mid-1999 release date was announced. Titled *Batman Triumphant*, Protosevich's script had the Scarecrow as the main villain. The Joker would return as a hallucination in Batman's mind caused by the Scarecrow's fear toxin. Harley Quinn appeared as a supporting character, written as the Joker's daughter trying to get revenge on Batman for the Joker's death. George Clooney and Chris O'Donnell were set to reprise the roles of Batman and Robin. However, when *Batman & Robin* received negative reviews and failed to outgross any of its predecessors, Warner Bros. was unsure of their plans for *Batman Triumphant*. The studio decided it was best to consider a live-action *Batman Beyond* film and an adaptation of Frank Miller's *Batman: Year One*. Warner Bros. would then greenlight whichever idea suited them the most. Schumacher felt he "owe[d] the Batman culture a real *Batman* movie. I would go back to the basics and make a dark portrayal of the Dark Knight." He approached Warner Bros. of doing *Batman: Year One* in mid-1998.

Batman: DarKnight

Despite Warner Bros. and Schumacher's interest with *Year One*, Lee Shapiro, a comic book fan, and Stephen Wise pitched the studio with a script titled *Batman: DarKnight* in mid-1998. *DarKnight* had Bruce Wayne giving up his crime fighting career and Dick Grayson attending Gotham University. Dr. Jonathan Crane uses his position as professor of psychology at Gotham University and as head psychiatrist at Arkham Asylum to conduct his experiments into fear (this element would later appear in *Batman Begins*). During a vengeful confrontation with a colleague, Dr. Kirk Langstrom, Crane unknowingly initiates Kirk's transformation into the creature known as Man-Bat. Citizens of Gotham believe Man-Bat's nightly activities to be Batman's "bloodthirsty" return. Bruce becomes Batman "to clear his name" and solve the mystery of Man-Bat. Kirk struggles with his "man vs. monster" syndrome as he longs to both reunite with his wife and get revenge on Crane, while Crane exacts revenge on those responsible for his dismissal from both Arkham and the university while encountering truths about his past. Warner Bros. decided not to move forward, and passed on *Batman: DarKnight* in favor of *Year One* and *Batman Beyond*.

Year One and *Beyond*

In January 2000, Scott Rosenberg turned down the chance to write the script for *Batman: Year One*. In mid-2000, Paul Dini, Neal Stephenson and Boaz Yakin were hired to write a script for *Batman Beyond*, with Yakin to direct. The film was based on the Warner Bros. animated television series of the same name. However, Warner Bros. abandoned *Batman Beyond* almost instantly in favor of *Batman: Year One*.

Around the same time, Warner Bros. hired Darren Aronofsky to write and direct *Year One*, despite interest from Joel Schumacher. Aronofsky, who collaborated with Frank Miller on an unproduced script for *Ronin*, brought Miller to co-write *Year One* with him. They intended to reboot the *Batman* franchise, "it's *somewhat* based on the comic book," Aronofsky said. "Toss out everything you can imagine about Batman! Everything! We're starting completely anew." Regular Aronofsky collaborator, Matthew Libatique, was set as cinematographer, and Aronofsky had also approached Christian Bale for the role of Batman. Coincidentally, Bale would be cast in the role for *Batman Begins*. At the same time, Warner Bros. was moving forward on a *Catwoman* spin-off. However, by June 2002, the studio decided to move forward on *Batman vs. Superman* and abandon *Year One*.

Batman vs. Superman

Warner Bros. abandoned J. J. Abrams' script for *Superman: Flyby*, which had been greenlighted with McG to direct. When McG dropped out in favor of *Charlie's Angels: Full Throttle*, Warner Bros. approached Wolfgang Petersen to direct *Superman: Flyby*, however, in August 2001, Andrew Kevin Walker pitched Warner Bros. an idea titled *Batman vs Superman*, attaching Petersen as director. *Superman: Flyby* was put on hold, and Akiva Goldsman was hired to rewrite Walker's *Batman vs. Superman*.

Goldsman's draft, dated June 21, 2002, had Bruce Wayne going through a mental breakdown after his five year retirement of crime fighting. Dick Grayson, Alfred Pennyworth and Commissioner Gordon are all dead, but Bruce's depressed emotions become resolved with fiancée Elizabeth Miller. Meanwhile, Clark Kent is struggling by a recent divorce with Lois Lane. Clark and Bruce are close friends, and Clark is Bruce's best man. After the Joker kills Elizabeth at the honeymoon, Bruce plots a revenge scheme, while Clark tries to hold him back. In return, Bruce blames Clark for her death, and the two go against one another. Part of the script took place in Smallville, where Clark goes into exile with Lana Lang. However, Lex Luthor is held to be responsible for the entire plot of Batman and Superman destroying each other. The two decide to team up and stop Luthor.

Christian Bale and Josh Hartnett had turned down the roles of Batman and Superman. Bale would eventually portray the same role in *Batman Begins*. Principal photography was to start in early-2003, with plans for a five–six month shoot. The release date was set for mid-2004. Within a month of Warner Bros. greenlighting *Batman vs. Superman*, Petersen left in favor of *Troy* (2004). Warner Bros. decided to move forward on *Superman: Flyby* and on a *Batman* reboot. Petersen and Bryan Singer are interested in directing the project sometime in the future, with Bale as Batman.

Aftermath

In December 2002, writer/filmmaker Joss Whedon pitched an origin story that was met with negative feedback from Warner Bros. Whedon's version had "a Hannibal Lecter-type villain in Arkham Asylum that Bruce went and sort of studied with," Whedon said. "It was set in Bruce's early years in Gotham City. I get very emotional about it, I still love the story. Maybe I'll get to do it as a comic one day." In January 2003, Christopher Nolan was hired to take over the *Batman* franchise, resulting in the rebooted *Batman Begins*.

Batman Begins (2005)

Main article: Batman Begins

Director/writer Christopher Nolan and co-writer David S. Goyer began work on *Batman Begins* in early 2003 and aimed for a darker and more realistic tone, with humanity and realism being the basis of the film. The film, which was primarily shot in England and Chicago, relied on traditional stunts and scale models — computer-generated imagery was used minimally. Christian Bale starred as Batman. Liam Neeson starred as Ra's al Ghul (albeit masquerading as Henri Ducard) and Cillian Murphy starred as The Scarecrow. Katie Holmes also starred in the movie as Bruce's love interest, Rachel Dawes. A new Batmobile (called the Tumbler) and a more mobile Batsuit were both created specifically for the film. *Batman Begins* was critically and commercially successful. The film opened on June 15, 2005 in the United States and Canada in 3,858 theaters. It grossed US$48 million in its opening weekend, eventually earning $370 million worldwide. The film received an 84% overall approval rating from Rotten Tomatoes, and was nominated for the Academy Award for Best Cinematography. Critics noted that fear was a common theme throughout the film, and remarked that it had a darker tone compared to previous *Batman* films. *Batman Begins* has also popularized the notion of reboots in Hollywood.

The Dark Knight (2008)

Main article: The Dark Knight (film)

Christopher Nolan reprised his duties as director, and brought his brother, Jonathan, to co-write the script. *The Dark Knight* featured Christian Bale reprising his role as Batman/Bruce Wayne, Heath Ledger as The Joker and Aaron Eckhart as Harvey Dent / Two-Face. Principal photography began in April 2007 in Chicago. Other locations included Pinewood Studios and Hong Kong. On January 22, 2008, after he had completed filming *The Dark Knight*, Ledger died of a sleeping pill overdose, leading to intense attention from the press and more people showing interest in the film. Warner Bros. had created a viral marketing campaign for *The Dark Knight*, developing promotional websites and trailers highlighting screen shots of Ledger as the Joker, but after Ledger's death, the studio refocused its promotional campaign. The film was released on July 16, 2008 (in Australia) and July 18, 2008 (in

North America); the film was met with positive reviews upon release, and became the second film ever to earn more than $500 million at the box office, the fourth film to gross over a billion dollars worldwide, and set numerous other records in the process. It received eight Academy Award nominations, and at the 81st Academy Awards it won two: Best Sound Editing and Best Supporting Actor (a posthumous win for Heath Ledger), making it the second Batman film ever to win at the Academy Awards.

Untitled third installment (2012)

Warner Bros. president of production Jeff Robinov hopes a third film will be released in 2011 or 2012. Nolan had originally not committed to another sequel, explaining that he does not normally line up projects right after completing a film, noting "Is there a story that's going to keep me emotionally invested for the couple of years that it will take to make another one? That's the overriding question. On a more superficial level, I have to ask the question: How many good third movies in a franchise can people name?" He added the only reason he would return would be if he found a necessary way to continue the story, but he feared midway through filming another installment he would find it redundant. Nolan had written a rough story outline and made some notes by December 2008, despite his uncertainty in returning for the sequel. Later in December, Alan F. Horn confirmed that while discussions with Nolan about a third film were ongoing, no casting had been done, and Horn categorically denied all such rumors.

Before Nolan confirmed his involvement, Gary Oldman had said he was confident Nolan would return. Oldman hinted that, in the third film, Commissioner Gordon would have to "hunt down Batman". He has also speculated that the villain of the upcoming film might be the Riddler. Nolan explained that as long as he is directing, Robin will not be appearing in the franchise because Bale is still portraying a "young Batman", which meant "Robin's not for a few films". Christian Bale said he would leave the franchise if Robin was introduced. In addition, Nolan considers the Penguin difficult to portray on film, explaining, "There are certain characters that are easier to mesh with the more real take on Batman we're doing. The Penguin would be tricky."

Gary Oldman, while taking questions from an audience at the 2009 San Diego Comic Con, was asked about a third film, in which he replied, "We start shooting next year. You didn't hear that from me." He subsequently clarified his comment, saying, "... well, I'm sure they want to do another one... it might [be] 2 or 3 years." However, in 2009, Michael Caine had told MTV News that the film was not being worked on and he did not know any details. On February 9, 2010, it was announced that Christopher Nolan has "cracked" the story of a sequel to *The Dark Knight* and has committed to return to that project. Jonathan Nolan and David S. Goyer worked on the script for the upcoming film.

On March 10, 2010, Nolan confirmed his involvement in the project and gave some information regarding the story. The next *Batman* film will be Nolan's last and a conclusion to the story. Nolan says, "Without getting into specifics, the key thing that makes the third film a great possibility for us is that we want to finish our story. And in viewing it as the finishing of a story rather than infinitely blowing up the balloon and expanding the story . . . I'm very excited about the end of the film, the conclusion, and what we've done with the characters. My brother has come up with some pretty exciting stuff. Unlike the comics, these things don't go on forever in film and viewing it as a story with an end is useful. Viewing it as an ending, that sets you very much on the right track about the appropriate conclusion and the essence of what tale we're telling. And it hearkens back to that priority of trying to find the reality in these fantastic stories. That's what we do." Nolan has also confirmed that Jonathan Nolan is writing the script and that the villain of the film "won't be Mr. Freeze."

In April 2010, Warner Bros. announced the film will be released on July 20, 2012. In June 2010, Nolan confirmed that the Joker will not return in the third film. On June 30, 2010, Nolan confirmed that the script written by Jonathan Nolan has been finished. The film will begin shooting in April 2011. Christopher Nolan's long-time cinematographer Wally Pfister has expressed interest in shooting the entirety of the next Batman movie in the IMAX format, as both Pfister and Nolan have expressed distaste for shooting the film in 3-D. Nolan has confirmed that he will be directing the film and stated that he is currently polishing Jonathan Nolan's screenplay.

Without a finished story in place, casting at this stage cannot be attributed to anything beyond rumor or suggestion. Bale said he would return if Nolan did. Aaron Eckhart had expressed his enthusiasm that he would reprise his role for a sequel if asked, although he later confirmed that, in talks with Nolan, the director confirmed his character is dead. Nolan confirmed that the ensemble cast from the first two films will be returning. On October 13, 2010, it was reported that Tom Hardy has been cast in an unnamed role.

Animated films

DC Animated Universe

Main article: DC animated universe

- 1993: *Batman: Mask of the Phantasm*, a theatrical feature based on *Batman: The Animated Series*.
- 1998: *Batman & Mr. Freeze: SubZero*, a direct-to-video feature also based on *Batman: The Animated Series*.
- 2000: *Batman Beyond: Return of the Joker*, a direct-to-video feature based on *Batman Beyond*.
- 2003: *Batman: Mystery of the Batwoman*, a direct-to-video feature based on *The New Batman Adventures*.

The DVD of the three part *Starcrossed* story arc from the *Justice League* animated series was labelled *Starcrossed: The Movie*. A similar case was applied with the three-part episode of *Superman: The Animated Series*, *World's Finest*, which was released as *The Batman/Superman Movie*.

Batman in film

The Batman

Main article: The Batman (TV series)

- 2005: *The Batman vs. Dracula*, a direct-to-video feature.

DC Universe Animated Original Movies

Main article: DC Universe Animated Original Movies

- 2008: *Justice League: The New Frontier*, based on the comic book
- 2008: *Batman: Gotham Knight*, a collection of six short films based on *Batman Begins* and *The Dark Knight*
- 2009: *Superman/Batman: Public Enemies*, based on the comic book
- 2010: *Justice League: Crisis on Two Earths*, inspired by *JLA: Earth 2*
- 2010: *Batman: Under the Red Hood*, based on *Batman: Under the Hood*
- 2010: *Superman/Batman: Apocalypse*, based on the comic book

Note that DC Universe Animated Original Movies are in fact each set in *separate* fictional universes, with the possible exception of the Superman/Batman films.

Cast and characters

Main article: List of Batman films cast members

Reception

Box office performance

Film	Release date		Box office revenue			Box office ranking		Budget	Reference
	United States	Worldwide	Domestic	Foreign	Worldwide	All time domestic	All time worldwide		
Batman	June 23, 1989	June 23, 1989	$251,188,924	$160,160,000	$411,348,924	#58 #49(A)	#121	$35,000,000	
Batman Returns	June 19, 1992	June 19, 1992	$162,831,698	$103,990,656	$266,822,354	#173 #162(A)	#276	$80,000,000	
Batman: Mask of the Phantasm	December 25, 1993	December 25, 1993	$5,617,391			#4,304			
Batman Forever	June 16, 1995	June 16, 1995	$184,031,112	$152,498,032	$336,529,144	#125 #134(A)	#187	$100,000,000	

Batman & Robin	June 20, 1997	June 20, 1997	$107,325,195	$130,881,927	$238,207,122	#400	#329	$125,000,000
Batman Begins	June 15, 2005	June 15, 2005	$205,343,774	$167,366,241	$372,710,015	#103	#145	$150,000,000
The Dark Knight	July 18, 2008	July 16, 2008	$533,345,358	$468,576,467	$1,001,921,825	#3 #28[(A)]	#7	$185,000,000
Total			$1,449,683,452	$1,183,473,323	$2,633,156,775			$675,000,000

List indicator(s)

- A light grey cell indicates information is not available.
- [(A)] indicates the adjusted totals based on current ticket prices (calculated by Box Office Mojo).

Critical reaction

Film	Rotten Tomatoes		Metacritic	Yahoo! Movies
	Overall	Top Critics		
Batman	71% (51 reviews)	57% (7 reviews)	66 (17 reviews)	B- (5 reviews)
Batman Returns	78% (46 reviews)	67% (9 reviews)		B (5 reviews)
Batman: Mask of the Phantasm	87% (23 reviews)			
Batman Forever	43% (54 reviews)	71% (14 reviews)	51 (23 reviews)	B- (9 reviews)
Batman & Robin	11% (62 reviews)	19% (16 reviews)	28 (21 reviews)	C- (9 reviews)
Batman Begins	84% (257 reviews)	60% (43 reviews)	70 (41 reviews)	B+ (15 reviews)
The Dark Knight	93% (275 reviews)	91% (44 reviews)	82 (39 reviews)	A- (14 reviews)
Average ratings	**67%**	**61%**	**59**	**N/A**

See also

- Batman franchise media
- Category:Batman fan films

External links

- "Batman Battle" [1] at Box Office Mojo
- *Batman film series* [2] at Allmovie
- *Batman: Year One* news archive [3]
- Michael Fleming (October 2000). "George Clooney Pitches the Next *Batman*" [4]. *Movieline*.
- Marc Graser (2009-07-25). "WB still seeking DC strategy" [5]. *Variety*.

The Batman Serial

Batman (serial)

Batman	
Promotional poster	
Directed by	Lambert Hillyer
Produced by	Rudolph C. Flothow
Written by	Victor McLeod Leslie Swabacker Harry L. Fraser Bob Kane *(character)*
Starring	Lewis Wilson Douglas Croft J. Carrol Naish Shirley Patterson
Music by	Lee Zahler
Cinematography	James S. Brown Jr.
Editing by	Dwight Caldwell Earl Turner
Distributed by	Columbia Pictures
Release date(s)	April 15, 1943 (United States)
Running time	15 chapters (260 minutes)
Country	United States
Language	English
Followed by	*Batman and Robin*

Batman was a 15-chapter serial released in 1943 by Columbia Pictures. The serial starred Lewis Wilson as Batman and Douglas Croft as Robin. J. Carrol Naish played the villain, an original character named Dr. Daka. Rounding out the cast were Shirley Patterson as Linda Page (Bruce Wayne's love interest), and William Austin as Alfred the butler. The plot is based on Batman, a US government agent, attempting to defeat the Japanese agent Dr. Daka, at the height of World War II.

The film is notable for being the first filmed appearance of Batman and for providing two core elements of the Batman mythos. It introduced "The Bat's Cave" and its entrance through a grandfather clock, which subsequently appeared in the comics. The serial also had an effect on the depiction of the Alfred character in later *Batman* works. Alfred was overweight and clean-shaven in contemporary comics, but the later comics portrayed him as trim and sporting a thin mustache following William Austin's appearance. The serial was successful in its day, and was followed by a sequel, *Batman and Robin*, in 1949. However, its low production value and over-the-top action and dialogue caused later audiences and reviewers to find it ridiculous. It was re-released in 1965 to capitalize on its camp value. The re-released version, called *An Evening with Batman and Robin*, proved very popular, and its success inspired the intentionally campy *Batman* television series starring Adam West and Burt Ward.

Plot

The serial's plot deals with Batman and Robin's struggle against Dr. Daka, a Japanese scientist who has invented a device that turns people into pseudo-zombies.

Cast

- Lewis Wilson as Batman/Bruce Wayne
- Douglas Croft as Robin/Richard 'Dick' Grayson
- J. Carrol Naish as Dr. Tito Daka/Prince Daka
- Shirley Patterson as Linda Page
- William Austin as Alfred Pennyworth

Production

The film was made at the height of World War II, and like numerous works of popular American fiction of the time, contains anti-German and, in this case, anti-Japanese ethnic slurs and comments (in one scene, one of Daka's henchmen turns on him, saying, "That's the kind of answer that fits the color of your skin."). The film also suffered from a low budget, just like other contemporary serials. No attempt was made to create a bona fide Batmobile, so a black Cadillac was used by Bruce Wayne and Dick Grayson, as well as Batman and Robin. Alfred chauffeured the Dynamic Duo in both identities.

While many serials made changes during adaptation, to the extent that they were "often 'improved' almost out of recognition", Batman "fared better than most" and the changes were minor. A normal limousine replaced the Batmobile, the utility belts are present but unused and Batman is a secret government agent in this serial instead of an independent vigilante. This last change was due to the film censors, who would not allow the hero to be seen taking the law into his own hands.

Several continuity errors occur in the serial, such as Batman losing his cape in a fight but wearing it again after the film only briefly cut away.

Press releases announced it as a "Super Serial" and it was Columbia's largest-scale serial production to date. The studio gave it publicity campaign equivalent to a feature film.

Cliffhangers

The quality of the cliffhangers varies according to episode. Chapter ten ends with Batman in a plane crash. In the resolution, Batman simply staggers out of the wreckage, slightly dazed but otherwise unhurt. In the words of Jim Harmon and Donald Glut, this "might as well have been a silent comedy."

Release

Theatrical

Batman was first released in theaters on July 16, 1943.

In 1965, the serial was re-released in theaters as *An Evening with Batman and Robin*, in one complete marathon showing, to capitalize on its camp value. This re-release was successful enough that it inspired the creation of the 1960s television series *Batman*, series starring Adam West and Burt Ward, which was intentionally campy.

Home media

The serial was released on home video in the late 1980s in a heavily edited format that removed the offensive racial content. A reviewer for the magazine *Cinefantastique* commented, "The changes aren't surprising when you see that Columbia is now owned by Japan's Sony Corporation. It appears that some of Daka's operatives escaped Batman's justice and were rewarded with positions at the new George Orwell department at Columbia."[citation needed]

However, in 1989, the cable network The Comedy Channel (United States) aired the serial uncut and uncensored. The cable network American Movie Classics did the same in the early 1990s on Saturday mornings.

Sony released the serial on DVD in October 2005. The DVD release is an unedited version, with the exception of Chapter 2, which is missing its "next Chapter" sequence.

The serial was also released on home movie formats in the 1960s and 1970s:

The 1960s: A Silent abridged version. The complete serial edited into 6 Chapters (available in 8mm and Super-8) running 10 minutes each. Also a 7th 3-minute reel titled "Batman's Last Chance" with action scenes was also issued.

The 1970s: The complete 15 chapter serial (in its original unaltered format) was released in a Super-8 Sound edition.

Critical reception

Stedman notes that the serial "gained good press notices" but "scarcely deserves them," going on to describe it as an "unintentional farce." Harmon and Glut describe Batman as "one of the most ludicrous serials ever made" despite its "forthright simplicity." It was, nevertheless, popular enough for a sequel, Batman and Robin, to be approved. Lewis Wilson's face resembled that of Bruce Wayne and he played his part with sincerity. However, his physique was unathletic and "thick about the middle" while his voice was both too high and had a Boston accent. Both the actors and their stunt doubles lacked the "style and grace" of either the comic characters they were portraying or their equivalents at Republic Pictures. Although the Batman costume was based on his first appearance both costumes were unconvincing. The Batman costume was baggy and "topped by pair of devils horns."

Influence

An Evening with Batman and Robin was especially popular in college towns, where theaters were booked solid. The success of this led to the creation of the *Batman* series. The breathless opening and closing narration of each chapter in this and other Columbia serials was to some extent the model that was parodied in the series.

The success of both the re-release and the subsequent TV series prompted the production of another serial based series, the Green Hornet TV series. It was played as a straight action mystery series, "in the tradition of its former presentations," and was also very popular with audiences but lasted only one season due to significantly higher production costs. As a result, serial revivals were not believed to be possible at that time.

Although the serial was set in Gotham City and several references were made to various Gotham establishments, Bruce Wayne's address was given as "1918 Hill Road, Los Angeles, Calif."

Chapter titles

1. *The Electrical Brain*
2. *The Bat's Cave*
3. *The Mark of the Zombies*
4. *Slaves of the Rising Sun*
5. *The Living Corpse*
6. *Poison Peril*
7. *The Phoney Doctor*
8. *Lured by Radium*
9. *The Sign of the Sphinx*
10. *Flying Spies*
11. *A Nipponese Trap*

12. *Embers of Evil*
13. *Eight Steps Down*
14. *The Executioner Strikes*
15. *The Doom of the Rising Sun*

Source:

See also

- List of film serials
- List of film serials by studio
- List of films based on English-language comics

External links

- *Batman* [1] at the Internet Movie Database
- *Batman* [2] at Allmovie
- Batman Serials & Interviews @ Legions Of Gotham [3]
- Serials @ Batman: Yesterday, Today, & Beyond [4]
- Batman Site www.GothamCity.com.br [5]
- "BATMAN ON FILM" – The 40s Serials [6]

Lewis Wilson

Lewis Gilbert Wilson (January 28, 1920 - August 9, 2000) was an American actor from New York City who was most famous for being the first actor to play the DC Comics character Batman in live action (1943's *Batman*).

He graduated from Worcester Academy in Worcester, Massachusetts in 1939. His family had long roots with the school and his father and even grandfather were graduates. He left acting in order to support his family soon after the Batman series. He worked for General Foods for many years.

In retirement, he lived in North Hollywood, California. He died in Los Angeles, California, aged 80.

He was married to novelist and occasional actress Dana Broccoli (née Natol) (also deceased). Their son, film producer Michael G. Wilson, is best known for his work on the James Bond film series.

External links

- Lewis Wilson [1] at the Internet Movie Database

Batman and Robin Serial

Batman and Robin (serial)

Batman and Robin	
Screen capture	
Directed by	Spencer Gordon Bennet
Produced by	Sam Katzman
Written by	George H. Plympton Joseph F. Poland Royal K. Cole Bob Kane *(character)*
Starring	Robert Lowery Johnny Duncan Jane Adams Lyle Talbot Ralph Graves Don C. Harvey William Fawcett Leonard Penn
Music by	Mischa Bakaleinikoff
Cinematography	Ira H. Morgan
Editing by	Dwight Caldwell Earl Turner
Distributed by	Columbia Pictures
Release date(s)	May 26, 1949 (United States)
Running time	15 chapters (263 minutes)
Country	United States
Language	English
Preceded by	*Batman*

Batman and Robin (1949) is a 15-chapter serial released by Columbia Pictures.

Robert Lowery played Batman, while Johnny Duncan played Robin. Supporting players included Jane Adams as Vicki Vale and veteran character actor Lyle Talbot as Commissioner Gordon.

Plot

The plot dealt with the Dynamic Duo facing off against the Wizard, a hooded villain whose identity remains a mystery throughout the serial until the end.

Cast

- Robert Lowery as Batman/Bruce Wayne
- Johnny Duncan as Robin/Dick Grayson
- Jane Adams as Vicki Vale
- Lyle Talbot as Commissioner Jim Gordon
- Ralph Graves as Winslow Harrison
- Don C. Harvey as Nolan, a henchman
- William Fawcett as Professor Hammil
- Leonard Penn as Carter, Hammil's valet and The Wizard
- Rick Vallin as Barry Brown, a radio announcer
- Michael Whalen as Dunne, a private investigator
- Greg McClure as Evans, a henchman
- House Peters, Jr. as Earl, a henchman
- Jim Diehl as Jason, a henchman
- Rusty Wescoatt as Ives, a henchman
- Eric Wilton as Alfred Pennyworth, (uncredited)
- uncredited as Jimmie Vale, Vicki's brother and henchman

Production

"As usual on a Katzman production," note Harmon and Glut, "the low budget showed everywhere in money-saving shortcuts, and inadequacies." The Batman costume had a poorly fitting cowl and the Robin costume added pink tights to cover the "hairy-legs" of both the actor and stuntman. The Batmobile is again excluded, but instead of a limousine, as in the first serial, the duo drive around in a 1949 Mercury.

Several mistakes and failures of logic occur in the serial. One example of this is that the film shows the Batsignal working in broad daylight. Another occurs despite the fact that the heroes' utility belts had been replaced by normal belts for this serial, with no pockets or pouches. Nevertheless, in order to escape from a vault, Batman pulls the nozzle and hose of a oxy-acetylene torch from his belt to cut through a steel door. (The tanks for the torch are not shown.) To compound this mistake, it is a full-sized oxy-acetylene torch that would have been impossible to carry unseen on his person. Harmon and Glut suggest that this was probably scripted to be a miniaturised 3-inch torch, as used in the comics, but the film-makers improvised in following the directions for a "blowtorch".

Release

Home media

The serial was released on DVD in 2005 to promote *Batman Begins*.

Chapter titles

1. *Batman Takes Over*
2. *Tunnel of Terror*
3. *Robin's Wild Ride*
4. *Batman Trapped*
5. *Robin Rescues Batman*
6. *Target - Robin!*
7. *The Fatal Blast*
8. *Robin Meets the Wizard*
9. *The Wizard Strikes Back*
10. *Batman's Last Chance*
11. *Robin's Ruse*
12. *Robin Rides the Wind*
13. *The Wizard's Challenge*
14. *Batman vs. Wizard*
15. *Batman Victorious*

Source:

See also

- List of film serials
- List of film serials by studio
- List of films based on English-language comics

External links

- *Batman and Robin* [1] at the Internet Movie Database
- *Batman and Robin* [2] at Allmovie

Robert Lowery (actor)

Robert Lowery	
Born	Robert Larkin Hanks October 17, 1913 Kansas City, Missouri
Died	December 26, 1971 (aged 58) Los Angeles, California
Other names	Bob Lowery Bob Lowry
Occupation	Actor
Years active	1936-1967
Spouse	Jean Parker (1951-1957) (divorced) 1 son Vivan Wilcox (?-?) (divorced) Rusty Farrell (?-?) (divorced)

Robert Lowery (October 17, 1913 – December 26, 1971) was an American motion picture, television, and stage actor who appeared in over seventy films.

Early life

Born **Robert Larkin Hanks** in Kansas City, Missouri, Lowery grew up on Wayne Avenue near the long-demolished Electric Park. Lowery's father was a local attorney and oil investor who worked several years for the Pullman Corporation as a railroad agent; his mother, Leah Thompson Hanks, was a concert pianist.

He graduated from Paseo High School in Kansas City, and soon was invited to sing with the Slats Randall Orchestra in the early 1930s. Lowery played on the Kansas City Blues minor league baseball team and was overall considered a versatile athlete; his physique and strength was gained from a stint working in a paper factory as a teenager. After the death of his father in 1935, he traveled to Hollywood with his mother and their housekeeper, and enrolled in the Lila Bliss acting school before being signed by Twentieth Century Fox in 1937.

Career

During his career, Lowery was primarily known for roles in action movies such as *The Mark of Zorro* (1940), *The Mummy's Ghost* (1944), and *Dangerous Passage* (1944). He became the second actor to play DC Comics' Batman, starring in a 1949's *Batman and Robin* serial. Lowery also had roles in a number of Western films including *The Homesteaders* (1953), *The Parson and the Outlaw* (1957), *Young Guns of Texas* (1962), and *Johnny Reno* (1966). He was also an accomplished stage actor and appeared in *Born Yesterday*, *The Caine Mutiny*, and in several other productions.

On television, Lowery was best known for the role of Big Tim Champion on the series *Circus Boy* (1956-1957). In 1956, he guest starred in an episode of *The Adventures of Superman* (the first time a Batman actor shared screen time with a Superman actor). Lowery also had guest roles on *Playhouse 90* ("The Helen Morgan Story"), *Cowboy G-Men*, *Maverick*, *Tales of Wells Fargo*, *Rawhide*, *77 Sunset Strip*, *Hawaiian Eye*, and *Pistols 'n' Petticoats*. He made his last onscreen appearance in the 1967 comedy/Western film *The Ballad of Josie*, opposite Doris Day and Peter Graves.

Personal life and death

He was married three times, to three different actresses: to Jean Parker, to Vivan Wilcox, and to Rusty Farrell. He had one child, Robert, who lives in Redondo Beach, California; and two grandchildren.

Lowery died of heart failure at the age of 58 in his Los Angeles, California apartment on December 26, 1971.

Selected filmography

	Film		
Year	Film	Role	Notes
1936	*Great Guy*	Mr. Parker	Uncredited
1937	*Second Honeymoon*	Reporter	Uncredited
1938	*Rebecca of Sunnybrook Farm*	Attendant	Uncredited
1939	*Young Mr. Lincoln*	Juror Bill Killian	Uncredited
1940	*Charlie Chan's Murder Cruise*	Dick Kenyon	
1941	*Remember the Day*	Hotel P.A. Announcer	Uncredited
1942	*My Gal Sal*	Sally's friend	Uncredited
1943	*Tarzan's Desert Mystery*	Prince Selim	
1945	*The Monster and the Ape*	Ken Morgan	
1946	*They Made Me a Killer*	Tom Durling	

1947	Queen of the Amazons	Gary Lambert	
1953	Jalopy (film)	Skid Wilson	with The Bowery Boys
1963	McLintock!	Gov. Cuthbert H. Humphrey	
1966	Johnny Reno	Jake Reed	
1967	The Ballad of Josie	Whit Minick, Town Drunk	

Television			
Year	Title	Role	Notes
1954	The Joe Palooka Story	Don Jackson	1 episode
	The Pepsi-Cola Playhouse	George Loring	1 episode
1955	Letter to Loretta	Gordy	1 episode
1956	The Millionaire	David Hanley	1 episode
1958	Casey Jones	Greg Pontus	1 episode
	26 Men	Red Tanner	3 episodes
	Yancy Derringer	Blair Devon	2 episodes
1959	The Texan	Coy Bennet	1 episode
	Bronco	Mike Kirk	1 episode
	Cimarron City	Harris	1 episode
1960	Richard Diamond, Private Detective	Mark Sutro	1 episode
	Hotel de Paree	Trent	1 episode
	COronado 9	Miller	1 episode
1961	Whispering Smith	Dave Markson	1 episode
1962	Frontier Circus	Marshal Taggert	1 episode
	Gunsmoke	Idaho Smith	1 episode

External links

- Robert Lowery [1] at the Internet Movie Database
- Robert Lowery [2] at TV.com
- Robert Lowery [3] at Find a Grave

Batman with Adam West

Batman (1966 film)

\	***Batman***
\	Theatrical release poster
Directed by	Leslie H. Martinson
Produced by	William Dozier
Screenplay by	Lorenzo Semple, Jr.
Story by	Lorenzo Semple, Jr. **Characters:** Bob Kane Bill Finger
Starring	Adam West Burt Ward Lee Meriwether Cesar Romero Burgess Meredith Frank Gorshin
Music by	Nelson Riddle *(incidental music)* **Theme:** Neal Hefti
Cinematography	Howard Schwartz
Editing by	Harry Gerstad
Studio	Twentieth Century-Fox Film Corporation William Dozier Productions Greenlawn Productions
Distributed by	20th Century Fox
Release date(s)	July 20, 1966
Running time	105 minutes
Country	United States
Language	English

| Budget | US$ 1,400,000 *(est.)* |

Batman, often promoted as ***Batman: The Movie***, is a 1966 film based on the television series and the first full-length theatrical adaptation of the DC Comics character of the same name. Released by 20th Century Fox, the film starred Adam West as Batman and Burt Ward as Robin.

The film was directed by Leslie H. Martinson, who also directed a pair of *Batman* episodes; "The Penguin Goes Straight" and "Not Yet, He Ain't", both from season one.

Plot

When Batman (West) and Robin (Ward) get a tip that Commodore Schmidlapp (the final role of actor Reginald Denny) is in danger aboard his yacht, they launch a rescue mission using the Batcopter. After a tangle with an exploding shark, Batman and Robin head back to Commissioner Gordon's office where, through deduction and wisdom, they figure out that the tip was a set-up by The United Underworld, a gathering of four of the most powerful villains in Gotham City (Joker, Penguin, Riddler and Catwoman), who plan to defeat The Dynamic Duo once and for all.

Armed with a dehydrator that can turn humans into dust, a World War II "Pre-Atomic" Submarine made to resemble a penguin, and their three pirate henchmen (Bluebeard, Morgan and Quetch), The United Underworld intends to take over the world, and Batman and Robin must stop them. Catwoman, disguised as the Soviet journalist "Miss KITKA" (short for Kitanya Irenia Tatanya Kerenska Alisoff), lures Bruce Wayne into a trap, little suspecting that Wayne is Batman's alter-ego, and Penguin even schemes his way into the Batcave, leaving the Duo unable to prevent the kidnapping of the dehydrated United World Organization's Security Council.

After giving chase in the Batboat, the Caped Crusader and Boy Wonder use a sonic charge weapon called "Bat-Charges" to disable Penguin's submarine and bring it to the surface, where a grand fistfight ensues. Although Commodore Schmidlapp sneezes on and scatters the powdered members of the dehydrated Council, mixing them together – which would normally spell their doom – Batman constructs an elaborate filter to separate the mingled dust.

Prior to this process, Robin asks Batman if it might not be in the world's best interests for them to alter the dust samples so that humans can no longer harm one another. In response, Batman says that they cannot do so and can only hope for people, in general, to learn to live together peacefully on their own.

However, in the final scene, Robin's wishes are ironically fulfilled when the Security Council is improperly re-hydrated. While all of the members are alive and well, continuing to squabble among themselves and totally oblivious of their surroundings, each of them now speaks a completely different language than their original native tongue. As the world looks on in disbelief at this development, Batman and Robin quietly climb out of the United World Headquarters to an uncertain future. Batman's final words express his sincere hope that this "mixing of minds" does more good than it does harm.

Cast

- Adam West as Bruce Wayne/Batman
- Burt Ward as Dick Grayson/Robin
- Cesar Romero as The Joker
- Frank Gorshin as The Riddler
- Burgess Meredith as The Penguin
- Lee Meriwether as Catwoman/Miss Kitka Karenska
- Alan Napier as Alfred Pennyworth
- Neil Hamilton as Commissioner Gordon
- Stafford Repp as Chief O'Hara
- Madge Blake as Aunt Harriet
- Reginald Denny as Commodore Schmidlapp
- Milton Frome as Vice Admiral Fangschleister
- Gil Perkins as Bluebeard
- Dick Crockett as Morgan
- George Sawaya as Quetch
- William Dozier as Desmond Doomsday the Narrator *(uncredited)*
- Van Williams as the President (*voice*; *uncredited*)

Though Julie Newmar played the Catwoman in the TV series, she had other commitments at that time and was replaced by Lee Meriwether in this movie. In his autobiography, Adam West writes of his asking for more money to do the film and that the producers countered with the fact that another actor would be hired.

Production

William Dozier wanted to make a big-screen film to generate interest in his proposed Batman TV series, to have the feature in theaters while the first season of the series was rolling before the cameras. The studio, 20th Century Fox, refused because while a network would have to cover the entire cost of a movie, they would only have to share the cost of a TV series (a much less risky proposition). So it was not filmed until the end of the first season of *Batman* the TV series (between April 25 and May 31, 1966 at an estimated $1,377,800). This movie featured four criminals from the show, including the Joker (Cesar Romero), Riddler (Frank Gorshin), Penguin (Burgess Meredith), and Catwoman (Lee Meriwether). It was written by series writer Lorenzo Semple, Jr. and directed by series director Leslie H. Martinson, who won a Golden Gryphon.

The 105-minute *Batman* opened at The Paramount Theatre in Austin, Texas on Saturday, July 30, 1966 (between the first and second seasons of the TV series).

The movie was moderately successful at the box office. It had its nationwide television debut as an *ABC Sunday Night Movie*, at 9:00 Eastern/8:00 Central, on July 4, 1971.

Tone

Like the television series, the movie featured saturated colors, campy dialogue and special effects, and exaggeration in acting performances, as well as the occasional breaking of the fourth wall, effectively being a tongue-in-cheek parody.

Though it is often described (like many contemporary shows) as a parody of a popular comic-book character, some commentators believe that its comedy is not so tightly confined. Some commentators felt the film's depiction of the Caped Crusader "captured the feel of the contemporary comics perfectly". The film was, they remind us, made at a time when "the Batman of the Golden Age comics was already essentially neutered".

Certain elements verge into direct parody of the history of Batman. The movie, like the TV series, is strongly influenced by the comparatively obscure 1940s serials of Batman, such as the escapes done almost out of luck. The penchant for giving devices a "Bat-" prefix, and the dramatic use of stylized title cards during fight scenes, acknowledge some of the conventions that the character had accumulated in various media. However, the majority of *Batman*'s campier moments can be read as a broader parody on contemporary mid-1960s culture in general.

Vehicles

Besides the Batmobile, other vehicles used by The Dynamic Duo:

- Batcycle with side car
- Batboat, provided by Glastron
- Batcopter

The Batmobile as seen in the 1960s *Batman* TV series.

Of the three new Batvehicles which first appeared in the *Batman* movie, only the Batcycle crossed over into the *TV series*, as the budgetary limits of the TV series precluded the use of the others. Instead, snippets of the Batcopter and Batboat from the movie were stitched into episodes.

Release

The film was in released on VHS in 1985 by Playhouse Video, in 1989 by CBS/Fox Video, and in 1994 by Fox Video. On August 21, 2001 this film was released on DVD; it was re-released July 1, 2008 on DVD and on Blu-ray for the 42nd anniversary of the film's release and to take advantage of *The Dark Knight's* release on July 18. The Blu-ray added several features in addition to those found on the original DVD, however the 2008 DVD is identical to the 2001 release, except for the disk artwork, which had a darker feel than the 2001 release and did not include Robin, probably to tie in with *The Dark Knight*.

Reception

Batman: The Movie has received positive reviews over the years, with an 82% rating on Rotten Tomatoes. Bill Gibron of Filmcritic.com gave the film 3 out of 5 stars and commented that "unlike other attempts at bringing these characters to life...the TV cast really captures the inherent insanity of the roles." *Variety* magazine stated on their review that "the intense innocent enthusiasm of Cesar Romero, Burgess Meredith and Frank Gorshin as the three criminals is balanced against the innocent calm of Adam West and Burt Ward, Batman and Robin respectively."

External links

- *Batman* [1] at the Internet Movie Database
- *Batman* [2] at Allmovie
- *Batman: The Movie* [3] at Rotten Tomatoes
- Batman The Movie @ BYTB: Batman Yesterday, Today and Beyond [4]
- Batmania UK: 1966 Batman [5]
- "Strange new Batman/White Stripes link" [6] Article on Batman: The Movie's pop culture influence
- kiddiematinee.com: BATMAN (1966, U.S.) [7]

Adam West

Adam West	
West at WonderCon 2009	
Born	William West Anderson September 19, 1928 Seattle, Washington, U.S.
Occupation	Actor, voice actor
Years active	1954–present
Spouse	Billie Lou Yeager (1950–1956) Frisbie Dawson (1957–1962) Marcelle Tagand Lear (1970–present)
Website	
http://www.adamwest.com	

Adam West (born September 19, 1928) is an American actor best known for his lead role in the 1960s TV series *Batman* and the film of the same name. He is currently known for portraying eccentric versions of himself, as well as his voice work on animated series such as *The Fairly OddParents* and *Family Guy*.

Early life

West was born **William West Anderson** in Seattle, Washington to Otto West Anderson and Audrey V. Speer. He has a younger brother named John. He attended Walla Walla High School during his freshman and sophomore years, and later enrolled in Lakeside School in Seattle. He graduated with a Bachelor of Arts degree in Literature and a minor in Psychology from Whitman College in Walla Walla where he was a member of the Beta Theta Pi fraternity and participated on the speech and debate team.

Early roles

In Hawaii, West landed a role as the sidekick on a children's show called *El Kini Popo Show*, which featured a chimp. West later took over as star of the show.

In 1959, the actor moved to Hollywood and took the stage name "Adam West." In his autobiography *Back to the Batcave* he explains that he chose "Adam" simply because he liked the way it looked and sounded with "West", his mother's maiden name. His close friends and family still call him "Bill".

He appeared in the film *The Young Philadelphians* with Paul Newman, and guest-starred in a number of television Westerns. He guest starred on Edmond O'Brien's syndicated crime drama *Johnny Midnight* and soon snagged a supporting role as police Sergeant Steve Nelson in the crime drama, *The Detectives Starring Robert Taylor*. He portrayed Wild Bill Hickok in the episode "Westbound Stage" of the 1960 NBC western series *Overland Trail*, with William Bendix and Doug McClure. He starred in an episode of the original television series *The Outer Limits* titled "The Invisible Enemy". He made a brief appearance in the film *Soldier in the Rain* starring Jackie Gleason and Steve McQueen and in the 1964 film *Robinson Crusoe on Mars*. In 1965, he starred in the comedy western *The Outlaws Is Coming*, the last feature film starring The Three Stooges.

Batman

Main articles: Batman (TV series) and Batman (1966 film)

Producer William Dozier cast West as Batman and his alter ego, Bruce Wayne, in the hit television series *Batman*, in part after seeing West perform as the James Bond-like spy Captain Q in a Nestlé Quik television ad. West beat out Lyle Waggoner for the Batman role.

The popular, campy show ran on ABC from 1966 to 1968; a film version was released in 1966.

In 1970, West was offered the role of James Bond by Cubby Broccoli for the film *Diamonds Are Forever*. West declined, later stating in his autobiography that he believed the role should always be played by someone British (despite the fact that an Australian had already played him).

Post-Batman career

After his high-profile role, West, along with Burt Ward and Yvonne Craig (who played crimefighting sidekicks Robin and Batgirl), was severely typecast. West's first post-Caped Crusader role was in the 1969 release *The Girl Who Knew Too Much*. His lead performance against type as cynical tough guy Johnny Cain did not erode his Batman image; the movie was a box office disappointment.

West in 1989 at the 41st Primetime Emmy Awards.

For a time, West made a living doing personal appearances as Batman. In 1972, when Ward and Craig reprised their *Batman* roles for a TV public-service announcement about equal pay for women, West was absent. Instead, Dick Gautier filled in as Batman. One of his more memorable Batman appearances post-series was when he made an appearance in the Memphis, Tennessee based United States Wrestling Association to engage in a war of words with Jerry "The King" Lawler while wearing the cowl and a track suit and even name-dropping Spider-Man, though he is a Marvel Comics hero.

West subsequently appeared in the theatrical films *The Marriage of a Young Stockbrocker* (1971), *The Curse of the Moon Child* (1972), *Partizani/Hell River* (1974), *The Specialist* (1975), *Hardcore* (1977), *Hooper* (as himself; 1978), *The Happy Hooker Goes Hollywood* (1980) and *One Dark Night* (1983). West also appeared in television films as *The Eyes of Charles Sand* (1972), *Poor Devil* (1973), *Nevada Smith* (1975), *For the Love of It* (1980) and *I Take These Men* (1983).

He did guest shots on the TV shows *Love, American Style*, *The Big Valley*, *Night Gallery*, *Alias Smith and Jones*, *Mannix*, *Emergency!*, *Alice*, *Police Woman*, *Operation Petticoat*, *The American Girls*, *Vegas*, *Big Shamus Little Shamus*, *Laverne & Shirley*, *Bewitched*, *Fantasy Island*, *The Love Boat*, *Hart to Hart*, *Zorro*, *King of Queens*, and *George Lopez*.

His typecasting kept him from landing more substantial roles. In recent years, West has exploited his fate to poke fun at his status as a pop culture icon.

Return to Batman

West often reprised his role as Batman/Bruce Wayne, first in the short-lived animated series, *The New Adventures of Batman*, and in other shows such as *Super Friends: The Legendary Super Powers Show*, *The Super Powers Team: Galactic Guardians* (succeeding Olan Soule in the role). In 1979, West once again put on the Batsuit for the live-action TV special *Legends of the Superheroes*.

West made an appearance in a 1992 episode of *Batman: The Animated Series* on Fox, but not as Batman (as the role of Batman was already being played by Kevin Conroy). Instead, he portrayed Simon Trent, a washed-up actor who used to play a superhero in a TV series called "The Gray Ghost" and who now has difficulty finding work. West later had a recurring role as the voice of Mayor Grange in the WB animated series *The Batman*.

The actor vocally reprised his role as Batman for the CGI animated short film *Batman: New Times*. He co-starred with Mark Hamill, who vocally portrayed The Joker and had originally played the role on *Batman: The Animated Series*. West also voiced Thomas Wayne, Bruce Wayne's father, in an episode of the animated series *Batman: The Brave and the Bold*.

1990s – 2000s

During the 1990s, West's status as a pop culture icon led to appearances as himself in the film *Drop Dead Gorgeous* and in several television series, including *NewsRadio*, *Murphy Brown*, *The Adventures of Pete and Pete*, *The Ben Stiller Show* and *The Drew Carey Show*. In 1991, he starred in the pilot episode of *Lookwell*, in which he portrayed a has-been TV action hero who falsely believes he can solve crimes in real life. The pilot, written by Conan O'Brien and Robert Smigel in their pre-*Late Night* period, aired on NBC that summer but was not picked up as a series. It was later broadcast on the Trio channel, under the "Brilliant But Cancelled" imprint.

Noticeably, he played a washed up superhero in the *Goosebumps* television series episode "Attack of the Mutant". The boy hero is a comic book geek whose favorite superhero, Galloping Gazelle (West's character), is portrayed as fading and on the verge of retirement. Towards the end, the boy is shocked to learn that the Gazelle is real, though he must save the day by himself.

In 1994, West, with Jeff Rovin, wrote his autobiography, *Back to the Batcave* published by Berkeley Books. He also appeared as a guest in the animated talk show *Space Ghost Coast to Coast* in an episode titled "Batmantis," where he displayed his book.

In 2003, West and Burt Ward starred in the TV-movie *Return to the Batcave: The Misadventures of Adam and Burt*, alongside Frank Gorshin, Julie Newmar, and Lee Meriwether. Jack Brewer portrayed West in flashbacks to the production of *Batman*.

In 2005, West appeared in the CBS show *The King of Queens*. In the episode, Spence first asks Lou Ferrigno to go to a sci-fi convention. But when Spence meets West (playing himself), he leaves Ferrigno and asks West to come with him.

West appears prominently in the 2006 video for California band STEFY's song "Chelsea" as "Judge Adam West", presiding over the courtroom scene.

In 2007, Adam West portrayed a defense attorney for Benny on the show *George Lopez*, and starred as "The Boss" in the movie comedy *Sexina: Popstar PI*.

Following the release of a Batman game, a host of the show *X-Play* visited Adam West on the show.

In 2009, West played himself in the episode "Apollo, Apollo" of *30 Rock*.

Voice-over work

Having a distinctive voice, West built a career doing voice-over work on a number of animated series (often as himself), including appearances on *The Simpsons*, *The Critic*, *The Boondocks*, *Histeria!*, *Kim Possible*, and *Johnny Bravo*. He also appeared in five episodes of Nickelodeon's cartoon, *The Fairly OddParents*, as a cat-obsessed version of himself who is famous for playing a superhero called Catman, and who actually believes he is Catman. Catman is a parody of his earlier character as Batman. A later appearance of Adam West in *The Fairly OddParents* world was a parody of himself, hired to play the role of the Crimson Chin in the movie of the same name. West also voiced many characters related to his famous Batman character, as mentioned above in the typecasting section.

Since 2000, West has made regular appearances on the animated series *Family Guy*, on which he plays Mayor Adam West, a parody of West himself, the lunatic mayor of Quahog, Rhode Island. His role has given him a new wave of popularity since Batman. Some of his latest voice-over performances were playing the role of Uncle Art in the Disney film *Meet the Robinsons*, and voicing the young Mermaid Man (along with Burt Ward, who voiced the young Barnacle Boy) in the cartoon show SpongeBob SquarePants.

West also played the voice of General Carrington in the video game *XIII*, and has voiced other video games like *Marc Ecko's Getting Up: Contents Under Pressure*, *Chicken Little: Ace in Action*, *Scooby Doo! Unmasked* and *Goosebumps: Attack of the Mutant*.

West has also done voice-over work for superhero-themed commercials for the investment firm The LendingTree.

He also spent a month doing radio commercials, entitled, "What's Adam West Watching?", promoting Fox Broadcasting Company shows.

Filmography

- *Voodoo Island* (1957)
- *Ghost of the China Sea* (1958)
- *The Young Philadelphians* (1959)
- *The FBI Story* (1959)
- *Geronimo* (1962)
- *Tammy and the Doctor* (1963)
- *Soldier in the Rain* (1963)
- *Robinson Crusoe on Mars* (1964)
- *The Outlaws Is Coming* (1965)
- *Mara of the Wilderness* (1965)

- *The Relentless Four* (1965)
- *Batman* (1966)
- *The Girl Who Knew Too Much* (1969)
- *Hollywood Blue* (documentary, 1970)
- *The Marriage of a Young Stockbroker* (1971)
- Curse of the Moon Child (1972)
- *Partizani* (1974)
- *The Specialist* (1975)
- *Hardcore* (1977)
- *Hooper* (1978)
- *The Happy Hooker Goes Hollywood* (1980)
- *One Dark Night* (1983)
- *Hell Riders* (1984)
- *Young Lady Chatterley II* (1985)
- *Zombie Nightmare* (1986)
- *Night of the Kickfighters* (1988)
- *Doing Time on Planet Earth* (1988)
- *Yellow Pages* (1988)
- *Return Fire* (1988)
- *Omega Cop* (1990)
- *Mad About You* (1990)
- *Maxim Xul* (1991)
- *The Best Movie Ever Made* (1994)
- *The New Age* (1994)
- *Not This Part of the World* (1994)
- *Run for Cover* (1995)
- *Race For Your Life: An Interactive Movie* (1995)
- *The Clinic* (1995)
- *The Size of Watermelons* (1996)
- *Joyride* (1996)
- *American Vampire (film)* (1997)
- *Drop Dead Gorgeous* (1999)
- *Séance* (2001)
- *Nuclear Rescue 911* (2001)
- *From Heaven to Hell* (2002)
- *BAADASSSSS!* (2003)
- *Tales from Beyond* (2004)
- *Stewie Griffin: The Untold Story* (2005, direct-to-DVD, voice)

- *Blue Harvest* (2007, Grand Moff Tarkin)
- *Aloha, Scooby-Doo!* (2005, direct-to-DVD, voice)
- *Buckaroo: The Movie* (2005)
- *Chicken Little* (2005, voice)
- *Angels with Angles* (2005)
- *Sexina: Popstar P.I.* (2006)
- *Meet the Robinsons* (2007, voice)
- *Ratko: The Dictator's Son* (2007)
- *Super Capers* (2009)

Short Subjects

- *Ride for Your Life* (1995)
- *Redux Riding Hood* (1997) (voice)
- *Batman: New Times* (2005) (voice)

Television

- *The Detectives Starring Robert Taylor* (1961–1962)
- *Bewitched* (1964) Darrin's friend Kermit
- *Batman* (1966–1968)
- *Batman: The Brave and the Bold* (Thomas Wayne, episode "Chill of the Night")
- *Alexander the Great* (1968, unsold pilot)
- *How I Got You* (1969)
- *The Eyes of Charles Sand* (1972)
- *Poor Devil* (1973)
- *Shazam!* (1974–1975, voice)
- *Nevada Smith* (1975)
- *The New Adventures of Batman* (1977–1978, voice)
- *Tarzan and the Super 7* (1978–1980, voice)
- *Legends of the Superheroes* (1979)
- *For the Love of It* (1980)
- *Warp Speed* (1981)
- *Time Warp* (1981)
- *I Take These Men* (1983)
- *Ace Diamond Private Eye* (1983, unsold pilot)
- *Batman: The Animated Series* (1992, voice, episode "Beware of the Grey Ghost")
- *The Ben Stiller Show* (1992, guest star)
- *Danger Theatre* (1993)
- *Space Ghost Coast to Coast* (1994, himself)
- *The Simpsons* (1994, 2002, voice)
- *The Adventures of Pete & Pete* (1993–1996)
- *Goosebumps (1995, Episode:* Attack of the Mutant, *as The Galloping Gazell)*
- *Johnny Bravo* (1997)
- *The Wayans Bros* (1997, himself)
- *The Secret Files of the Spy Dogs* (1998–1999, voice)
- *Histeria!* (1999, voice)
- *The Fairly OddParents* (recurring cast member, voice, himself)
- *Family Guy* (2000–present, voice, himself)
- *The Grim Adventures of Billy & Mandy* (2001, voices)
- *Return to the Batcave: The Misadventures of Adam and Burt* (2003)
- *Kim Possible* (2003, episode The Fearless Ferret, voice)
- *Monster Island* (2004)
- *Celebrity Deathmatch* (1998–2001, 2005–2006, himself)

- *Super Friends: The Legendary Super Powers Show* (1984–1985, voice)
- *The Super Powers Team: Galactic Guardians* (1985–1986, voice)
- *The Last Precinct* (1986, canceled after 7 episodes)
- *Zorro* (1990, episode "The Wizard")
- *Lookwell* (1991, unsold pilot)
- *1775* (1992, unsold pilot)
- *Rugrats* (1992, voice)
- *The Drew Carey Show* (2001)
- *Yes Dear* (2004)
- *George Lopez (TV series)* (2007)
- *Blue Harvest* (2007, Grand Moff Tarkin)
- *The Boondocks* (2006)
- *30 Rock* (2009, himself)
- *SpongeBob SquarePants* (2010, voice, young Mermaid Man)

References

Other sources

- West, Adam (1994). *Back to the Batcave*. Berkeley. ISBN 0-425-14370-8.
- Press kit notes for *The Girl Who Knew Too Much*

External links

- Adam West Official Website [1]
- Adam West [2] at the Internet Movie Database
- Adam West [3] at TV.com
- Adam West as Batman [4]
- Adam West interview in Dangerous Ink Magazine [5]
- Adam West gets back in the Batmobile [6]

Batman and Batman Returns

Batman (1989 film)

Batman	
Theatrical release poster	
Directed by	Tim Burton
Produced by	Peter Guber Jon Peters *Executive*: Benjamin Melniker Michael Uslan
Screenplay by	Sam Hamm Warren Skaaren
Story by	Sam Hamm *Comic book*: Bill Finger *(uncredited)* Bob Kane
Starring	Michael Keaton Jack Nicholson Kim Basinger Robert Wuhl Jack Palance
Music by	**Score:** Danny Elfman **Songs:** Prince
Cinematography	Roger Pratt
Editing by	Ray Lovejoy
Studio	PolyGram Filmed Entertainment The Guber-Peters Company
Distributed by	Warner Bros.
Release date(s)	June 23, 1989

Running time	126 minutes
Country	United States
Language	English
Budget	$48 million
Gross revenue	$411,348,924
Followed by	*Batman Returns*

Batman is a 1989 superhero film based on the DC Comics character of the same name, directed by Tim Burton. The film stars Michael Keaton in the title role, as well as Jack Nicholson, Kim Basinger, Robert Wuhl and Jack Palance. The film, in which Batman deals with the rise of a powerful villain known as "The Joker", is the first installment of Warner Bros.' *Batman* film series.

After Burton was hired as director, Steve Englehart and Julie Hickson wrote film treatments before Sam Hamm wrote the first screenplay. *Batman* was not greenlit until after the success of Burton's *Beetlejuice* (1988). Numerous A-list actors were considered for the role of Batman. Nicholson was cast as the Joker in a deal that included both salary and a portion of the box office profits.

Filming took place at Pinewood Studios from October 1988 to January 1989. The budget escalated from $30 million to $48 million, while the 1988 Writers Guild of America strike forced Hamm to drop out. Uncredited rewrites were performed by Warren Skaaren, Charles McKeown and Jonathan Gems. *Batman* was a critical and financial success, earning over $400 million in box office totals. The film received several Saturn Award nominations and was nominated for an Academy Award and a Golden Globe. It also inspired the Emmy Award-winning *Batman: The Animated Series*, paving the way for the DC Animated Universe, and has left a legacy over the modern perception of the superhero film genre.

Plot

As a child, Bruce Wayne (Michael Keaton) witnessed his parents' murder at the hands of a mugger. He vows to avenge their deaths in a lifelong battle against crime in the guise of Batman while concealing his secret identity, working in Wayne Enterprises and using its vast resources to build his crime-fighting arsenal. Years later, Gotham is under the control of crime boss Carl Grissom (Jack Palance). Despite the best efforts of newly-elected district attorney Harvey Dent (Billy Dee Williams) and police commissioner James Gordon (Pat Hingle), the city's police department and administration remain in Grissom's pocket. Reporter Alexander Knox (Robert Wuhl) and photo-journalist Vicki Vale (Kim Basinger) begin investigating the rumors of a mysterious vigilante dressed as a bat who has been terrifying criminals throughout the city.

Vicki and Knox attend a benefit at Wayne Manor, where Bruce is taken by Vicki's charms. That same night, Grissom sends his second-in-command Jack Napier (Jack Nicholson) to raid the Axis Chemical plant. After the police receive a tip-off and arrive to arrest him and his henchmen, Jack realizes he has been set-up by his boss, angered by his affair with Grissom's mistress. In the midst of the shoot-out, Batman arrives and takes out Napier's henchmen.

In a bizarre accident caused by his own ricocheting bullet, deflected by Batman's metal-reinforced gauntlet, Napier's face is ripped open. Reeling from the pain, he topples over a platform rail but manages to grab a lower rail with one hand. Batman momentarily clutches Jack's free hand, but the grip is soon broken, and he falls into a large vat of toxic waste. Shortly thereafter, he emerges from an adjacent reservoir, his hair and skin discolored. Following a botched surgical attempt to repair his face, Jack is left with a permanent and twisted grin, giving him the appearance of an evil clown. Driven insane by his reflection, he fashions himself as "the Joker".

After killing Grissom, the Joker takes over his empire and holds the city at his mercy by poisoning everyday hygiene products with "Smilex", causing those using a certain combination of products to laugh to death. Batman attempts to track down the Joker, who has become obsessed with Vicki. During an altercation, Batman recognizes the Joker as the criminal who who killed his parents years before. Batman destroys the factory the Joker used to make the poisoned products.

The Joker holds a parade through Gotham, luring its citizens on to its streets by dispensing money, intending to kill them with lethal gas. Batman foils his plan, but the Joker kidnaps Vicki and takes her to the roof of a cathedral. After Batman fights with the Joker and his henchmen, he says to his opponent that they "made each other" — Batman would not exist had Napier not murdered his parents, and the Joker would not exist had Batman never met Napier. As the Joker tries to escape in a helicopter, Batman attaches a grappling hook to his foot and ties it to a gargoyle; the Joker falls to his death when the gargoyle comes loose from its moorings. As Vicki rides back to Wayne Manor, Commissioner Gordon unveils the Bat-Signal along with a note from Batman read by Harvey Dent, promising to defend Gotham whenever crime strikes again.

Production

Development

Further information: Batman in film#Warner Bros. live-action productions

After the financial success of *Pee-wee's Big Adventure* (1985), Warner Bros. hired Tim Burton to direct *Batman*. Burton had then-girlfriend Julie Hickson write a new 30-page film treatment, feeling the previous script by Tom Mankiewicz was campy. The success of *The Dark Knight Returns* and *The Killing Joke* prompted Warner Bros. to give the film a darker, more serious tone. Although Burton was initially not a comic book fan, he enjoyed *The Killing Joke*. Warner Bros. enlisted the aid of Steve Englehart to write a new treatment in March 1986. His first treatment included the Joker and Rupert Thorne as the main villains, with a cameo appearance by the Penguin. Silver St. Cloud and Dick Grayson were key supporting roles. It followed the similar storyline from Englehart's own limited series *Strange Apparitions* (ISBN 1-56389-500-5). Warner Bros. was impressed, but Englehart felt there were too many characters. He removed the Penguin and Dick Grayson in his second treatment, finishing in May 1986.

Burton approached Sam Hamm, a comic book fan, to write the screenplay. Hamm decided not to use an origin story, feeling that flashbacks would be more suitable and that "unlocking the mystery" would become part of the storyline. He reasoned, "You totally destroy your credibility if you show the literal process by which Bruce Wayne becomes Batman." Hamm replaced Silver St. Cloud with Vicki Vale and Rupert Thorne with his own creation, Carl Grissom. He completed his script in October 1986, which demoted Dick Grayson to a cameo, and not a supporting character. One scene in Hamm's script had James Gordon on duty the night of the murder of Bruce Wayne's parents. When Hamm's script was rewritten, the scene was deleted.

Warner Bros. was less willing to move forward on development, despite their enthusiasm for Hamm's script, which Batman co-creator Bob Kane greeted with positive feedback. Hamm's script then became largely bootlegged at various comic book stores across America. *Batman* was finally given the greenlight to commence pre-production in April 1988, after the surprising success of Burton's *Beetlejuice* (1988). When comic book fans found out about Burton directing the film and Michael Keaton starring in the lead role, controversy arose over the tone and direction *Batman* was going in. Hamm explained, "they hear Tim Burton's name and they think of *Pee-wee's Big Adventure*. They hear Keaton's name and they think of any number of Michael Keaton comedies. You think of the 1960s version of Batman, and it was the complete opposite. We tried to market it with a typical dark and serious tone, but the fans didn't believe us." To combat negative reports on the film's production, Batman co-creator Bob Kane was hired as creative consultant.

Casting

Mel Gibson, Kevin Costner, Charlie Sheen, Pierce Brosnan, Tom Selleck and Bill Murray were all considered for Batman. Tim Burton was pressured to cast an obvious action movie star. Producer Jon Peters favored Michael Keaton, arguing he had the right "edgy, tormented quality." Having directed Keaton in *Beetlejuice*, Burton agreed.

Keaton's casting caused a controversy among comic book fans, with 50,000 protest letters sent to Warner Bros. offices. Bob Kane, Sam Hamm and Michael Uslan also heavily questioned the casting, while Adam West felt himself to be a better choice. Burton acknowledged, "Obviously there was a negative response from the comic book people. I think they thought we were going to make it like the 1960s TV series, and make it campy, because they thought of Michael Keaton from *Mr. Mom* and *Night Shift* and stuff like that." Keaton studied *The Dark Knight Returns* for inspiration.

Tim Curry, Willem Dafoe, David Bowie and James Woods were considered for the Joker. Robin Williams lobbied hard for the part. Jack Nicholson was producer Michael Uslan's and Bob Kane's choice since 1980. Peters approached Nicholson as far back as 1986, during filming of *The Witches of*

Eastwick. Nicholson had what was known as an "off-the-clock" agreement. His contract specified the number of hours he was entitled to have off each day, from the time he left the set to the time he reported back for filming. Nicholson demanded to have all of his scenes shot in a three-week block, but the schedule lapsed into 106 days. He received a $6 million salary, as well as a large percentage of the box office gross. The fee is reported to be as high as $50 million.

Sean Young was originally cast as Vicki Vale, but was injured during filming. Burton suggested replacing Young with Michelle Pfeiffer but Keaton, who was in a relationship with Pfeiffer, believed it would be too awkward. She went on to portray Catwoman in *Batman Returns*. Peters suggested Kim Basinger, and she was cast. As a fan of Michael Gough's work in various Hammer Film Productions, Burton cast Gough as Bruce Wayne's butler, Alfred Pennyworth. Robert Wuhl was cast as reporter Alexander Knox. His character was originally supposed to die by the Joker's poison gas in the climax, but the filmmakers "liked [my] character so much," Wuhl said "that they decided to let me live." Billy Dee Williams took the role of Harvey Dent because he was looking forward to portray Two-Face in a sequel. Tommy Lee Jones was later cast in the role for *Batman Forever*. Williams was mildly disappointed by the casting decision. Nicholson convinced the filmmakers to cast Tracey Walter as the Joker's henchman, Bob; in real life, Nicholson and Walter are close friends. The rest of the cast included Pat Hingle as Commissioner Gordon, Jack Palance as Carl Grissom, Jerry Hall as Alicia Hunt, Lee Wallace as Mayor Borg, and William Hootkins as Lt. Max Eckhardt.

Filming

The filmmakers considered filming *Batman* entirely in Hollywood, California, but media interest in the film made them change the location to England. It was shot at Pinewood Studios in England from October 1988 to January 1989. 18 sound stages were used, almost the entirety of Pinewood's 95-acre backlot. Locations included Knebworth House and Hatfield House doubling for Wayne Manor, plus Acton Lane Power Station and Little Barford Power Station. The original production budget escalated from $30 million to $48 million. Filming was highly secretive. The unit publicist was offered and refused £10,000 for the first pictures of Jack Nicholson as the Joker. The police were later called in when two reels of footage (about 20 minutes' worth) were stolen. With various problems during filming, Burton called it "torture. The worst period of my life!"

Hamm was not allowed to perform rewrites during the 1988 Writers Guild of America strike. Jonathan Gems, Warren Skaaren and Charles McKeown rewrote the script during filming. Hamm criticized the rewrites, but blamed the changes on Warner Bros. Burton explained, "I don't understand why that became such a problem. We started out with a script that everyone liked, although we recognized it needed a little work." Dick Grayson appeared in the shooting script but was deleted, as the filmmakers felt he was irrelevant to the plot. Bob Kane supported this decision.

Originally in the climax, the Joker was to kill Vicki Vale, sending Batman into a vengeful fury. Jon Peters reworked the climax without telling Burton and commissioned production designer Anton Furst to create a 38-foot (12 m) model of the cathedral. This cost $100,000 when the film was already well over budget. Burton disliked the idea, having no clue how the scene would end: "Here were Jack Nicholson and Kim Basinger walking up this cathedral, and halfway up Jack turns around and says, 'Why am I walking up all these stairs? Where am I going?' 'We'll talk about it when you get to the top!' I had to tell him that I didn't know."

Design

"I envisaged Gotham the way I see it now at Pinewood. They've got it, every building, every trash can, every brick."

—Batman co-creator Bob Kane when looking at the buildings at Pinewood Studios

Burton was impressed with Anton Furst's designs in *The Company of Wolves*, and previously failed to hire Furst as production designer for *Beetlejuice*. Furst had been too committed on *High Spirits*, a choice he later regretted. Furst enjoyed working with Burton. "I don't think I've ever felt so naturally in tune with a director," he felt. "Conceptually, spiritually, visually, or artistically. There was never any problem because we never fought over anything. Texture, attitude and feelings are what [Burton] is a master at."

Furst and the art department deliberately mixed clashing architectural styles to "make Gotham City the ugliest and bleakest metropolis imaginable." Furst continued, "we imagined what New York City might have become without a planning commission. A city run by crime, with a riot of architectural styles. An essay in ugliness. As if hell erupted through the pavement and kept on going.'" Derek Meddings served as the visual effects supervisor, while Keith Short helped construct the newly-created 1989 Batmobile, adding two Browning machine guns. On designing the Batmobile, Furst explained, "We looked at jet aircraft components, we looked at war machines, we looked at all sorts of things. In the end, we went into pure expressionism, taking the Salt Flat Racers of the 30s and the Stingray macho machines of the 50s." The car was built upon a Chevrolet Impala when previous development with a Jaguar and Ford Mustang failed.

Costume designer Bob Ringwood (*A.I. Artificial Intelligence*, *Troy*) turned down the chance to work on *Licence to Kill* in favor of *Batman*. Ringwood found it difficult designing the Batsuit because "the image of Batman in the comics is this huge, big six-foot-four hunk with a dimpled chin. Michael Keaton is a guy with average build," He stated. "The problem was to make somebody who was average-sized and ordinary looking into this bigger-than-life creature." Burton commented, "Michael is a bit claustrophobic, which made it worse for him. The costume put him in a dark, Batman-like mood though, so he was able to use it to his advantage." Burton's idea was to use an all-black suit, and was met with positive feedback by Bob Kane. Jon Peters wanted to use a Nike product placement with the Batsuit. Ringwood studied over 200 comic book issues for inspiration. 28 sculpted latex designs were created; 25 different cape looks and 6 different heads were made, accumulating a total cost of $250,000. Comic book fans initially expressed negative feedback against the Batsuit. Burton opted not to use tights, spandex or underpants as seen in the comic book, feeling it was not intimidating.

Prosthetic makeup designer Nick Dudman (*Harry Potter* film series, *Legend*) used acrylic paint for Nicholson's chalk-white face. Part of Nicholson's contract was approval over the makeup designer.

Music

See also: Batman (album) and Batman (score)

Burton hired Danny Elfman, his collaborator on *Pee-wee's Big Adventure* and *Beetlejuice*, to compose the music score. For inspiration Elfman was given *The Dark Knight Returns*. Elfman was worried, as he never had worked on a production this large in budget and scale. In addition, producer Jon Peters was skeptical of hiring Elfman, but was later convinced when he heard the opening number. Peters and Peter Guber wanted Prince to write music for the Joker and Michael Jackson to do the romance songs. Elfman would then combine the style of Prince and Jackson's songs together for the entire film score.

Burton protested the ideas, citing "my movies aren't commercial like *Top Gun*." Elfman enlisted the help of Oingo Boingo lead guitarist Steve Bartek and Shirley Walker to arrange the compositions for the orchestra. Elfman later was displeased with the audio mixing of his film score. "*Batman* was done in England by technicians who didn't care, and the non-caring showed," he stated. "I'm not putting down England because they've done gorgeous dubs there, but this particular crew elected not to." *Batman* was one of the first films to spawn two soundtracks. One of them featured songs written by Prince while the other showcased Elfman's score. Both were successful, and compilations of Elfman's opening credits were used in the title sequence theme for *Batman: The Animated Series*, also composed by Shirley Walker.

Themes

When discussing the central theme of *Batman*, director Tim Burton explained, "the whole film and mythology of the character is a complete duel of the freaks. It's a fight between two disturbed people." He continued, "The Joker is such a great character because there's a complete freedom to him. Any character who operates on the outside of society and is deemed a freak and an outcast then has the freedom to do what they want." "They are the darker sides of freedom. Insanity is in some scary way the most freedom you can have, because you're not bound by the laws of society."

Burton saw Bruce Wayne as two people at one time and a symbol of America. Bruce has pretense of appearing to be one image, while hiding the reality from the world. Burton biographer Ken Hanke wrote that Bruce Wayne, struggling with his alter-ego as Batman, is depicted as an antihero. Hanke felt that Batman has to push the boundaries of civil justice to deal with certain criminals, such as the Joker. Kim Newman theorized that "Burton and the writers saw Batman and the Joker as a dramatic antithesis, and the film deals with their intertwined origins and fates to an even greater extent."

A visual motif is present in the scene of Batman's first major act of vigilantism at Axis Chemicals. He is carefully framed so that the single word AXIS, in gigantic red neon letters, looms over him. This parallels his actions and those of the totalitarian governments of World War II. The dangers inherent in these actions include the transformation of Jack Napier into the Joker. *Batman* also conveys trademarks found in 1930s pulp magazines, notably the design of Gotham City stylized with Art Deco design. Richard Corliss, writing for *Time*, observed that Gotham's design was a reference to films such as *Metropolis* (1927) and *The Cabinet of Dr. Caligari* (1920). "Gotham City, despite being shot on a studio backlot," he continued, "is literally another character in the script. It has the demeaning presence of German Expressionism and fascist architecture, staring down at the citizens." Hanke further addressed the notions of *Batman* being a period piece. "The citizens, cops, people and the black-and-white television looks like it takes place in 1939." However, Hanke later said. "Had the filmmakers made Vicki Vale a femme fatale rather than a damsel in distress, this could have made *Batman* as a homage and tribute to classic film noir. Portions of the climax pay homage to *Vertigo*.

Release

Marketing

Production designer Anton Furst designed the poster, which he called "evocative but ubiquitous. Only featuring the Bat-Symbol. Not too much and not too little." Earlier designs "had the word 'Batman' spelled in *RoboCop* or *Conan the Barbarian*-type font." Jon Peters unified all the film's tie-ins, even turning down $6 million from General Motors to build the Batmobile because the car company would not relinquish creative control.

During production, Peters read in *The Wall Street Journal* that comic book fans were unsatisfied with the casting of Michael Keaton. In response, Peters rushed the first film trailer that played in thousands of theaters during Christmas. It was simply an assemblage of scenes without music, but happened to create enormous anticipation for the film. DC Comics allowed screenwriter Sam Hamm to write his own comic book miniseries. Hamm's stories were collected in the graphic novel *Batman: Blind Justice* (ISBN 978-1563890475). Denys Cowan and Dick Giordano illustrated the artwork. *Blind Justice* tells the story of Bruce Wayne trying to solve a series of murders connected to Wayne Enterprises. It also marks the first appearance of Henri Ducard, who was later used in the rebooted *Batman Begins*, albeit as an alias for the more notable Ra's al Ghul.

In the months pre-dating *Batman*'s release in June 1989, a popular culture phenomenon rose known as "Batmania". Over $750 million worth of merchandise was sold. Cult filmmaker and comic book writer Kevin Smith remembered, "That summer was huge. You couldn't turn around without seeing the Bat-Signal somewhere. People were cutting it into their fucking heads. It was just the summer of Batman and if you were a comic book fan it was pretty hot." Hachette Book Group USA published a novelization, written by Craig Shaw Gardner. It remained on the *New York Times* Best Seller list throughout June 1989. Burton admitted he was annoyed by the publicity. David Handelman of *The New York Observer* categorized *Batman* as a high concept film. He believed "it is less movie than a corporate behemoth."

Reaction

Batman opened on June 23, 1989, grossing $43.6 million in 2,194 theaters during its opening weekend. This broke the opening weekend record, set by *Ghostbusters II* one week earlier, with $29.4 million. *Batman* would eventually gross $251.2 million in North America and $160.15 million internationally, totaling $411.35 million. *Batman* was the first film to earn $100 million in its first ten days of release, and was the highest grossing film based on a DC comic book, until 2008's *The Dark Knight*. The film is 58th highest ever in North American ranks. Although *Indiana Jones and the Last Crusade* made the most money worldwide in 1989, *Batman* was able to beat *The Last Crusade* in North America, and made a further $150 million in home video sales.

Many observed that Burton was more interested in the Joker rather than Batman in terms of characterization and screen time. Comic book fans reacted negatively over the Joker murdering Thomas and Martha Wayne. In the comic book, Joe Chill is responsible. Writer Sam Hamm, who is a comic book fan, said it was Burton's idea to have the Joker murder Wayne's parents. "The Writer's Strike was going on," Hamm continued, "and Tim had the other writers do that. I also hold innocent to Alfred letting Vicki Vale into the Batcave," he reasoned. "Fans were ticked off with that, and I agree. That would have been Alfred's last day of employment at Wayne Manor."

The songs written by Prince were criticized for being "too out of place". While Burton has stated he had no problem with the Prince songs, he was less enthusiastic with their use in the film. On the film, Burton remarked "I liked parts of it, but the whole movie is mainly boring to me. It's OK, but it was more of a cultural phenomenon than a great movie." Nonetheless, the film received generally favorable reviews from critics. Based on 51 reviews collected by Rotten Tomatoes, 71% of reviewers have enjoyed *Batman*. By comparison, Metacritic has collected an average score of 66, based on 17 reviews.

Burton biographer Alison McMahan wrote, "fans of the *Batman* franchise complained when they heard of Michael Keaton's casting. However, no one complained when they saw his performance." James Berardinelli called the film entertaining, with the highlight being the production design. However, he concluded, "the best thing that can be said about *Batman* is that it led to *Batman Returns*, which was a far superior effort." *Variety* felt "Jack Nicholson stole every scene" but still greeted the film with positive feedback. Roger Ebert was highly impressed with the production design, but claimed "*Batman* is a triumph of design over story, style over substance, a great-looking movie with a plot you can't care much about." His reviewing partner, Gene Siskel, disagreed, however, describing the film as having a 'refreshingly adult' approach with performances, direction and set design that 'draws you into a psychological world'. Jonathan Rosenbaum of the *Chicago Reader* called it "watchable enough".

Legacy

Anton Furst and Peter Young won the Academy Award for Best Art Direction, while Nicholson was nominated for the Golden Globe Award for Best Actor (Musical or Comedy). The British Academy of Film and Television Arts nominated *Batman* in six categories (Production Design, Visual Effects, Costume Design, Makeup, Sound and Actor in a Supporting Role for Nicholson), but it won none of the categories. Nicholson, Basinger, the make-up department and costume designer Bob Ringwood all received nominations at the Saturn Awards. The film was nominated the Saturn Award for Best Fantasy Film and the Hugo Award for Best Dramatic Presentation.

The success of *Batman* prompted Warner Bros. Animation to create the Emmy Award-winning *Batman: The Animated Series*, as a result beginning the long-running DC Animated Universe. Series co-creator Bruce Timm stated the television show's Art Deco design was inspired from the film. Timm commented, "our show would never have gotten made if it hadn't been for that first *Batman* movie." *Batman* initiated the original *Batman* film series and helped establish the modern day superhero film genre. Burton joked, "ever since I did *Batman*, it was like the first dark comic book movie. Now everyone wants to do a dark and serious superhero movie. I guess I'm the one responsible for that trend."

Producers Michael Uslan and Benjamin Melniker filed a breach of contract lawsuit in Los Angeles County Superior Court on March 26, 1992. Uslan and Melniker claimed to be "the victims of a sinister campaign of fraud and coercion that has cheated them out of continuing involvement in the production of *Batman* and its sequels. We were denied proper credits, and deprived of any financial rewards for our indispensable creative contribution to the success of *Batman*." A superior court judge rejected the lawsuit. Total revenues of *Batman* have topped $2 billion, with Uslan claiming to have "not seen a penny more than that since our net profit participation has proved worthless." Warner Bros. offered the pair a out-of-court pay-off, a sum described by Uslan and Melniker's attorney as "two popcorns and two Cokes".

Reflecting on the twentieth anniversary of its release in a retrospective article on Salon.com, film commentator Scott Mendelson noted that continuing impact that *Batman* has had on the motion film industry, including the increasing importance of opening weekend box office receipts; the narrowing window between a film's debut and its video release that caused the demise of second-run movie theaters; the accelerated acquisition of pre-existing, pre-sold properties for film adaptation that can be readily leveraged for merchandizing tie-ins; the primacy of the MPAA PG-13 as the target rating for film producers; and more off-beat, non-traditional casting opportunities for genre films.

The film also received recognition from the American Film Institute. Batman was anointed the 46th greatest movie hero on AFI's *100 Years... 100 Heroes and Villains*. The Joker was anointed the 45th greatest movie villain on the same list. In 2008, *Batman* was selected by Empire Magazine as number 458 of *The 500 Greatest Movies of All Time*.

Home video

Many versions of the film have been released. Included are VHS, Laserdisc, single disc DVD, Special Edition DVD and an anthology set. The *Batman: The Motion Picture Anthology* released in 2005 included 2-Disc Special Edition DVDs of the Tim Burton/Joel Schumacher Batman films. This anthology set was re-released on Blu-ray on March 10, 2009.

On May 19, 2009 a 20th anniversary stand-alone edition was released. This stand-alone version contains the exact same special features as its anthology set (both DVD and Blu-ray) counterparts. There are two differences: This version includes a 50-page booklet guide to the film, and a slight variation in packaging from normal Blu-ray cases (Warner Bros. *Digibook*) They both include a digital copy of the film.

Further reading

- Janet K. Halfyard, (28 October 2004) (Paperback). *Danny Elfman's Batman: A Film Score Guide*. A careful study of Elfman's scoring technique with a detailed analysis of the film itself. Scarecrow Press. ISBN 0810851261.
- Craig Shaw Gardner (1 June 1989) (Mass Market Paperback). *Batman*. Novelization of the film. Hachette Book Group USA. ISBN 0446354872.

External links

- Script review of *The Batman* [1] *IGN* reviews Tom Mankiewicz's unproduced script
- Sam Hamm's Batman script draft 1986 [2]
- Behind-the-scenes photos [3]
- Screenshots [4]
- *Batman* [5] at the Internet Movie Database
- *Batman* [6] at Allmovie
- *Batman* [7] at Rotten Tomatoes
- *Batman* [8] at Metacritic
- *Batman* [9] at Box Office Mojo

Batman Returns

Batman Returns	
Theatrical release poster	
Directed by	Tim Burton
Produced by	Tim Burton Denise Di Novi *Executive*: Benjamin Melniker Michael Uslan Peter Guber Jon Peters
Screenplay by	Daniel Waters
Story by	Sam Hamm Daniel Waters *Comic book*: Bill Finger *(uncredited)* Bob Kane
Starring	Michael Keaton Danny DeVito Michelle Pfeiffer Christopher Walken Michael Murphy
Music by	Danny Elfman
Cinematography	Stefan Czapsky
Editing by	Chris Lebenzon Bob Badami
Distributed by	Warner Bros.
Release date(s)	June 19, 1992
Running time	126 minutes
Country	United States
Language	English
Budget	$80 million
Gross revenue	$266,822,354

Preceded by	*Batman*
Followed by	*Batman Forever*

Batman Returns is a 1992 American superhero film directed by Tim Burton. Based on the DC Comics character Batman, it is the sequel to Burton's *Batman* (1989), and features Michael Keaton reprising the title role, with Danny DeVito as the Penguin and Michelle Pfeiffer as Catwoman.

Burton originally did not want to direct a sequel because of his mixed emotions toward the previous film. Daniel Waters delivered a script that satisfied Burton; Wesley Strick did an uncredited rewrite, deleting the character of Robin and rewriting the climax. Filming started at Burbank, California in June 1991. *Batman Returns* was released to financial and critical success, though it caused some controversy for being darker than its predecessor.

Plot

A hideously deformed baby is born to a wealthy aristocratic couple, who—after a short-lived attempt to cope with their child's unnatural deformity—decide to dispose of the infant into the sewers beneath the Gotham Zoo, where he is found and raised by a group of penguins.

Thirty-three years later, business tycoon Max Shreck (Christopher Walken) proposes to build a new power plant to save Gotham City from a possible power failure in the future, although the Mayor and other city officials question Shreck's motives. Meanwhile, during a public speech from Shreck, a group of rogue circus clowns, known as the Red Triangle Gang, disrupt the gathering, setting many buildings afire. Shreck escapes and falls into the sewers and is introduced to the legendary Penguin (Danny DeVito), the deformed boy, now an adult, who blackmails Shreck with incriminating evidence of past crimes into helping him emerge from the sewers to become a public hero. Shreck accepts, planning to use the penguin-man to his own advantage.

Shreck discovers that his secretary, Selina Kyle (Michelle Pfeiffer), has learned the true nature of his proposed power plant: it will drain and store the power of Gotham City and make a huge profit for the Shreck family. Shreck attempts to kill Selina by pushing her out of the window of the office, but she survives the fall, though unconscious. Mysteriously revived by alley cats, she goes back home and causes great destruction out of sudden insanity. She then becomes Catwoman, making her costume from a leather coat and dedicating her life to feminism in an exceedingly aggressive manner.

Meanwhile, Penguin, with the help of a Red Triangle acrobat, stages a kidnapping of the Mayor's infant son into the sewers, where the child is subsequently "rescued" by Penguin. Now a media sensation, Penguin is granted private access into the Hall of Records to discover his parents' identity and learn his real name: Oswald Chesterfield Cobblepot. He publicly forgives his now-deceased parents for abandoning him, and wins the sympathy of the public, except for Bruce Wayne (Michael Keaton), who is skeptical of Penguin's heroics and eventually links Cobblepot to several child disappearances over the past few years. Bruce soon realizes that Cobblepot is the leader of the Red Triangle gang and attempts to confront Shreck with his suspicions during an intended business meeting. However, Shreck, who is in on Cobblepot's plans, takes offense at Bruce's accusations, and bluntly dismisses Bruce from his office.

Shortly thereafter, Shreck hatches a plan with Cobblepot that would exploit the gang's past crimes to defame the Mayor and propose a recall election, making Cobblepot the ideal replacement candidate. During the next attack by the Red Triangle gang, Catwoman runs into Batman and Penguin, after having destroyed a part of Shreck's department store. Batman pursues her atop a building, and the two fight. Catwoman overcomes Batman and casually threatens his life while dangling him off a high ledge with her whip. During this opportune moment, Batman throws at her a concealed chemical vial from his utility belt and knocks her off the building, where she lands safely but injured into a kitty-litter-filled truck bed leaving the area.

Catwoman joins forces with Penguin to devise a plan to frame Batman and destroy him; at the same time, Selina begins a romantic relationship with Bruce Wayne. While Bruce and Selina are sharing a passionate moment at Wayne Manor, an unexpected news bulletin catches their attention in which the beautiful holiday Ice Princess (Cristi Conaway), is abducted, with Batman as the main suspect. Both Selina and Bruce abruptly cancel their evening plans and part ways, unaware that they're both going to the same destination. Bruce, as Batman, heads to rescue the Princess and clear his name, but is met with both the Penguin and Catwoman. The confrontation on the building rooftop ends with Penguin causing the Princess to fall to her death with the public below believing Batman was responsible. When Batman tries to escape, he discovers that the Batmobile has been sabotaged and that Penguin has remote control over its operation. During the destructive rampage throughout the city while trying to evade the police, Batman pinpoints the remote transmitter overriding the Batmobile and removes it, all the while recording Cobblepot's callous remarks about the city and the naiveté of its people. Batman narrowly escapes the police and returns to Wayne Manor with the Batmobile heavily damaged. Penguin seeks to celebrate his victory with Catwoman, but the alliance soon ends when she rebuffs a sexual advance from him, which leads to Penguin using his flying umbrella to drop her into a Greenhouse below to leave her for dead.

The following day, Bruce Wayne uses his radio machinery at the Batcave to interrupt Cobblepot's campaign speech and play back the harsh, subversive statements made about Gotham, revealing Cobblepot's treachery. After hearing the recording, the crowd heckles and condemns Cobblepot, forcing him to retreat to the sewers after Shreck also abandons him. Enraged, Cobblepot reverts to his master plan: to abduct and murder all the first-born sons of Gotham City using information he acquired from the Hall of Records. At a ball hosted by Shreck in which Bruce and Selina meet and accidentally discover their dual identities, Penguin makes an unexpected entrance by exploding the glass center of the floor and announces his plan, with Shreck's son Chip to be the first victim. Shreck insists on being taken instead, and Penguin reluctantly agrees. In the meantime, Batman stops Penguin's men from kidnapping the children and learns of Penguin's sewer hideout. Angered at being foiled once again,

Penguin instead plans to destroy Gotham completely using his (real) penguins to fire missiles into the heart of the city. Batman, with help from his butler Alfred (Michael Gough), jams the penguins' communicators and makes them return to the sewers.

Penguin attempts to flee from the sewer through the zoo, but Batman catches up with him and they fight until Batman tricks him into firing all the penguins' missiles at the abandoned zoo. In the fray, Penguin is attacked by bats that were hidden inside Batman's watercraft and falls through the glass ceiling, plummeting into the toxic waste-contaminated pool in which he planned to drown Gotham's children. Meanwhile, Shreck escapes but is ambushed by Catwoman. Batman intervenes by removing his mask to talk Catwoman out of her desire for vengeance, and although she claims that she does indeed love him, she refuses to listen, claiming that she "Just couldn't live with herself." Shreck pulls out a gun and shoots Batman, then shoots Catwoman, but continues to shoot at her three more times since she does not fall from the wounds. Claiming she has two lives left, she ignites an electrical surge that kills Shreck and destroys the giant air-conditioning/cooling system within the lair. Batman, who was wearing body armor, tries to find Selina in the wreckage, but only finds Max Shreck's charred corpse. Meanwhile, a fatally-injured Penguin emerges from the toxic water and tries to shoot Batman from behind using one of his umbrellas, but picks up the wrong one, choosing "The Cute One" which he planned to use to lure Gotham's children into the pool. With his last few breaths he declares that he thirsts for some ice water, then collapses and dies. Three Emperor penguins and three King penguins gather around him, in a fashion similar to pallbearers, to push his corpse into the water.

On the way back home, Bruce glimpses Catwoman's shadow in an alley and looks for her, but only finds a cat. He subsequently takes the cat home with him, wishing Alfred a Merry Christmas. In the distance, the Bat-Signal lights up in the night sky and Catwoman's silhouette is seen glaring up towards the glowing emblem, as if to taunt Batman once again.

Cast

- Michael Keaton as Bruce Wayne / Batman. After ending The Joker's reign of terror, Batman continues his quest as Gotham City's sole protector, in his wake he meets Selina Kyle, and clashes with new anti-heroine Catwoman. His situation becomes complicated due to the arrival of a mysterious "Penguin-like Man" spotted throughout Gotham.
- Danny DeVito as Oswald Cobblepot / The Penguin . Abandoned at birth due to his hideous appearance by his aristocratic parents, he spends his life living in the sewers of Gotham City. His real intentions are to dispose of every first born son in Gotham City out of vengeance against his parents for abandoning him as a child.
- Michelle Pfeiffer as Selina Kyle / Catwoman. Formerly a quiet and shy secretary for Max Shreck, Selina transforms into Catwoman after an attempt on her life. She becomes a romantic interest for Bruce Wayne and a deadly adversary for Batman. She has nine lives, manifesting as a supernatural ability to live through mortal injuries eight times.

- Christopher Walken as Max Shreck: A powerful business mogul who serves as the boss of Selina Kyle and unusual ally to the Penguin.
- Michael Gough as Alfred Pennyworth: Bruce Wayne's faithful butler.
- Pat Hingle as Commissioner Gordon: Police Commissioner of Gotham City.
- Michael Murphy as The Mayor: Gotham's unpopular Mayor whose position is challenged by the Penguin at the urging of Max Shreck.
- Vincent Schiavelli as The Organ Grinder: Head of The Penguin's Red Triangle Circus Gang.
- Andrew Bryniarski as Charles "Chip" Shreck: Max Shreck's son and right-hand man.
- Cristi Conaway as The Ice Princess: A beauty queen who is kidnapped and eventually killed by the Penguin.
- Jan Hooks as Jen: Image Consultant to Max Shreck.
- Steve Witting as Josh: Image Consultant to Max Shreck.
- Paul Reubens as Tucker Cobblepot: The Penguin's Father.
- Diane Salinger as Esther Cobblepot: The Penguin's Mother.
- Anna Katarina as Poodle Lady: Red Triangle Circus Gang member.
- John Strong as Sword Swallower: Red Triangle Circus Gang member.
- Rick Zumwalt as Tattooed Strongman: Red Triangle Circus Gang member.

Production

Development

After the success of *Batman*, Warner Bros. was hoping for a sequel to start filming in May 1990 at Pinewood Studios. They spent $250,000 storing the sets from the first film. Tim Burton had mixed emotions from the previous film. "I will return if the sequel offers something new and exciting," he said in 1989. "Otherwise it's a most-dumbfounded idea." Burton decided to direct *Edward Scissorhands* for 20th Century Fox. Meanwhile, Sam Hamm from the previous film delivered the first two drafts of the script, while Bob Kane was brought back as a creative consultant. Hamm's script had Penguin and Catwoman going after hidden treasure.

Burton was impressed with Daniel Waters' work on *Heathers*; Burton originally brought Waters aboard on a sequel to *Beetlejuice*. Warner Bros. then granted Burton a large amount of creative control, demoting producers Jon Peters and Peter Guber to executive producers. Dissatisfied with the Hamm script, Burton commissioned a rewrite from Waters. Waters "came up with a social satire that had an evil mogul backing a bid for the Mayor's office by the Penguin," Waters reported. "I wanted to show that the true villains of our world don't necessarily wear costumes." The plot device of Penguin running for Mayor came from the 1960s TV series episodes "Hizzoner the Penguin" and "Dizzoner the Penguin". Waters wrote a total of five drafts.

On the characterization of Catwoman, Waters explained "Sam Hamm went back to the way comic books in general treat women, like fetishy sexual fantasy. I wanted to start off just at the lowest point in society, a very beaten down secretary." Harvey Dent appeared in early drafts of the script, but was deleted. Waters quoted, "Sam Hamm definitely planned that. I flirted with it, having Harvey start to come back and have one scene of him where he flips a coin and it's the good side of the coin, deciding not to do anything, so you had to wait for the next movie." In early scripts Max Shreck was the "golden boy" of the Cobblepot family, whereas Penguin was the deformed outsider. It turned out that Shreck would be the Penguin's long-lost brother. Max Shreck was also a reference to actor Max Schreck, known for his role as Count Orlok in *Nosferatu*.

Burton hired Wesley Strick to do an uncredited rewrite. Strick recalled, "When I was hired to write *Batman Returns* (*Batman II* at the time), the big problem of the script was Penguin's lack of a 'master plan'." Warner Bros. presented Strick with warming or freezing Gotham City (later to be used in *Batman & Robin*). Strick gained inspiration from a Moses parallel that had Penguin killing the firstborn sons of Gotham. A similar notion was used when the Penguin's parents threw him into a river as a baby. Robin appeared in the script, but was deleted due to too many characters. Waters feels Robin is "the most worthless character in the world, especially with [Batman as] the loner of loners." Robin started out as a juvenile gang leader, who becomes an ally to Batman. Robin was later changed to a black teenager who's also a garage mechanic. Waters explained, "He's wearing this old-fashioned garage mechanic uniform and it has an 'R' on it. He drives the Batmobile, which I notice they used in the third film!" Marlon Wayans was cast, and signed for a sequel. Wayans had attended a wardrobe fitting, but it was decided to save the character for a third installment.

Michael Keaton returned after a significant increase in his salary at $10 million. Annette Bening was cast as Catwoman after Burton saw her performance in *The Grifters*, but dropped out due to pregnancy. Raquel Welch, Jennifer Jason Leigh, Lena Olin, Ellen Barkin, Cher, Bridget Fonda and Susan Sarandon were then in competition for the role. Sean Young, who was originally cast as Vicki Vale in the first film, believed the role should have gone to her. Young visited production offices dressed in a homemade Catwoman costume, demanding an audition. Burton was unfamiliar with Michelle Pfeiffer's work, but was convinced to cast her after one meeting. Pfeiffer received a $3 million salary ($2 million more than Bening) and a percentage of the box office. Pfeiffer took kickboxing lessons for the role. Kathy Long served as Pfeiffer's body double. On Danny DeVito's casting, Waters explained, "I kind of knew that DeVito was going to play The Penguin. We didn't really officially cast it, but for a short nasty little guy, it's a short list. I ended up writing the character for Danny DeVito."

Filming

In early-1991, two of Hollywood's largest sound stages (Stage 16 at Warner Bros. and Stage 12 at Universal Studios) were being prepared for the filming of *Batman Returns*. Filming started in June 1991. Stage 16 held Gotham Plaza, based on Rockefeller Center. Universal's Stage 12 housed Penguin's underground lair. A half-a-million gallon tank filled with water was used. Burton wanted to make sure that the penguins felt comfortable. Eight other locations on the Warner Bros. lot were used, over 50% of their property was occupied by Gotham City sets.

Animal rights groups started protesting the film after finding out that penguins would have rockets strapped on their backs. Richard Hill, the curator of the penguins explained that Warner Bros. was very helpful in making sure the penguins were comfortable. "On the flight over the plane was refrigerated down to 45 degrees," recalls Hill. "In Hollywood, they were given a refrigerated trailer, their own swimming pool, half-a-ton of ice each day, and they had fresh fish delivered daily straight from the docks. Even though it was 100 degrees outside, the entire set was refrigerated down to 35 degrees."

Warner Bros. devoted a large amount of secrecy for *Batman Returns*. The art department was required to keep their office blinds pulled down. Cast and crew had to have photo ID badges with the movie's fake working title *Dictel* to go anywhere near the sets. Kevin Costner was refused a chance to visit the set. An entertainment magazine leaked the first photos of Danny DeVito as the Penguin; in response Warner Bros. employed a private investigator to track down the accomplice. $65 million was spent during the production of *Batman Returns*, while $15 million was used for marketing, coming to a total cost of $80 million. The final shot of Catwoman looking at the Bat-Signal was completed during post-production and was not part of the shooting script. After *Batman Returns* was completed Warner Bros. felt it was best for Catwoman to survive, saving more characterizations in a future installment. Pfeiffer was unavailable and a body double was chosen.

Danny Elfman had great enthusiasm for returning because "I didn't have to prove myself from the first film. I remember Jon Peters was very skeptical at first to hire me." Elfman's work schedule was 12 hours a day, 7 days a week. "When completing this movie I realized it was something of a film score and an opera. It was 95 minutes long, twice the amount of the average of film score." Elfman co-orchestrated *Face to Face*, which was written and performed by Siouxsie and the Banshees. The song can be heard in one scene during the film and during the end credits.

Design and effects

Bo Welch, Burton's collaborator on *Beetlejuice* and *Edward Scissorhands*, replaced Anton Furst as production designer. Welch blended "Fascist architecture with World's Fair architecture" for Gotham City. Russian architecture and German Expressionism were also studied. An iron maiden was used for Bruce Wayne's entry into the batcave. Stan Winston, who worked with Burton on *Edward Scissorhands*, designed Danny DeVito's prosthetic makeup, which took two hours to apply. The Penguin's design was based on the titular character of the German Expressionist silent film *The Cabinet of Dr. Caligari*, similar to how the silent film's Somnambulist was referenced for *Edward Scissorhands*. DeVito put a combination of mouthwash and red/green food coloring in his mouth "to create a grotesque texture of some weird ooze."

More than 60 Catsuits were designed in the six-month shoot at $1,000 each. The Batsuit was updated, which was made out of a thinner, slightly more flexible foam rubber material than the suit from *Batman*. DeVito was uncomfortable with his costume, but this made it easy for him to get into character. J. P. Morgan's wardrobe was used for inspiration on Max Shreck's costume design.

The bats were entirely composed of computer-generated imagery since it was decided directing real bats on set would be problematic. The Penguin's "bird army" was a combination of CGI, robotic creatures, men in suits and even real penguins. Robotic penguin puppets were commissioned by Stan Winston. In total 30 African Penguins and 12 King Penguins were used. A miniature effect was used for the exteriors of the Cobblepot Mansion in the opening scene and for Wayne Manor. The same method was used for the Bat Ski-boat and the exterior shots of the Gotham Zoo.

Reception

Reaction

Batman Returns was released in America on June 19, 1992, earning $45.69 million in 2,644 theaters on its opening weekend. This was the highest opening weekend in 1992 and the highest opening weekend of any film up to that point. The film went on to gross $162.83 million in North America, and $104 million in foreign countries, coming to a worldwide total of $266.83 million. *Batman Returns* was the third highest grossing film in America of 1992, and sixth highest in worldwide totals. The film was declared a financial success, but Warner Bros. felt the film should have been more successful. A "parental backlash" criticized *Batman Returns* with violence and sexual references that were unsuitable for children. McDonald's shut down their Happy Meal tie-in for the film. Burton responded, "I like *Batman Returns* better than the first one. There was this big backlash that it was too dark, but I found this movie much less dark."

Based on 46 reviews collected by Rotten Tomatoes, 78% of reviewers enjoyed the film.

Janet Maslin in *The New York Times* thought that "Mr. Burton creates a wicked world of misfits, all of them rendered with the mixture of horror, sympathy and playfulness that has become this director's hallmark." She described Michael Keaton as showing "appropriate earnestness," Danny Devito as "conveying verve," Christopher Walken as "wonderfully debonair," Michelle Pfeiffer as "captivating... fierce, seductive," Bo Welch's production design as "dazzling," Stefan Czapsky's cinematography as "crisp," and Daniel Waters's screenplay as "sharp."

Peter Travers in *Rolling Stone* wrote: "Burton uses the summer's most explosively entertaining movie to lead us back into the liberating darkness of dreams." He praised the performances: "Pfeiffer gives this feminist avenger a tough core of intelligence and wit; she's a classic dazzler... Michael Keaton's manic-depressive hero remains a remarkably rich creation. And Danny DeVito's mutant Penguin - a balloon-bellied *Richard III* with a kingdom of sewer freaks - is as hilariously warped as Jack Nicholson's Joker and even quicker with the quips."

Desson Howe in the *Washington Post* wrote: "Director Burton not only re-creates his one-of-a-kind atmosphere, he one-ups it, even two-ups it. He's best at evoking the psycho-murky worlds in which his characters reside. The Penguin holds court in a penguin-crowded, *Phantom of the Opera*-like sewer home. Keaton hides in a castlelike mansion, which perfectly mirrors its owner's inner remoteness. Comic strip purists will probably never be happy with a Batman movie. But *Returns* comes closer than ever to Bob Kane's dark, original strip, which began in 1939." He described Walken as "engaging," DeVito as "exquisite" and Pfeiffer as "deliciously purry."

Todd McCarthy in *Variety* wrote that "the real accomplishment of the film lies in the amazing physical realization of an imaginative universe. Where Burton's ideas end and those of his collaborators begin is impossible to know, but the result is a seamless, utterly consistent universe full of nasty notions about societal deterioration, greed and other base impulses." He praised the contributions of Stan Winston, Danny Elfman, Bo Welch and cinematographer Stefan Czapsky, and in terms of performances, opined that "the deck is stacked entirely in favor of the villains," calling DeVito "fascinating" and Pfeiffer "very tasty."

Roger Ebert in the *Chicago Sun-Times* wrote: "I give the movie a negative review, and yet I don't think it's a bad movie; it's more misguided, made with great creativity, but denying us what we more or less deserve from a Batman story. No matter how hard you try, superheroes and film noir don't go together; the very essence of noir is that there are no more heroes." He compared the Penguin negatively with the Joker of the first film, writing that "the Penguin is a curiously meager and depressing creature; I pitied him, but did not fear him or find him funny. The genius of Danny DeVito is all but swallowed up in the paraphernalia of the role. *Batman Returns* is odd and sad, but not exhilarating."

Jonathan Rosenbaum called DeVito "a pale substitute for Jack Nicholson from the first film" and felt that "there's no suspense in *Batman Returns* whatsoever". Batman comic book writer/artist Matt Wagner was quoted as saying: "I hated how *Batman Returns* made Batman little more than just another costumed creep, little better than the villains he's pursuing. Additionally, Burton is so blatantly not an action director. That aspect of both his films just sucked."

Awards and nominations

Batman Returns was nominated for two Academy Awards in the categories of Best Visual Effects and Best Makeup. It was also nominated for two British Academy Film Awards (BAFTAs) in the same categories, and the Hugo Award for Best Dramatic Presentation.

Stan Winston and Ve Neill won the Saturn Award for Best Make-up, and the film was nominated in a further four categories: Best Fantasy Film, Best Director (Tim Burton), Best Supporting Actor (Danny DeVito) and Best Costumes.

Danny Elfman won the BMI Film Music Award.

At the MTV Movie Awards 1993, the film was nominated in three categories: Best Kiss (Michael Keaton and Michelle Pfeiffer), Best Villain (Danny DeVito) and Most Desirable Female (Michelle Pfeiffer). Danny DeVito was also nominated for the Golden Raspberry Award (Razzie) for Worst Supporting Actor.

Awarding Body	Award	Nominee	Result
Academy Awards	Best Visual Effects	Michael L. Fink, Craig Barron, John Bruno, Dennis Skotak	nomination
	Best Makeup	Ve Neill, Ronnie Specter, Stan Winston	nomination
British Academy Film Awards (BAFTAs)	Best Makeup Artist	Ve Neill, Stan Winston	nomination
	Best Special Effects	Michael L. Fink, Craig Barron, John Bruno, Dennis Skotak	nomination
BMI Film & TV Awards	**BMI Film Music Award**	**Danny Elfman**	**winner**
Golden Raspberry Awards (Razzies)	Worst Supporting Actor	Danny DeVito	nomination
Hugo Awards	Best Dramatic Presentation		nomination
MTV Movie Awards	Best Kiss	Michael Keaton, Michelle Pfeiffer	nomination
	Best Villain	Danny DeVito	nomination
	Most Desirable Female	Michelle Pfeiffer	nomination

Saturn Awards	Best Fantasy Film		nomination
	Best Director	Tim Burton	nomination
	Best Supporting Actor	Danny DeVito	nomination
	Best Make-Up	**Stan Winston, Ve Neill**	**winner**
	Best Costumes	Bob Ringwood, Mary E. Vogt, Vin Burnham	nomination

Legacy

"After the traumas of the *Batman Returns* she has amnesia, and she doesn't really remember why she has all these bullet holes in her body, so she goes to relax in Oasisburg. What Gotham City is to New York, Oasisburg is to Las Vegas-Los Angeles-Palm Springs. [It's a] resort area in the middle of the desert. It's run by superheroes, and the movie has great fun at making fun at the whole male superhero mythos. Then they end up being not very good at all deep down, and she's got to go back to that whole Catwoman thing."

—Daniel Waters on his script for *Catwoman*

Batman Returns would be the last film in the *Batman* film series that featured Tim Burton and Michael Keaton as director and leading actor, respectively. With *Batman Forever*, Warner Bros. decided to go in a "lighter" direction to be more mainstream in the process of a family film. Burton had no interest in returning to direct a sequel, but he did serve as a producer. With Warner Bros. moving on development for *Batman Forever* in June 1993, a *Catwoman* spin-off was announced. Michelle Pfeiffer was to reprise her role, with the character not to appear in *Forever* because of "her own little movie".

Burton became attached as director, while producer Denise Di Novi and writer Daniel Waters also returned to the *Catwoman* spin-off with Burton. In January 1994, Burton was unsure of his plans to direct *Catwoman* or an adaptation of *The Fall of the House of Usher*. On June 6, 1995, Waters turned in his *Catwoman* script to Warner Bros., the same day *Batman Forever* was released. Burton was still being courted to direct. Waters joked, "turning it in the day *Batman Forever* opened may not have been my best logistical move, in that it's the celebration of the fun-for-the-whole-family Batman. *Catwoman* is definitely not a fun-for-the-whole-family script." The film labored in development hell for years, with Pfeiffer getting replaced by Ashley Judd. The film ended up becoming the critically-panned *Catwoman* (2004) starring Halle Berry.

Despite its mixed reception on initial release, *Batman Returns* has attracted a cult following among fans due to its striking production design and gloomy tone. For example, animation director Satoshi Kon has cited it as one of his 100 favorite movies.

The idea of Penguin taking over the Batmobile was later used in the episode "The Mechanic" of *Batman: The Animated Series*.

External links

- Official website [1]
- *Batman Returns* [2] at the Internet Movie Database
- *Batman Returns* [3] at Allmovie
- *Batman Returns* [4] at Box Office Mojo
- *Batman Returns* [5] at Rotten Tomatoes
- http://www.variety.com/article/VR103029.html?categoryid=13&cs=1

Michael Keaton

Michael Keaton	
Keaton at the 2004 Dallas Comic Convention	
Born	Michael John Douglas September 5, 1951 Coraopolis, Pennsylvania, U.S.
Occupation	Actor
Years active	1975–present
Spouse	Caroline McWilliams (1982-1990)

Michael John Douglas (born September 5, 1951), better known as **Michael Keaton**, is an American actor, well known for his early comedic roles in films such as *Night Shift*, *Mr. Mom*, *Johnny Dangerously*, *Beetlejuice*, and for his dramatic portrayal of Batman in Tim Burton's *Batman* and *Batman Returns*, as well as lead roles in other films including *The Paper*, *Jackie Brown*, *Jack Frost* and *White Noise*.

Personal life

Keaton, the youngest of seven children, was born in Coraopolis, Pennsylvania, and lived in Robinson Township, Allegheny County, Pennsylvania. His father, George A. Douglas, worked as a civil engineer and surveyor, and his mother, Leona Elizabeth (née Loftus), a homemaker, came from a Scots-Irish community in McKees Rocks, Pennsylvania. Keaton was raised in a large Catholic family and attended Montour High School in Pennsylvania. He studied speech for two years at Kent State before dropping out and moving to Pittsburgh. Keaton was married to actress Caroline McWilliams from 1982 until 1990. They have one son, Sean Maxwell (born May 27, 1983). He also had a six-year relationship with actress Courteney Cox from 1989 to 1995. Michael was a contributor to the John Kerry for President campaign in 2004.

Career

1970s and 1980s

An unsuccessful attempt at stand-up comedy led Keaton to working as a TV cameraman at public television station WQED (TV) in Pittsburgh. Keaton first appeared on TV in the Pittsburgh-based public television program *Mister Rogers' Neighborhood* (1975), as one of the "Flying Zucchini Brothers." He also served as a full-time production assistant on the show. (In 2003, following Rogers' death, Keaton hosted the PBS memorial tribute program, *Fred Rogers: Everybody's Favorite Neighbor*.)

Keaton left Pittsburgh and moved to Los Angeles to begin auditioning for various TV parts. He popped up in various popular TV shows including *Maude* and *The Mary Tyler Moore Hour*. Around this time Keaton decided to use an alternative surname to remove confusion with well-known actor Michael Douglas, as well as satisfying SAG rules, and after reading an article on actress Diane Keaton, he decided on "Michael Keaton."

His next key break was working alongside James Belushi in the short-lived comedy series *Working Stiffs*, which showcased his comedic talent and led to a co-starring role in the comedy *Night Shift* directed by Ron Howard. His role as the hilariously fast-talking schemer Bill "Blaze" Blazejowski alongside nerdish morgue attendant Henry Winkler earned Keaton some critical acclaim, and he scored leads in the subsequent comedy hits *Mr. Mom*, *Johnny Dangerously*, and *Gung Ho*.

Keaton's role as the title character in the 1988 Tim Burton horror-comedy *Beetlejuice*, which co-starred Alec Baldwin, Geena Davis, Catherine O'Hara, and Winona Ryder, earned Keaton widespread acclaim and boosted him to movieland's A-list. He was originally turned down for the title role in *Beetlejuice* but was reconsidered by director Burton. Keaton now considers *Beetlejuice* his favorite of his own films. That same year, Keaton also gave an acclaimed dramatic performance as a drug-addicted businessman in *Clean and Sober*. *Newsweek* featured him in a story during this time.

Batman

Michael Keaton's career was given another major boost when he was again cast by Tim Burton, this time as the title superhero of the 1989 blockbuster *Batman*. Burton cast him because he thought that Keaton was the only actor who could believably portray someone who has the kind of darkly obsessive personality that the character demands.[citation needed] Warner Bros. received thousands of letters of complaint by fans commenting that the comedic Keaton was the wrong choice for Gotham City's creature of the night, given his prior work in comedies and the fact that he lacked the suave, handsome features and tall, muscular physicality often attributed to the character in the comic books.[citation needed] However, Keaton's sophisticated performance earned universal acclaim from critics and audiences alike, and *Batman* became one of the most successful films of the year.

According to Keaton, he was astounded when he was first considered as Batman since he was only familiar with the 1960s *Batman* television series starring Adam West, but it was not until Burton introduced Keaton to Frank Miller's *Batman: The Dark Knight Returns* that Keaton really understood the dark and brooding side of Batman that he portrayed to much fan approval. Keaton later returned to wear the cape and cowl again in *Batman Returns* (1992), which was another financial success, though controversial for being darker than the original.

He was prepared to return for *Batman Forever* (1995), even going so far as to show up for costume fitting. However, when Burton was dropped by Warner Bros., Keaton left the franchise. He was reportedly dissatisfied with the screenplay approved by the new director, Joel Schumacher, which Keaton considered to be lighter in tone than the past two Batman movies. According to the A&E *Biography* episode on Keaton, after he had refused the first time (after meetings with Schumacher), Warner Brothers offered him $35,000,000 (one of the highest salaries offered to an actor at the time), but Keaton steadfastly refused. He was subsequently succeeded as Batman by Val Kilmer and later on by George Clooney in *Batman & Robin* (1997), which became the least successful Batman film both critically and commercially. It was not until the success of *Batman Begins* (2005), a reboot starring Christian Bale as the Dark Knight, that the franchise was continued.

1990s and 2000s

Keaton remained in demand during the 1990s, appearing in a wide range of films including *Pacific Heights*, *One Good Cop*, *My Life*, and the star-studded Shakespearian story *Much Ado About Nothing*. He also starred in another Ron Howard film, *The Paper*, as well as with Andie MacDowell in *Multiplicity* and twice in the same role, Elmore Leonard character Agent Ray Nicolette, in *Jackie Brown* and *Out of Sight*. The actor also made *Jack Frost* and the thriller *Desperate Measures*.

Keaton starred in *Speechless* with Geena Davis (his co-star in *Beetlejuice*) and Christopher Reeve (who, like Keaton, also portrayed a famous DC Comics superhero on film; Superman), as a political candidate's speechwriter.

Since 2000, Keaton has appeared in several films with mixed success including *Live From Baghdad* for which he was nominated for a Golden Globe award, *First Daughter*, *White Noise*, and *Herbie: Fully Loaded*. While he continued to receive good notices from the critics (particularly for *Jackie Brown*), he was not able to approach the box-office success of *Batman* until the release of *Cars*, in which he played the part of Chick Hicks, in 2006. On New Years Day of 2004, he hosted the PBS TV special *Mr. Rogers: America's Favorite Neighbor*. It was released by Triumph Marketing LLC on DVD September 28 that year.

In 2006, Keaton starred in an independent film called *Game 6*, a semi-thriller based around the infamous 1986 World Series bid by the Boston Red Sox. He had a cameo in the Tenacious D short film, *Time Fixers*, an iTunes exclusive. The 9-minute film was released to coincide with *Tenacious D in The Pick of Destiny*. Keaton was announced to be the lead in Media 8 Entertainment's film *Reaper*, a supernatural thriller. He reportedly agreed to star as John Target in the Matt Evans scripted *No Rule To Make Target,* and he has directed a drama, *The Merry Gentleman.*

Keaton reportedly was cast as Dr. Jack Shephard in the series *Lost,* understanding that the role of Jack would be a brief one. Once the role was retooled to be a long-running series regular, Keaton withdrew. The part was given to actor Matthew Fox.

Keaton starred in the 2007 TV mini-series *The Company,* set during the Cold War, in which he portrayed the real-life CIA counterintelligence chief James Jesus Angleton. The role garnered Keaton a 2008 SAG nomination for Outstanding Performance by a Male Actor in a Television Movie or Miniseries. *The Company* also starred Chris O'Donnell, who portrayed Batman's crime fighting sidekick Robin (the Boy Wonder was absent from the two Batman films that Keaton starred in) in *Batman Forever* and *Batman & Robin.*

Keaton most recently provided the voice of Ken, Barbie's friend, in *Toy Story 3*. He announced in June 2010 his interest in returning for a *Beetlejuice* sequel.

Filmography

Film

Year	Film	Role	Notes
1982	*Night Shift*	Bill Blazejowski	**Won** Kansas City Film Critics Circle Award for Best Supporting Actor
1983	*Mr. Mom*	Jack Butler	
1984	*Johnny Dangerously*	Jonathan "Johnny" Kelly (a.k.a. Johnny Dangerously)	
1986	*Gung Ho*	Hunt Stevenson	
	Touch and Go	Robert "Bobby" Barbato	
1987	*The Squeeze*	Harold "Harry" Berg	
1988	*She's Having a Baby*	Himself	uncredited cameo
	Beetlejuice	Betelgeuse (pronounced "Beetlejuice")	**Won** National Society of Film Critics Award for Best Actor (also for *Clean and Sober*) Nominated - Saturn Award for Best Supporting Actor
	Clean and Sober	Daryl Poynter	National Society of Film Critics Award for Best Actor (also for *Beetlejuice*)
1989	*The Dream Team*	William "Billy" Caufield	
	Batman	Bruce Wayne / Batman	
1990	*Pacific Heights*	Carter Hayes	

Year	Title	Role	Notes
1991	One Good Cop	Arthur "Artie" Lewis	
1992	Batman Returns	Bruce Wayne / Batman	Nominated MTV Movie Award (shared with *Michelle Pfeiffer*)
	Porco Rosso	Porco Rosso	voice in 2003 English dubbed version
1993	Much Ado About Nothing	Dogberry	
	My Life	Robert "Bob" Jones	
1994	The Paper	Henry Hackett	
	Speechless	Kevin Vallick	
1996	Multiplicity	Douglas "Doug" Kinney	
1997	Inventing the Abbotts	Narrator / Older Doug	uncredited
	Jackie Brown	Raymond "Ray" Nicolette	
1998	Desperate Measures	Peter McCabe	
	Out of Sight	Raymond "Ray" Nicolette	Cameo
	Jack Frost	Jack Frost	
2000	A Shot at Glory	Peter Cameron	
2002	Live From Baghdad	Robert Wiener	Nominated for a Golden Globe
2003	Quicksand	Martin Raikes	
2004	First Daughter	President Mackenzie	
2005	White Noise	Jonathan Rivers	
	Game 6	Nicholas "Nicky" Rogan	
	Herbie: Fully Loaded	Raymond "Ray" Peyton, Sr.	
2006	Cars	Chick Hicks	voice
	The Last Time	Ted "Theodore"	
2009	The Merry Gentleman	Franklin "Frank" Logan	
	Post Grad	Walter Malby	
	Noah's Ark: The New Beginning	Noah	voice
2010	Toy Story 3	Ken	
	The Other Guys	Captain Mauch	
2011	Cars 2	Chick Hicks	voice

Television

Year	Production	Role	Other notes
1976	All's Fair	Lannie Wolf	
1977	Klein Time	Various	
	Maude	Chip Winston	
1978	Mary (1978)	Skit characters	
	The Tony Randall Show	Zeke	
1979	The Mary Tyler Moore Hour	Kenneth Christy	
	Working Stiffs	Mike O'Rourke	
1982	Report To Murphy	Murphy	
2002	Frasier	Blaine Sternin	
	Live from Baghdad	Robert Wiener	Nominated - Golden Globe Award for Best Performance by an Actor in a Mini-Series or Motion Picture Made for Television
2001	The Simpsons	Jack Crowley	1 episode guest star
2002	King of the Hill	Trip Larsen	
2004	Fred Rogers: America's Favorite Neighbor	Host	Nominated - Emmy Award for Outstanding Nonfiction Special
2007	The Company	James Angleton	Nominated - Screen Actors Guild Award for Outstanding Performance by a Male Actor in a Miniseries or Television Movie

External links

- Michael Keaton [1] at the Internet Movie Database
- Story on Michael Keaton and his hometown [[Pittsburgh Pirates [2]] opening day controversy]

Batman Forever

Batman Forever

Batman Forever	
Theatrical release poster	
Directed by	Joel Schumacher
Produced by	Tim Burton Peter Macgregor-Scott *Executive*: Benjamin Melniker Michael Uslan
Screenplay by	Lee Batchler Janet Scott-Batchler Akiva Goldsman
Story by	Lee Batchler Janet Scott-Batchler *Comic book*: Bill Finger *(uncredited)* Bob Kane
Starring	Val Kilmer Tommy Lee Jones Jim Carrey Nicole Kidman Chris O'Donnell
Music by	Elliot Goldenthal
Cinematography	Stephen Goldblatt
Editing by	Dennis Virkler Mark Stevens
Distributed by	Warner Bros.
Release date(s)	June 16, 1995
Running time	122 minutes
Country	United States

Language	English
Budget	US$100 million
Gross revenue	$336,529,844
Preceded by	*Batman Returns*
Followed by	*Batman & Robin*

Batman Forever is a 1995 American superhero film directed by Joel Schumacher and produced by Tim Burton. It is the third installment of the *Batman* film series and stars Val Kilmer as Batman. The plot focuses on Batman trying to stop Two-Face (Tommy Lee Jones) and the Riddler (Jim Carrey) in their villainous scheme to drain information from all the brains in Gotham City. He gains allegiance from psychiatrist Chase Meridian (Nicole Kidman) and orphaned ward Dick Grayson (Chris O'Donnell).

The film had a change in tone compared to the previous installments, more family-friendly, since Warner Bros. considered that the previous film, *Batman Returns*, underperformed at the box office due to its violence and dark overtones. Production was troubled, with many actors considered for the main roles, and Kilmer entering in conflicts with the director and the rest of the crew. *Batman Forever* received mixed reviews upon release, but was a success with audiences, outgrossing *Returns* with over $336 million worldwide and becoming the second-highest grossing film of 1995.

Plot

The movie opens with Batman (Val Kilmer) stopping a hostage situation in a bank caused by Two-Face (Tommy Lee Jones), who had once been Gotham City District Attorney Harvey Dent until a mobster threw acid in his face, scarring him and creating a split personality, who decides his every move by flipping a coin. Two-Face escapes after defacing Gotham's Statue of Liberty. Meanwhile, Edward Nygma (Jim Carrey), a researcher at Wayne Enterprises, has been developing a device to beam television directly to a person's brain. When put on the spot, Bruce Wayne rejects the invention, noting that its admitted manipulation of brainwaves "raises too many questions". Hurt by Wayne's disapproval, Edward becomes determined to upstage him. He works after hours to perfect the device, but is caught by his supervisor. After testing the machine on him, Edward kills his supervisor, hacks into the security cameras to make it look like a suicide, and then resigns from his post.

After meeting psychiatrist Dr. Chase Meridian (Nicole Kidman), Bruce invites her to a charity circus event. While there, Two-Face and his henchmen storm the event in an attempt to discover Batman's secret identity, threatening to set off a bomb. An acrobat, Dick (Chris O'Donnell), manages to throw Two-Face's bomb into the river, but returns to find Two-Face had caused his family to fall to their deaths. Bruce assumes responsibility for Dick and allows him to stay at Wayne Manor. Dick declares his intention to kill Two-Face and avenge his family's murder, and later discovers the existence of the Batcave, even going as far as to take the Batmobile for a joy ride.

Meanwhile, Edward has become obsessed with Bruce, and he begins to leave riddles for him. He takes up the mantle of "The Riddler" and approaches Two-Face with a deal: Two-Face will provide Riddler with funding for his experiments, and in return, the Riddler will find out Batman's identity for Two-Face. Using his invention that Bruce had rejected earlier, Edward discovers a way to read people's minds and steal their intelligence quotient (although it does not decrease the victim's IQ, only increasing Edward's). At a business party, Edward discovers Bruce's secret identity before Two-Face attacks the party and nearly kills Batman, but Dick comes just in time to save his life. Dick hassles Bruce to make him his partner, but Bruce responds by expressing his intention to quit being Batman. However, whilst Bruce invites Chase over for dinner, revealing his identity to her, Two-Face and the Riddler attack Wayne Manor, knocking Bruce unconscious, kidnapping Chase and destroying the Batcave. After Bruce and Alfred solve the Riddler's clues, identifying him as Edward Nygma, Batman accepts Dick, now calling himself Robin, as his partner and the two head towards Riddler's Lair.

Batman and Robin survive the Riddler's sea mines; evil frogmen and anti-aircraft beam and locate the Riddler's Lair, where both are separated upon reaching the island. Robin then encounters Two-Face and manages to beat him to the ground, but is taken captive when he saves him from falling to his death. Meanwhile, Batman makes his way into the Riddler's lair and meets the Riddler himself, who gives Batman the choice to save either Robin or Chase before they are dropped into a watery grave. Unable to simply choose one to save, Batman asks the Riddler a riddle, which buys him enough time to destroy the Superbox with a Sonar Batarang, causing it to malfunction and driving Riddler mad in the process. Before he goes completely insane, Riddler sends Chase and Robin plummeting, but Batman manages to save them in time. Two-Face appears out of nowhere and flips his coin to determine the heroes' fate. However, Batman throws several other coins in the air, causing Two-Face to lose his balance and fall to his death. As a result of the machine's malfunction and Batman's fear, Riddler becomes insane, forgetting Batman's true identity, and is admitted into Arkham Asylum. Chase then meets Bruce Wayne outside and tells him his secret is safe. The movie ends showing Batman and Robin running to a crime scene.

Cast

- Val Kilmer as Bruce Wayne / Batman: After coming across the journal of his father, he starts questioning his act of vengeance. Bruce struggles with his dual identity as a crime fighter, becoming romantically involved with Dr. Chase Meridian.
- Tommy Lee Jones as Harvey Dent / Two-Face: Formerly the good district attorney of Gotham City, half of Harvey's face is scarred with acid during the conviction of a crime boss. Driven insane, he becomes the criminal Two-Face.
- Jim Carrey as Dr. Edward Nygma / The Riddler: A former Wayne Enterprises employee, Edward resigns after his newest invention is personally rejected by Bruce Wayne. He becomes the villainous Riddler, leaving riddles and puzzles at scenes of crime.

- Nicole Kidman as Dr. Chase Meridian: A psychologist and love interest of Bruce Wayne. Chase is fascinated by the dual nature of Batman. She's held as a damsel in distress in the climax.
- Chris O'Donnell as Dick Grayson / Robin: Once a circus acrobat, Dick is taken in by Bruce after Two-Face murders his parents and brother at a circus event. Bruce is reminded when his parents were murdered when he sees the same vengeance in Dick, and decides to take him in as his ward. He eventually discovers the Batcave and learns Bruce's secret identity. In his wake, he becomes the crime fighting partner, Robin.
- Michael Gough as Alfred Pennyworth: The Wayne family's faithful butler and Bruce's confidant. Alfred also befriends the young Dick Grayson.
- Pat Hingle as James Gordon: The Police Commissioner of Gotham City.
- Drew Barrymore and Debi Mazar as Sugar and Spice: Two-Face's "good" and "bad" henchwomen; they were created specifically for the film.
- Ed Begley, Jr. as Fred Stickley: Edward Nygma's ill-tempered supervisor at Wayne Enterprises. After Stickley discovers the true nature of Nygma's invention, Nygma kills him and makes it look like suicide. Begley was uncredited for this role.
- Ofer Samra as Harvey's Thug.
- Elizabeth Sanders as Gossip Gerty: Gotham's top gossip columnist.
- René Auberjonois as Dr. Burton: Head Doctor of Arkham Asylum.
- Joe Grifasi as The Bank Guard: Two-Face's hostage during the opening scene.

Production

Development

Even though *Batman Returns* was a financial success, Warner Bros. felt the film should have made more money and decided to make the film series more mainstream. Tim Burton, who had directed the two previous installments, was asked to restrict himself to the role of producer and approved of Joel Schumacher as director. Schumacher originally had in mind an adaptation of Frank Miller's *Batman: Year One*. The studio rejected the idea as they wanted a sequel, not a prequel, though Schumacher was able to include very brief events in Batman's past. Burton and Schumacher together hired Lee and Janet Scott-Batchler to write the script which introduced a psychotic Riddler with a pet rat accompanying him. The story elements and much of the dialogue still remained in the finished film, though Schumacher felt it could be "lighted down." He hired Akiva Goldsman, whom he previously had worked for on *The Client* to write the second draft.

Production went on fast track with Rene Russo cast as Dr. Chase Meridian. Michael Keaton decided not to reprise Batman because he did not like the new direction the film series was heading in. Keaton also wanted to pursue "more interesting roles", turning down $15 million to appear in *Batman Forever*. Val Kilmer was cast days later, and the filmmakers decided that Russo was too old for Kilmer, replacing her with a different actress. Schumacher got interested in Kilmer for Batman after seeing him in *Tombstone*, and the actor accepted the role without even reading the script or knowing who the new director was. Before Val Kilmer was cast, Daniel Day-Lewis, Ralph Fiennes, William Baldwin and Johnny Depp were all under consideration to replace Michael Keaton.

Robin Wright Penn, Jeanne Tripplehorn and Linda Hamilton were in competition for Dr. Chase Meridian, with Penn appearing as the favorable choice. Nicole Kidman was eventually cast. Even though Billy Dee Williams took the role of Harvey Dent in *Batman* because he was looking forward to portray Two-Face in a sequel, the producers cast Tommy Lee Jones in the role. Jones was always Schumacher's first choice for the role after working with him on *The Client*. Jones claims he was sent the script and was very cautious to accept, but accepted the part because Two-Face was his son's favorite character. Robin Williams was considered to play the Riddler, but Jim Carrey was eventually cast. Robin appeared in the shooting script of *Batman Returns*. Tim Burton cast Marlon Wayans in the role at the time, but later decided there were too many characters in the film and dropped the minor scene from production. Wayans also signed on for *Batman Forever*. When Schumacher took over, he decided Wayans was not the right actor to play Robin for his production. Wayans was paid out and replaced with a different actor. Leonardo DiCaprio and Chris O'Donnell became the top two choices, with O'Donnell winning the part. Mitchell Gaylord served as O'Donnell's stunt double.

Filming

Filming started in September 1994. Schumacher hired Barbara Ling for production design, claiming that the film needed a "force" and felt Ling could "advance on it." Schumacher wanted a design that was not to be any way connected to the previous films, and instead was to be inspired by the images from the Batman comic books seen in the 1940s/early 1950s and taken from that of New York City architecture in the 1930s, with a combination of modern Tokyo. He also wanted a "city with personality", with more statues, as well as various amounts of neon. The Batmobile was also given a makeover, with two cars being constructed, one for stunt purposes and one for close ups with both showcasing a V8 engine.

Schumacher had problems filming with Kilmer, whom he described as "childish and impossible", reporting that he fought with various crewmen, and refused to speak to Schumacher during two weeks after the director told him to stop behaving in a rude way. Schumacher also mentioned Tommy Lee Jones as source of trouble: "Jim Carrey was a gentleman, and Tommy Lee was threatened by him. I'm tired of defending overpaid, overprivileged actors. I pray I don't work with them again."

Design and effects

Rick Baker designed the prosthetic makeup. John Dykstra, Andrew Adamson and Jim Rygiel served as visual effects supervisors, with Pacific Data Images also contributing with visual effects work. PDI provided a computer-generated Batman for complicated stunts. For the costume design, producer Peter MacGregor-Scott claimed that 146 workers were at one point working together. Batman's costume was redesigned along the lines of a more "MTV organic, and edgier feel" to the suit, as were the Batcave and Batmobile (which had been destroyed in Batman Returns). Various suits were designed for specific purposes, such as one where as Val Kilmer sits in the Batmobile and various others for stunts and close ups.

Music

Elliot Goldenthal was hired to compose the film score even before the first draft of the script was written. He stated he was told by Schumacher as not to listen to Danny Elfman's previous score, and instead compose a different orchestral piece. An album featuring over 40 minutes of Elliot Goldenthal's Original Motion Picture Score, was released two weeks after the soundtrack album.

The soundtrack was also hugely successful, selling almost as many copies as Prince's soundtrack to the 1989 Batman film. Only five of the songs on the soundtrack are actually featured in the movie, the rest are strictly 'inspired by'. Hit singles from the soundtrack include "Hold Me, Thrill Me, Kiss Me, Kill Me" by U2 and "Kiss from a Rose" by Seal, both of which were nominated for MTV Movie Awards. "Kiss From a Rose" (whose video was also directed by Joel Schumacher) reached #1 in the U.S. charts as well. The soundtrack itself, featuring additional songs by The Flaming Lips, Brandy (both songs also included in the film), Method Man, Nick Cave, Michael Hutchence (of INXS), PJ Harvey, and Massive Attack, was an attempt to (in producer Peter MacGregor-Scott's words) make the film more "pop".

Release

Batman Forever went through a few major edits before its release. Originally darker than the final product, the movie's original length was closer to 2 hours and 40 minutes according to director Joel Schumacher. There was talk of an extended cut being released to DVD for the film's 10th anniversary in 2005. While all four previous Batman films were given Special Edition DVD releases on the same day as the *Batman Begins*' DVD release, the version of *Batman Forever* released was the original, although some of the following scenes were in a deleted scenes section in the special features.

Many scenes were filmed but deleted from the film. These included:

- The escape of Two-Face from Arkham Asylum. Rene Auberjonois had more scenes filmed here, playing Doctor Burton but his role was reduced to a cameo in the final film. He encounters the escape with the psychologist killed and hanged in Two-Face's cell with his blood smeared on the wall, written as "The Bat Must Die." This was supposed to begin the picture but producers decided

this was far too dark for a family audience. As this was cut, it made the editing of the final film somewhat muddled to the fans of the original script as later scenes were re-arranged. This scene appears in a rough edit on the Special Edition DVD. Segments of the scene also appears on the U2 music video "Hold Me, Thrill Me, Kiss Me, Kill Me."
- The construction of NygmaTech was more in-depth. There were scenes shot that appear in publicity stills of Edward Nygma with a hard hat helping with the construction of his headquarters on Claw Island. This scene does not appear on the new Special Edition release but is shown in the sticker album published by Merlin Collections.
- Sugar and Spice, played by Drew Barrymore and Debi Mazar, try out the Riddler's device during the montage when it goes on sale. They are seated with the Riddler and Two-Face on the couch where Chase is handcuffed later in the film. This scene appears in the comic adaptation but not in the final film.
- The most known deleted scene involved further backstory to the film which screenwriter Akiva Goldsman believed would have improved the quality of the film considerably.[citation needed] It involved Bruce waking up after being shot in the head by Two-Face, temporarily wiping a part of his memory; he has forgotten his origin and life as the Dark Knight. Alfred takes him to the Batcave, which has been destroyed by the Riddler. They stand on the platform where the Batmobile was and Alfred says "Funny they did not know about the cave beneath the cave." The platform then rotates downward to another level where the sonar-modification equipment is kept, from the special batsuit to the hi-tech weaponry. Bruce then discovers the cavern where he first saw the image that would make him become Batman — a giant bat. The bat appears and Bruce raises his arms and the shot shows that they are one. Bruce now remembers who he is and goes with Alfred to solve the riddles left throughout the film. Akiva admitted the scene was very theatrical on the Special Edition DVD and felt the scene would have made a difference to the final cut. The bat was designed and created by Rick Baker, who was in charge of the make-up of Two-Face, played by Tommy Lee Jones. This scene appears in a rough form on the Special Edition DVD and is briefly mentioned in the comic adaptation.
- The original ending paid homage to the ending of the first film. When Alfred drives Doctor Chase Meridian back to Gotham she asks him "Does it ever end?" Alfred replies, "No, Doctor Meridian, not in this lifetime..." The Bat-Signal shines on the night sky and Batman and Robin are standing on a giant gargoyle overlooking the city. This scene, with Kilmer and O'Donnell, was shot in front of a blue screen. A rough edit of the first half of the ending scene appears on the Special Edition DVD, but not in its entirety. The sequence with Batman and Robin at the end of this scene is not to be confused with a commercial for the video game, which is on the VHS release of this film (released in the UK on December 3, 1995), with Batman standing on a pillar looking ahead. Robin then comes into the shot and joins his partner. Batman leaps off the pillar, towards the camera. This commercial was filmed with two stuntmen dressed in Batman and Robin outfits on a small sound stage.

Reception

Box office

Batman Forever opened in 2,842 theaters in the United States on June 16, 1995, making $52.78 million in its opening weekend. This was the highest opening weekend of 1995. The film went on to gross $184.03 million in North America, and $152.5 million in international countries, totaling $336.53 million. *Batman Forever* was declared a huge financial success. The film earned more money than its predecessor *Batman Returns*, and was the second-highest (behind *Toy Story*) grossing film of 1995, in North America.

Critical reaction

Batman Forever was released to mixed reviews. Based on 54 reviews collected by Rotten Tomatoes, 43% of reviewers enjoyed the film. The film was more balanced with 14 critics in Rotten Tomatoes's "Top Critics" poll, receiving a 71% approval rating. Metacritic collected an average score of 51, based on 23 reviews.

Peter Travers criticized the movie's blatant commercialism, but commented that "*Batman Forever* still gets in its licks. There's no fun machine this summer that packs more surprises. The script misses the pain Tim Burton caught in a man tormented by the long-ago murder of his parents." Brian Lowry of *Variety* believed "One does have to question the logic behind adding nipples to the hard-rubber batsuit. Whose idea was that supposed to be anyway, Alfred's? Some of the computer-generated Gotham cityscapes appear too obviously fake. Elliot Goldenthal's score, while serviceable, also isn't as stirring as Danny Elfman's work in the first two films."

James Berardinelli enjoyed the film. "It's lighter, brighter, funnier, faster-paced, and a whole lot more colorful than before." Scott Beatty felt "Tommy Lee Jones played Harvey Dent as a Joker knock-off rather than a multi-layered rogue." Lee Bermejo called *Batman Forever* "unbearable". Gene Siskel and Roger Ebert both gave the film mixed reviews, but with the former giving it a thumbs up and the latter a thumbs down. In his written review, Ebert wrote: "Is the movie better entertainment? Well, it's great bubblegum for the eyes. Younger children will be able to process it more easily, some kids were led bawling from *Batman Returns* where the PG-13 rating was a joke." Mick LaSalle had a mixed reaction, concluding "a shot of Kilmer's rubber buns at one point is guaranteed to bring squeals from the audience."

Awards

At the 68th Academy Awards, *Batman Forever* was nominated with Cinematography, Sound and Sound Editing. "Hold Me, Thrill Me, Kiss Me, Kill Me" by U2 was nominated for Golden Globe Award for Best Original Song, but was also nominated for the Worst Song Golden Raspberry Award. At the Saturn Awards, the film was nominated for Best Fantasy Film, Make-up, Special Effects and Costume Design. Composer Elliot Goldenthal was given a Grammy Award nomination. *Batman Forever* received six nominations at the 1996 MTV Movie Awards.

Merchandising

In addition to a large line of toys and action figures from Kenner, the McDonald's food chain released several collectibles and mugs to coincide with the release of the film. Peter David and Alan Grant wrote separate novelizations of the film. Dennis O'Neil authored a comic book adaptation, with art by Michal Dutkiewicz.

See also

- *Batman Forever* (score)
- *Batman Forever* (soundtrack)
- *Batman Forever* (video game)
- *Batman Forever: The Arcade Game*

External links

- Official website [1]
- *Batman Forever* [1] at the Internet Movie Database
- *Batman Forever* [2] at Allmovie
- *Batman Forever* [3] at Box Office Mojo
- *Batman Forever* [4] at Rotten Tomatoes

Val Kilmer

Val Kilmer	
Kilmer in June 2005	
Born	Val Edward Kilmer December 31, 1959 Los Angeles, California, U.S.
Occupation	Actor
Years active	1984–present
Spouse	Joanne Whalley (1988–1996) 2 children

Val Edward Kilmer (born December 31, 1959) is an American actor. Originally a stage actor, Kilmer became popular in the mid-1980s after a string of appearances in comedy films, starting with *Top Secret!* (1984), then the cult classic *Real Genius* (1985), as well as blockbuster action films, including a role in *Top Gun* and a lead role in *Willow*.

During the 1990s, Kilmer gained critical respect after a series of films that were also commercially successful, including his roles as Jim Morrison in *The Doors*, Doc Holliday in 1993's *Tombstone*, Batman in 1995's *Batman Forever*, Chris Shiherlis in 1995's *Heat* and Simon Templar in 1997's *The Saint*. During the early 2000s, Kilmer appeared in several well-received roles, including *The Salton Sea*, *Spartan*, and supporting performances in *Kiss Kiss Bang Bang*, *Alexander*, and as the voice of KITT in *Knight Rider*.

Early life

Kilmer was born in Los Angeles, California, the son of Gladys (*née* Ekstadt) and Eugene Kilmer, an aerospace equipment distributor and real estate developer. Kilmer's grandfather was a gold miner in New Mexico; the poet Joyce Kilmer is a second cousin of Kilmer's. Kilmer grew up in the San Fernando Valley with his two siblings, older brother Mark and younger brother Wesley, but says that even as a child growing up in California he did not like it there.[citation needed] Kilmer, who was raised a Christian Scientist, attended Chatsworth High School—where his classmates included Kevin Spacey and Mare Winningham—as well as Hollywood's Professional's School. He also attended Berkeley Hall School, a Christian Science school in Beverly Hills, California, from nursery school until graduation from the 9th grade. At the age of 17, he was at the time the youngest person to be accepted into Juilliard's drama program. He was in Group 10 of the Drama Division. His brother Wesley died as a teenager due to an epileptic seizure in a swimming pool.

Career

1980s

In 1981, Kilmer co-authored and starred in the play *How It All Began*, which was performed at the Public Theatre at the New York Shakespeare Festival. Kilmer turned down a role in Francis Ford Coppola's 1983 film, *The Outsiders*, as he had prior theatre commitments. That same year, his first off-stage acting role (excluding television commercials) came in the form of a television short titled *One Too Many*, which was an educational drama on drinking and driving; it also starred a young Michelle Pfeiffer. His big break came when he received top billing in the spoof comedy *Top Secret!*, where he played an American rock and roll star. Kilmer sang all the songs in the film and actually released an album under the film character's name, "Nick Rivers".

During a brief hiatus, he backpacked throughout Europe, before going on to play the lead character in the 1985 comedy *Real Genius*. He turned down roles in *Dune* and *Blue Velvet*, before being cast as naval aviator "Iceman" in the big budget action film *Top Gun*, alongside Tom Cruise. *Top Gun* grossed a total of $344,700,000 worldwide. Following roles in the television films *The Murders in the Rue Morgue* and *The Man Who Broke 1,000 Chains*, Kilmer played "Madmartigan" in the fantasy *Willow*; he met his future wife, co-star Joanne Whalley, on the film's set. Kilmer published a book of his poems, *My Edens After Burns*, in 1987, and starred in the Colorado Shakespeare Festival production of *Hamlet* in 1988. In 1989, Kilmer played the lead in both *Kill Me Again*, again opposite Whalley, and in TNT's *Billy the Kid*.

1990s

After several delays, director Oliver Stone finally started production on the film, *The Doors*, based on the band of the same name. Kilmer memorized the lyrics to all of lead singer Jim Morrison's songs prior to his audition, and sent a video of himself performing some Doors songs to director Stone. Stone was not impressed with the tape, but Paul Rothchild (the original producer of The Doors) said "I was shaken by it" and suggested they record Kilmer in the studio. After Kilmer was cast as Morrison, he prepared for the role by attending Doors tribute concerts and reading Morrison's poetry. He spent close to a year before production dressing in Morrison-like clothes, and spent time at Morrison's old hangouts along the Sunset Strip. His portrayal of Morrison was praised and members of The Doors noted that Kilmer did such a convincing job that they had trouble distinguishing his voice from Morrison's. Paul Rothchild played Val's version of 'The End' for Robby Krieger, and he told him "I'm really glad they got 'The End'. We never got a recording of that live with Jim and now we've got it." However, Doors keyboardist, Ray Manzarek, was less than enthusiastic with how Morrison was portrayed by director Oliver Stone's interpretation.[*citation needed*] In the early 1990s, Kilmer starred in the mystery thriller *Thunderheart*, action comedy *The Real McCoy* and again teamed with *Top Gun* director Tony Scott to play Elvis in *True Romance*, which was written by Quentin Tarantino.

In 1993, Kilmer played Doc Holliday in the western *Tombstone* alongside Kurt Russell, in what some say is one of Kilmer's finest performances.Wikipedia:Avoid weasel words 1995 saw Kilmer star in *Wings of Courage*, a 3D IMAX film, and that same year, he starred opposite Al Pacino and Robert De Niro in *Heat*, which is now considered one of the best crime/drama films of the 1990s. In 1996, he appeared in a largely unknown film, *Dead Girl*, and starred alongside Marlon Brando in the poorly received *The Island of Dr Moreau*. That year, Kilmer starred alongside Michael Douglas in the thriller *The Ghost and the Darkness*. The next year he played Simon Templar in the popular action film, *The Saint*. In 1998, he lent his voice to the animated film *The Prince of Egypt*, before starring in the independent film *Joe the King* (1999) and playing a blind man in the drama/romance *At First Sight*, which he described as of then, the hardest role he had ever had.

Batman

In December 1993, *Batman Forever* director Joel Schumacher had seen *Tombstone*, and was most impressed with Kilmer's performance as Doc Holliday. Schumacher felt for him to be perfect for the role of the Caped Crusader, though at the time, the role was still Michael Keaton's. Batman co-creator Bob Kane said he felt Kilmer was the best actor to portray Batman.

In July 1994, Michael Keaton decided not to return for a third Batman film after 1992's *Batman Returns*, due to "creative differences." William Baldwin (who previously worked with Schumacher on *Flatliners*) was reported to be a top contender, though just days after Keaton dropped out, Kilmer was cast. Kilmer took the role without even knowing who the new director was and without reading the script. Kilmer first learned that he was offered the role of Batman while he was literally in a bat cave in

Africa, doing research for *The Ghost and the Darkness* (1996). Released in June 1995, *Batman Forever* was a success at the box office, despite receiving mixed reviews from critics.

In February 1996, Kilmer decided not to return for a sequel (1997's *Batman & Robin*, in which George Clooney replaced Kilmer), feeling that Batman was being marginalized in favor of the villains. Kilmer went on to do *The Saint* with a salary of $6 million.

2000s

Kilmer's first role in 2000 was in the big budget Warner Bros. box office disaster *Red Planet*. That same year, he had a supporting role in the film *Pollock* and hosted *Saturday Night Live* for the first time. In 2002, he starred in the thriller *The Salton Sea*, which was generally well-reviewed, but received only a limited release. The same year, he teamed with his *True Romance* co-star, Christian Slater, and the two starred in the low budget film, *Hard Cash*, also known as *Run for the Money*.

In 2003, Kilmer starred alongside Kate Bosworth in the drama/thriller *Wonderland*, as well as appearing in *The Missing*, where he again worked with *Willow* director Ron Howard. The next year, he starred in *Spartan*, where he played a United States government secret agent who is assigned the task of rescuing the kidnapped daughter of the President. He received Delta Force-like training in preparation for the role. Subsequently, he had a role in the drama, *Stateside*, and starred (again with Slater) in the thriller *Mindhunters*, which was filmed in 2003 but not released until 2005. Kilmer next appeared in the big budget Oliver Stone production, *Alexander*, which received poor reviews. Also in 2004, Kilmer returned to the theatre to play Moses in a Los Angeles musical production of *The Ten Commandments: The Musical*, produced by BCBG founder Max Azria. The production played at the Kodak Theater in Hollywood. Kilmer had previously played Moses in the animated film *The Prince of Egypt*. Finally in 2004, Kilmer appeared in an episode of Entourage where he played a tripped-out Sherpa shaman whose primary source of income was the growing, harvesting and distributing high-quality marijuana all under a guise of hippy-dippy metaphysical insights.

Kilmer was in negotiations with Richard Dutcher (a leading director of Mormon-related films) to play the lead role in a film entitled *Prophet: The Story of Joseph Smith*, although the project never materialized. Kilmer performed in *The Postman Always Rings Twice* on the London stage from June to September 2005. In 2005, he co-starred with Robert Downey, Jr in the action-comedy film *Kiss Kiss Bang Bang*. His performance was praised and the film was well reviewed, but the film received only a limited release. It later won the award as "Overlooked Film of the Year" from the Phoenix Film Critics Society. In 2006, he reunited with director Tony Scott a third time for a supporting role opposite Denzel Washington in the box-office hit *Déjà Vu*. In 2007, he guest-starred in hit TV series *Numb3rs* episode "Trust Metric" as torture expert Mason Lancer. In 2008, Kilmer starred alongside Stephen Dorff in the Sony and Stage 6 film *Felon*. The film was given only a limited theatrical release in New York and Los Angeles in 2008, but it developed into a success secondary to positive word of mouth.

He next starred alongside Nicolas Cage in the Werner Herzog film *Bad Lieutenant: Port of Call New Orleans*, and alongside Curtis "50 Cent" Jackson in *Streets of Blood*. Both were released in 2009. He appeared as the main antagonist "Mongoose" in a live TV series adaptation of the comic/video game of *XIII* on NBC in 2009.

As of 2010, Kilmer was working on writing the movie about the life of Mary Baker Eddy, the founder of the Christian Science church. He starred in the 2010 thriller from Michael Oblowitz, *Mr. Nobody*, where he portrayed a Police Officer.

Knight Rider revival

He was the voice of KITT for the 2008 *Knight Rider* TV pilot movie and the following television series. He replaced Will Arnett, who had to step down from the role due to contractual conflict with General Motors.

In keeping with tradition established by the original *Knight Rider* series and original KITT actor William Daniels, Kilmer was uncredited for the role on-screen.

Personal life

Kilmer was married to Joanne Whalley, an actress, from March 1988 to February 1996. The two met while working together on the film *Willow*. They have two children, daughter Mercedes, born in 1991, and son Jack, born in 1995.

He dated supermodel Cindy Crawford in the 1990s. A noted incident in their dating life involved Crawford's advertising for a bar of which Kilmer did not approve. He admitted being unreasonable.

Warwick Davis, Kilmer's co-star from the 1988 fantasy *Willow*, in his audio commentary for the film described Kilmer as a very funny man and a hard working, dedicated actor. Kilmer is also an avid musician, and released a CD in the fall of 2007, proceeds of which went to his charity interests.

Other actors have noted that he prepares for his roles extensively and meticulously. Kevin Jarre, the original director of *Tombstone*, said that Kilmer once told him, "I have a reputation for being difficult. But only with stupid people." Irwin Winkler (director of *At First Sight*) talked about his decision to hire Kilmer. "I'd heard the stories, so I checked him out. I called Bob DeNiro and Michael Mann, who'd worked with him on *Heat*, and they both gave him raves... I had a wonderful experience in spite of all the naysayers."[*citation needed*] Jeffrey Katzenberg (director of *Prince of Egypt*) talks about the actor. "Val was one of the first people cast in *The Prince of Egypt*. He was there every step of the way; patient, understanding, and phenomenally generous with his time."[*citation needed*]

Following their appearance together in *Top Gun*, Kilmer and co-star Tom Cruise reportedly had taken their onscreen conflict offscreen. Reports classified the two as holding a vitriolic hatred of one another. Kilmer even refused to participate in a charity beach volleyball game with Cruise on the grounds that he was, quote, "dangerous", although Kilmer is noted to have knocked out Cruise when a fistfight between the two developed during the filming of *Top Gun*.

Kilmer owns a ranch in New Mexico, where he hunts, tracks, hikes, fishes, and raises buffalo. Kilmer is also involved with The Wildlife Center of New Mexico and assists in rescuing animals and releasing them on his ranch.

In 2009, Kilmer listed Pecos River Ranch [1] for sale for $33,000,000 with conservation real estate firm Orvis/Cushman & Wakefield [2].

He briefly flirted with running for Governor of New Mexico in 2010, but in the end declined to run. He made a donation to Ralph Nader's 2008 presidential campaign. On January 30, 2009, Kilmer was chosen to be the King of Bacchus, a parading Krewe in New Orleans, who in 1969, began the tradition of having celebrities ride in their parade as King.

Filmography

Year	Film	Role	Notes
1984	*Top Secret!*	Nick Rivers	Film debut
1985	*Real Genius*	Chris Knight	
1986	*Top Gun*	Lt. Tom 'Iceman' Kazanski	
	The Murders in the Rue Morgue	Phillipe Huron	TV film
1987	*The Man Who Broke 1,000 Chains*	Robert Eliot Burns/Eliot Roberts	TV film CableACE Award for Best Actor in a Movie or Miniseries
1988	*Willow*	Madmartigan	
1989	*Billy the Kid*	William Bonney	
	Kill Me Again	Jack Andrews	
1991	*The Doors*	Jim Morrison	Nominated – MTV Movie Award for Best Performance - Male
1992	*Thunderheart*	Ray Levoi	
1993	*The Real McCoy*	J.T. Barker	
	Tombstone	Doc Holliday	Based on a true story Nominated – MTV Movie Award for Most Desirable Male Nominated – MTV Movie Award for Best Performance - Male
	True Romance	Mentor	

Year	Title	Role	Notes
1995	Batman Forever	Bruce Wayne/Batman	Nominated – MTV Movie Award for Most Desirable Male also for *Heat*
	Heat	Chris Shiherlis	Nominated – MTV Movie Award for Most Desirable Male also for *Batman Forever* Nominated – Saturn Award for Best Supporting Actor
	Wings of Courage	Jean Mermoz	IMAX Film
1996	The Island of Dr Moreau	Montgomery	
	The Ghost and the Darkness	Col. John Henry Patterson	Based on a true story
	Dead Girl	Dr. Dark	
1997	The Saint	Simon Templar	
1998	The Prince of Egypt	Moses/God	Voice-over
1999	At First Sight	Virgil 'Virg' Adamson	
	Joe the King	Bob Henry	
2000	Pollock	Willem de Kooning	
	Red Planet	Robby Gallagher	
2002	The Salton Sea	Danny Parker / Tom Van Allen	Limited release Prism Award for Best Performance in a Theatrical Feature Film
	Hard Cash	FBI Agent Mark C. Cornell	a.k.a. *Run for the Money*
2003	Wonderland	John Holmes	Based on the Wonderland Murders
	The Missing	Lt. Jim Ducharme	
	Blind Horizon	Frank Kavanaugh	
	Masked and Anonymous	Animal Wrangler	
2004	Entourage	The Sherpa	Episode: "The Script and the Sherpa"
	Spartan	Robert Scott	
	Stateside	Staff Sergeant Skeer	
	Alexander	Philip	
	George and the Dragon	El Cabillo	uncredited
2005	Mindhunters	Jake Harris	
	Kiss Kiss Bang Bang	Perry Van Shrike/"Gay Perry"	Satellite Award for Best Supporting Actor - Motion Picture Nominated– Saturn Award for Best Supporting Actor

2006	*Summer Love*	The Wanted Man	a.k.a. *Dead Man's Bounty*
	Moscow Zero	Andrey	
	10th & Wolf	Murtha	
	Played	Dillon	
	Déjà Vu	Agent Andrew Pryzwarra	
	The Ten Commandments: The Musical	Moses	
2007	*Have Dreams, Will Travel*	Henderson	
	Numb3rs	Mason Lancer	Episode: "Trust Metric"
2008	*Comanche Moon*	Inish Scull	TV mini-series based on the book
	Knight Rider	voice of KITT	TV film based on 1980s TV series
	Conspiracy	MacPherson	direct-to-video
	Felon	John Smith	
	Delgo	Bogardus	voice only
	2:22	Maz	
	Columbus Day	John	
	XIII	Mongoose	based on Belgian comic book XIII
2008–2009	*Knight Rider*	voice of KITT	TV series based on the 2008 TV film
2009	*The Chaos Experiment*	James Pettis	a.k.a. *The Steam Experiment*
	Streets of Blood	Detective Andy Devereaux	
	American Cowslip	Todd Inglebrink	
	The Thaw	Dr. David Kruipen	
	Bad Lieutenant: Port of Call New Orleans	Stevie Pruit	
	Hardwired	Virgil	

2010	*Fake Identity* also known as *Double Identity*	Nick	
	The Traveler	The Stranger/Mr. Nobody	
	Provinces of Night	Warren Bloodworth	post-production
	The Irishman	Joe Manditski	post-production
	MacGruber	Dieter Von Cunth	
	Georgia	Dutch Journalist	Post-production
	Tales of an Ancient Empire	Rollo	Post-production
	Gun	Angel	Post-production
	Blood Out	Arturo	filming
	Riddle	Sheriff Richards	filming

External links

General

- Kilmer's Official website [3]
- Kilmer's Official Myspace [4]
- Val Kilmer [5] at the Internet Movie Database
- Val Kilmer [6] at the Internet Broadway Database
- Val Kilmer [7] at the Internet Off-Broadway Database

Interviews

- Maxim Online interview [8] (January, 2007)
- Tom Green Live [9] (November 6, 2006)
- UGO interview [10] (March, 2004)
- Deal Memo interview [11] (April 23, 2002)

Batman & Robin

Batman & Robin (film)

Batman & Robin	
Theatrical release poster	
Directed by	Joel Schumacher
Produced by	Peter MacGregor-Scott *Executive*: Benjamin Melniker Michael Uslan
Screenplay by	Akiva Goldsman
Story by	Akiva Goldsman *Comic book*: Bill Finger *(uncredited)* Bob Kane
Starring	George Clooney Chris O'Donnell Arnold Schwarzenegger Uma Thurman Alicia Silverstone
Music by	Elliot Goldenthal
Cinematography	Stephen Goldblatt
Editing by	Dennis Virkler Mark Stevens
Distributed by	Warner Bros.
Release date(s)	June 20, 1997
Running time	125 minutes
Country	United States
Language	English
Budget	$140 million

Gross revenue	$238,207,122
Preceded by	*Batman Forever*

Batman & Robin is a 1997 American superhero film directed by Joel Schumacher. Based on the DC Comics character Batman, the film is a sequel to *Batman Forever* (1995), with George Clooney replacing Val Kilmer as Batman. *Batman & Robin* also stars Arnold Schwarzenegger, Uma Thurman, Chris O'Donnell, Alicia Silverstone, and Michael Gough. The film tells the story of Batman and Robin struggling to keep their relationship together. At the same time, they have to stop Mr. Freeze, Poison Ivy and Bane from covering Gotham City with ice and vegetation.

Development for *Batman & Robin* started immediately after *Batman Forever*, and Warner Bros. commissioned the film for an adamant June 1997 release. Principal photography began in September 1996 and finished in January 1997, two weeks ahead of the shooting schedule. *Batman & Robin* was released on June 20, 1997, and was critically panned. Observers criticized the film for its toyetic and camp approach, as well as possible homosexual innuendo added by Schumacher. *Batman & Robin* received 11 nominations at the 1997 ceremony of the Razzie Awards, including one for Worst Picture, and frequently ranks among the worst superhero films of all time. After this, Warner Bros. canceled the unproduced *Batman Triumphant*, and the film series was eventually rebooted with *Batman Begins* (2005) by director Christopher Nolan.

Plot

In Gotham City, Batman and Robin attempt to stop Mr. Freeze from a robbery attempt, but he escapes. In South America, Pamela Isley is working under Dr. Jason Woodrue, experimenting with the Venom drug. She witnesses Woodrue use the formula to turn a diminutive convict into a hulking monstrosity dubbed "Bane". Woodrue and Isley argue over the use of the drug and Woodrue overturns a shelf of various toxins on to her. She transforms into the beautiful and seductive Poison Ivy before killing Woodrue. She finds that Wayne Enterprises funded Woodrue, thus she takes Bane with her to Gotham. Meanwhile, Alfred Pennyworth's niece, Barbara Wilson, makes a surprise visit and is invited by Bruce Wayne to stay at Wayne Manor until she goes back to school. Alfred is revealed to be suffering from the fictional MacGregor's Syndrome which will eventually kill him.

Wayne Enterprises presents a new telescope at a press conference interrupted by Isley. She proposes a project that could help the environment, but Bruce declines her offer, as it would kill millions of people. That night, a charity event is held by Wayne Enterprises with special guests, Batman and Robin, and she decides to use her abilities to seduce them. Freeze crashes the party and steals a diamond from the event. However, he is captured and sent to a chamber prison in Arkham Asylum, but escapes with the help of Ivy and Bane. Batman and Robin begin to have crime fighting relationship problems because of the presence of Ivy's seductive ability with Robin. Ivy is then able to contact Robin once more, but fails to seduce him. Robin becomes trapped. Batman shows up but is also captured. Batgirl shows up and begins duking it out with Ivy, eventually defeating the part plant menace. Batgirl reveals that she is Barbara and knows the location of the Batcave.

Batman, Robin, and Batgirl decide to go after Freeze together. By the time they get to the observatory where Freeze and Bane are, Gotham is completely frozen. Robin and Batgirl confront Bane and defeat him, while Batman and Freeze begin to fight each other, with Batman winning. Batgirl and Robin unfreeze Gotham and Batman shows Freeze a recording of Ivy during her fight with Batgirl. Freeze learns that Ivy has betrayed him over the death of his wife. Ivy blamed Batman for Nora's death, but she informs Batgirl that it was her idea. Freeze is angered by the betrayal and is informed by Batman that his wife is not dead; she is restored in cryogenic slumber and has been moved to Arkham waiting for him to finish his research. Batman proceeds to ask Freeze for the cure he has created for the first stage of MacGregor's Syndrome, the disease that Freeze's wife is suffering from, for Alfred. Freeze atones for his misunderstanding by giving him medicine he had developed. Ivy is shown imprisoned in Arkham with a vengeful Freeze as her cellmate. Alfred is eventually healed and everyone agrees to let Barbara stay at the mansion.

Cast

- George Clooney as Bruce Wayne / Batman: A billionaire industrialist whose parents were killed at a young age. At night, Bruce becomes Batman, Gotham City's vigilante protector. Eric Lloyd portrays him as a child in a flashback. Val Kilmer decided not to reprise the role from *Batman Forever*. Director Joel Schumacher admitted he had difficulty working with Kilmer on *Forever*. "He sort of quit," Schumacher said, "and we sort of fired him." Kilmer said he was not aware of the fast track production and was already committed to *The Saint* (1997). Schumacher cast Clooney in the role because he felt the actor could act less serious from the previous portrayals of Michael Keaton (in *Batman* and *Batman Returns*) and Kilmer. The shooting schedule allowed Clooney to simultaneously work on *ER* without any scheduling conflicts.
- Chris O'Donnell as Dick Grayson / Robin: The crime-fighting partner to Batman and legal ward to Bruce Wayne. He disagrees with some of Batman's tactics and considers having a solo crime fighting career.
- Arnold Schwarzenegger as Dr. Victor Fries / Mr. Freeze: A molecular biologist who suffers a terrible accident while trying to cryogenically preserve his ill wife. As a result, he is transformed into a deranged criminal forced to live in a sub-zero suit powered by diamonds. Patrick Stewart was considered for the role, before the script was rewritten to accommodate Schwarzenegger's casting. Schumacher decided that Mr. Freeze must be "big and strong like he was chiseled out of a glacier". Schwarzenegger was paid a $25 million salary for the role, while his prosthetic makeup and wardrobe took six hours to apply each day.
- Uma Thurman as Dr. Pamela Isley / Poison Ivy: A crazed botanist who after being pushed into vials of chemicals, poisons, and toxins becomes the beautiful, but deadly Poison Ivy, the ultimate eco-

terrorist. Demi Moore was considered for the role. Thurman took the role because she liked the femme fatale characterization of Poison Ivy.
- Alicia Silverstone as Barbara Wilson / Batgirl: Her parents died in a car accident and Alfred, her uncle, was very close to her mother, Margaret. Silverstone was the first and only choice for the role.
- Michael Gough as Alfred Pennyworth: The trusted butler for Bruce Wayne and Dick Grayson. Alfred is struggling with a rare disease that Mr. Freeze's wife also has.
- Pat Hingle as Commissioner James Gordon: the police commissioner of Gotham City. He is close to Batman and informs him of numerous crimes.
- John Glover as Dr. Jason Woodrue: a deranged scientist with a desire for world domination via his Venom-powered "supersoldiers". He is responsible for the creation of both Bane and Poison Ivy, the latter of whom kills him in revenge.
- Elle Macpherson as Julie Madison: Bruce Wayne's girlfriend. She proposes to Bruce, but he does not respond, fearing for her safety.
- Vivica A. Fox as Ms. B. Haven: Mr. Freeze's sexy assistant who flirts with him constantly. He is unresponsive, as he is still in love with his wife.
- Vendela Kirsebom as Nora Fries: Mr. Freeze's cryogenically frozen wife.
- Elizabeth Sanders as Gossip Gerty: Gotham's top gossip columnist.
- Jeep Swenson as Bane: Poison Ivy's bodyguard and muscle, who was originally a diminutive criminal named Antonio Diego. Transformed into a hugely powerful "Super-soldier" by the strength-enhancing drug "Venom", he was seen assisting the main villains in several ways, including getting Mr. Freeze's suit back from Arkham Asylum, and fighting against the main heroes several times, eventually being defeated by Robin and Batgirl after they found a way to stop the venom flow to his brain.

Production

With the box office success of *Batman Forever* in June 1995, Warner Bros. instantly commissioned a sequel. They hired director Joel Schumacher and writer Akiva Goldsman to reprise their duties the following August, and decided it was best to fast track production for a June 1997 target release date. Schumacher wanted to homage both the broad camp style of the 1960s television series and the work of Dick Sprang. The storyline of *Batman & Robin* was conceived by Schumacher and Goldsman during pre-production on *A Time to Kill*. Portions of Mr. Freeze's back-story were based on the *Batman: The Animated Series* episode "Heart of Ice", written by Paul Dini. The original start date was August 1996, but principal photography did not begin until September 12, 1996. *Batman & Robin* finished filming in late-January 1997, two weeks ahead of the shooting schedule. The film was mostly shot at Warner Bros. Studios in Burbank, California.

When comparing work on *Batman Forever*, Chris O'Donnell, who portrayed Robin, explained, "It just felt like everything got a little soft the second time. On *Batman Forever*, I felt like I was making a movie. The second time, I felt like I was making a kid's toy commercial." According to John Glover, who played Dr. Jason Woodrue, "Joel [Schumacher] would sit on a crane with a megaphone and yell before each take, 'Remember everyone, this is a cartoon'. It was hard to act because that kind of set the tone for the film." Production designer Barbara Ling admitted her influences for the Gotham City design came from "neon-ridden Tokyo and the Machine Age. Gotham is like a World's Fair on ecstasy." Rhythm and Hues and Pacific Data Images created the visual effects sequences, with John Dykstra and Andrew Adamson credited as the visual effects supervisors.

Release

Marketing

The *Batman & Robin* film trailer debuted on the February 19, 1997 episode of *Entertainment Tonight*. Warner Bros. spent $15 million to market and promote the film, bringing the total budget from $125 million to $140 million. The studio also brought in toy companies to be involved with pre-production, including the design of concept art and character illustrations. Director Joel Schumacher criticized Warner Bros.' strategy for *Batman & Robin* as being overtly toyetic. Various Six Flags parks (Six Flags Great Adventure, Six Flags Over Texas, and Six Flags St. Louis) all debuted coasters themed to the film.

Box office

Batman & Robin was released on June 20, 1997 in North America, earning $42,872,605 in its opening weekend, making it the third-highest opening weekend of 1997. However, the film rapidly declined with a 63% second week plunge. Many observers based the second week drop on negative word of mouth. In addition, *Batman & Robin* faced early competition with *Face/Off* and *Hercules*. Schumacher blamed it on yellow journalism started by Harry Knowles of Ain't It Cool News and other film websites such as Dark Horizons. The film went on to gross $107.3 million in North America and $130.9 million internationally, coming to a worldwide total of $238.2 million. Warner Bros. declared *Batman & Robin* a financial success, but not on the scale they were hoping for.

Critical analysis

"If there's anybody watching this, that... let's say, loved *Batman Forever*, and went into *Batman & Robin* with great anticipation, if I've disappointed them in any way, then I really want to apologize. Because it wasn't my intention. My intention was just to entertain them."

—Joel Schumacher's apology for his work on *Batman & Robin*

Despite being a box office success, *Batman & Robin* was a critical failure and received mainly negative reviews. Based on 62 reviews collected by Rotten Tomatoes, 11% of the critics gave *Batman & Robin* positive reviews, culminating in a "rotten" rating. By comparison Metacritic collected an average score of 28, based on 21 reviews.

Schumacher and producer Peter MacGregor-Scott blamed the negative reception of *Batman & Robin* on Warner Bros.' decision to fast track production. "There was a lot of pressure from Warner Bros. to make *Batman & Robin* more family-friendly," Schumacher explained. "We decided to do a less depressing *Batman* movie and less torture and more heroic. I know I have been criticized a lot for this, but I didn't see the harm in that approach at all." Roger Ebert criticized the toyetic approach and Mr. Freeze's one-liner jokes. Kenneth Turan of the *Los Angeles Times* believed the film "killed" the *Batman* film series, and felt *Batman & Robin* depended too much on visual effects. Desson Thomson of *The Washington Post* largely disapproved over Schumacher's direction and Akiva Goldsman's script. Mick LaSalle, writing in the *San Francisco Chronicle*, said, "George Clooney is the big zero of the film, and should go down in history as the George Lazenby of the series." However, Janet Maslin of *The New York Times* gave a positive review. She praised Uma Thurman's acting, as well as the production and costume design.

Batman & Robin was nominated the Saturn Award for Best Fantasy Film, as well as categories for Best Make-up and Best Costume. Alicia Silverstone won the Razzie Award for Worst Supporting Actress. Other nominations at the Razzie Awards included Schumacher (Worst Director), George Clooney and Chris O'Donnell (Worst Screen Couple), Akiva Goldsman (Worst Screenplay), both Chris O'Donnell and Arnold Schwarzenegger (Worst Supporting Actor), Uma Thurman (Worst Supporting Actress), and Billy Corgan (Worst Song for "The End Is the Beginning Is the End"). *Batman & Robin* received nominations for Worst Picture, Worst Remake or Sequel and Worst Reckless Disregard for Human Life and Public Property.

Homosexual interpretation

Further information: Homosexuality in the Batman franchise

Many observers accused Schumacher of adding possible homosexual innuendo in the storyline. James Berardinelli questioned the "random amount of rubber nipples and camera angle close-ups of the Dynamic Duo's butts and Bat-crotches." Similar to *Batman Forever*, this primarily included the decision to add nipples and enlarged codpieces to Batman and Robin suits. Schumacher stated, "I had no idea that putting nipples on the Batsuit and Robin suit were going to spark international headlines. The bodies of the suits come from ancient Greek statues, which display perfect bodies. They are anatomically erotic." Chris O'Donnell, who portrayed Robin, felt "it wasn't so much the nipples that bothered me. It was the codpiece. The press obviously played it up and made it a big deal, especially with Joel directing. I didn't think twice about the controversy, but going back and looking and seeing some of the pictures, it was very unusual." It should be noted that Batgirl was given a similarly designed suit. George Clooney joked, "Joel Schumacher told me we never made another *Batman* film because Batman was gay". Clooney himself has spoken critically of the film, saying "I think we might have killed the franchise", and called it "a waste of money".

Legacy

Further information: Batman in film#Proposals for fifth film

During the filming of *Batman & Robin*, Warner Bros. was impressed with the dailies. This prompted them to immediately hire Joel Schumacher to return as director for a sequel, but writer Akiva Goldsman, who worked on *Batman Forever* and *Batman & Robin* with Schumacher, turned down the chance to write the script. In late 1996, Warner Bros. and Schumacher hired Mark Protosevich to write the script for a fifth *Batman* film. A projected mid-1999 release date was announced. Titled *Batman Triumphant*, Protosevich's script had the Scarecrow as the main villain and had Steve Buscemi intended to play him. The Joker returned in the movie as a hallucination in Batman's mind caused by the Scarecrow's fear toxin. Harley Quinn appeared as a supporting character, written as the Joker's daughter. George Clooney and Chris O'Donnell were set to reprise the roles of Batman and Robin.

Nevertheless, when *Batman & Robin* received negative reviews and failed to outgross any of its predecessors, Warner Bros. was unsure of their plans for *Batman Triumphant*. The studio decided it was best to consider a live-action *Batman Beyond* film and an adaptation of Frank Miller's *Batman: Year One*. Warners would then greenlight whichever idea suited them the most. Schumacher felt he "owe[d] the Batman culture a real *Batman* movie. I would go back to the basics and make a dark portrayal of the Dark Knight." He approached Warner Bros. of doing *Batman: Year One* in mid-1998, but they were more interested in hiring Darren Aronofsky. Aronofsky and Frank Miller developed a *Year One* script with Aronofsky to direct, but it was ultimately canceled. Christopher Nolan was eventually hired to helm the next *Batman* film in January 2003, resulting in the rebooted *Batman Begins* (2005).

In "Legends of the Dark Knight", an episode of *The New Batman Adventures*, three teenagers discuss their ideas about what Batman is really like. They briefly meet an effeminate youth called *Joel* (in front of a *shoemaker*'s shop) whose idea of Batman consists mainly of a fascination with the tight rubber suits and a Batmobile that can drive up walls. The other three kids treat Joel's ideas with utter disdain. In *Watchmen*, director Zack Snyder and comic book artist Dave Gibbons choose to parody the molded muscle and nipple Batsuit design from *Batman & Robin* for the Ozymandias costume.

External links

- *Batman & Robin* [1] at the Internet Movie Database
- *Batman & Robin* [2] at Allmovie
- *Batman & Robin* [3] at Box Office Mojo
- *Batman & Robin* [4] at Rotten Tomatoes
- *Batman & Robin* [5] at RiffTrax

George Clooney

George Clooney	
Clooney at the 2009 Venice Film Festival	
Born	George Timothy Clooney May 6, 1961 Lexington, Kentucky, U.S.
Occupation	Actor, director, producer, screenwriter
Years active	1978–present
Spouse	Talia Balsam (1989-1993)

George Timothy Clooney (born May 6, 1961) is an American actor, film director, producer, and screenwriter. For his work as an actor, he has received two Golden Globe Awards and an Academy Award. Clooney is noted for parlaying his celebrity into social activism and has served as one of the United Nations Messengers of Peace since January 31, 2008.

Though he made his acting debut on television in 1978, Clooney gained fame and recognition by portraying Dr. Douglas "Doug" Ross on the long-running medical drama *ER* from 1994 to 1999. While working on *ER*, he started attracting a variety of leading roles in films including *Batman & Robin* (1997) and *Out of Sight* (1998), where he first teamed with long-term collaborator Steven Soderbergh. In 2001, Clooney's fame widened with the release of his biggest commercial success, *Ocean's Eleven*, the first of a profitable film trilogy, that is a remake of the movie from 1960 with the members of The Rat Pack with Frank Sinatra as Danny Ocean. He made his directorial debut a year later with the 2002 biographical thriller *Confessions of a Dangerous Mind* and has since directed *Good Night, and Good Luck* (2005) and *Leatherheads* (2008). He won the 2006 Academy Award for Best Supporting Actor for his work in the Middle East thriller *Syriana* (2005).

Clooney's humanitarian work includes his advocacy of finding a resolution for the Darfur conflict, raising funds for the 2010 Haiti earthquake, 2004 Tsunami and 9/11 victims, and creating documentaries such as *Sand and Sorrow* to raise awareness about international crises.

Early life

Clooney was born in Lexington, Kentucky. His mother, Nina Bruce (née Warren), was a former beauty pageant queen, and his father, Nick Clooney, was an anchorman, as well as game show and American Movie Classics host. Clooney is of Irish descent on his father's side; his paternal great-great-grandparents, Nicholas Clooney (of County Kilkenny) and Bridget Byron, immigrated to the United States from Ireland. Clooney was raised a strict Roman Catholic. He has an older sister, Adelia (also known as Ada), and his cousins include actors Miguel and Rafael Ferrer, who are the sons of his aunt, singer Rosemary Clooney, and actor José Ferrer. He is also related to another singer, Debby Boone, who married José Ferrer and Rosemary Clooney's son Gabriel. From an early age, Clooney would hang around his father's sets, often participating in shows, where he proved to be a crowd favorite.[citation needed]

Clooney began his education at the Blessed Sacrament School in Fort Mitchell, Kentucky. Spending part of his childhood in Ohio, he attended St. Michael's School in Columbus, and St. Susanna School in Mason, Ohio. In middle school, Clooney developed Bell's palsy, a debilitating condition that partially paralyzes the face. The malady went away within a year. "That was the worst time of my life," he told the *Daily Mirror* in 2003. "You know how cruel kids can be. I was mocked and taunted, but the experience made me stronger."

His parents eventually moved to Augusta, Kentucky, where Clooney attended Augusta High School. He has stated that he earned all As and a B in school, and was an enthusiastic baseball and basketball player. He tried out with the Cincinnati Reds in 1977 to play professional baseball, but was not offered a contract. He did not pass the first round of player cuts. He attended Northern Kentucky University from 1979 to 1981 majoring in History and Political Science and, very briefly, the University of Cincinnati, but did not graduate from either. He had such odd jobs as selling men's suits and cutting tobacco.

Career

Early work, 1978-1994

Clooney's first role was as an extra in the TV series Centennial in 1978. The series was based on the novel of the same name by James Michener and was partially filmed in Clooney's hometown of Augusta, Kentucky. Clooney's first major role came in 1984 in the short-lived sitcom *E/R* (not to be confused with *ER*, the better-known hospital drama, on which Clooney also costarred a decade later). He played a handyman on the series *The Facts of Life* and appeared as Bobby Hopkins, a detective, on an episode of *The Golden Girls*. His first significant break was a semi-regular supporting role in the sitcom *Roseanne*, playing Roseanne Barr's overbearing boss Booker Brooks, followed by the role of a construction worker on *Baby Talk* and then as a sexy detective on *Sisters*. In 1988, Clooney also played a role in *Return of the Killer Tomatoes*.

Breakthrough, 1994-2001

Clooney achieved stardom when he was selected to play Dr. Doug Ross, alongside Anthony Edwards's and Noah Wyle's characters on the hit NBC drama *ER* from 1994 to 1999. After leaving the series in 1999, he returned for a guest spot in the show's final season and also made a cameo appearance in the 6th season.

Clooney began appearing in movies while working on *ER*. His first major Hollywood role was in *From Dusk till Dawn*, directed by Robert Rodriguez. He followed its success with *One Fine Day* with Michelle Pfeiffer and *The Peacemaker* with Nicole Kidman. Clooney was then cast as the new Batman in *Batman & Robin*, which was a moderate box office success, but a critical failure (with Clooney himself calling the film "a waste of money"). In 1998, he starred in *Out of Sight* opposite Jennifer Lopez, marking the first of his many collaborations with director Steven Soderbergh. He also starred in *Three Kings* during the last weeks of his contract with *ER*.

International success, 2001-present

After leaving *ER*, Clooney starred in commercially successful projects such as *The Perfect Storm* and *O Brother, Where Art Thou?*. In 2001, he teamed up with Soderbergh again for *Ocean's Eleven*, a remake of the 1960s Rat Pack film of the same name. It remains Clooney's most commercially successful movie, earning more than $444 million worldwide.[*citation needed*] The film spawned two sequels starring Clooney, *Ocean's Twelve* in 2004 and *Ocean's Thirteen* in 2007.

George Clooney cast his feet and hands in the Grauman's Chinese Theatre in 2007.

In 2001, Clooney and director Steven Soderbergh co-founded the Section Eight Productions, for which Grant Heslov was president of television. He made his directorial debut in the 2002 film *Confessions of a Dangerous Mind*, an adaptation of the autobiography of TV producer Chuck Barris. Though the movie didn't do well at the box office, Clooney's direction was praised among critics and audiences alike.[*citation needed*]

In 2005, Clooney starred in *Syriana*, which was based loosely on former Central Intelligence Agency agent Robert Baer and his memoirs of being an agent in the Middle East. Clooney suffered an accident on the set of *Syriana*, which resulted in a brain injury with complications arising from a punctured dura. The same year he directed, produced, and starred in *Good Night, and Good Luck.*, a film about 1950s television journalist Edward R. Murrow's famous war of words with Senator Joseph McCarthy. Both films received critical acclaim and decent box-office returns despite being in limited release. At the 2006 Academy Awards, Clooney was nominated for Best Director and Best Original Screenplay for *Good Night, and Good Luck*, as well as Best Supporting Actor for *Syriana*. He became the first person in Oscar history to be nominated for directing one movie and acting in another in the same year. He won the Oscar for his role in *Syriana*.

George Clooney at the premiere of The Men Who Stare At Goats in the 2009 Toronto International Film Festival

Clooney next appeared in *The Good German* (2006), a film-noir directed by Soderbergh that is set in post-World War II Germany. Clooney also received the American Cinematheque Award in October 2006, an award that honors an artist in the entertainment industry who has made "a significant contribution to the art of motion pictures". In August 2006, Clooney and Grant Heslov started a new production company: *Smokehouse Pictures*.

On January 22, 2008, Clooney was nominated for an Academy Award (and many others awards) for Best Actor for his role in *Michael Clayton* (2007). Clooney then directed his third film, *Leatherheads* (2008), in which he also starred. It was reported on April 4, 2008 in *Variety* that Clooney had quietly resigned from the Writers Guild of America over controversy surrounding *Leatherheads*. Clooney, who is the director, producer, and star of the film, stated that he had contributed in writing, "all but two scenes," of the film and requested a writing credit, alongside Duncan Brantley and Rick Reilly, who had been working on the project for 17 years. In an arbitration vote, Clooney lost 2–1 and ultimately decided to withdraw from the union over the decision. Clooney is now technically a "financial core status" nonmember, meaning he loses his voting rights, and cannot run for office or attend membership meetings, according to the WGA's constitution.

Clooney next co-starred with Ewan McGregor and Kevin Spacey in *The Men Who Stare At Goats*, which was directed by his friend Grant Heslov and released in November 2009. Also in November 2009, he voiced Mr. Fox in Wes Anderson's *Fantastic Mr. Fox*. The same year, Clooney starred in *Up in the Air*, which was initially given limited release, and then wide-released on December 25, 2009. For his performance in the film, which was directed by Jason Reitman, he was nominated for a Golden Globe, a Screen Actors Guild Award, BAFTA and an Academy Award.

Clooney is represented by Bryan Lourd, Co-Chairman of Creative Artists Agency (CAA).

Humanitarian work

Clooney has been active in advocating a resolution of the Darfur conflict. His efforts include appearing on an episode of Oprah and speaking at the Save Darfur rally in Washington, D.C., on April 30, 2006. On March 25, 2007, he sent an open letter to German chancellor Angela Merkel, calling on the European Union to take "decisive action" in the region in the face of Omar al-Bashir's failure to respond to the UN resolutions. Author Ishmael Beah writes: "He has used his fame to speak wholeheartedly for those who cannot speak, with genuine concern and insight and a deep commitment and selflessness that is rare but does not have to be."[citation needed]

After making his first trip to Darfur in 2006 with his father Nick, Clooney made the TV special "A Journey to Darfur", and advocated for action in the US. The documentary was broadcast on American cable TV as well as in the UK and France. In 2008, it was released on DVD with the proceeds from its sale being donated to the International Rescue Committee.

In April 2006, he spent ten days in Chad and Sudan with his father to make a film in order to show the dramatic situation of Darfur's refugees. In September of the same year, he spoke in front of the Security Council of the UN with Nobel Prize-winner Elie Wiesel to ask the UN to find a solution to the conflict and to help the people of Darfur. In December, he made a trip to China and Egypt with Don Cheadle and two Olympic winners to ask both governments to pressure Sudan's government.

Clooney in Abéché, Chad in January 2008 with the UN

Clooney is involved with Not On Our Watch, an organization that focuses global attention and resources to stop and prevent mass atrocities, along with Brad Pitt, Matt Damon, Don Cheadle, and Jerry Weintraub. He narrated and was co-executor producer of the documentary *Sand and Sorrow*. Clooney also appeared in the documentary film *Darfur Now*, a call to action film for people all over the world to help stop the ongoing crisis in Darfur. The film was released on November 2, 2007. In February 2009, he visited Goz Beida, Chad with NY Times columnist Nicholas Kristof. In January 2010. he organized the Telethon Hope for Haiti Now, which collects donations for the 2010 Haiti earthquake victims.

On December 13, 2007, Clooney and fellow actor Don Cheadle were presented with the Summit Peace Award by the Nobel Peace Prize Laureates in Rome. In his acceptance speech, Clooney said that "Don and I...stand here before you as failures. The simple truth is that when it comes to the atrocities in Darfur...those people are not better off now than they were years ago." On January 18, 2008, the United Nations announced Clooney's appointment as a United Nations messenger of peace, effective from January 31.

In the media

Clooney is one of three people to have been given the title of "Sexiest Man Alive" twice by *People Magazine*, first in 1997 and again in 2006. Clooney has appeared in commercials outside the US for products like Fiat, Nespresso and Martini vermouth, and has lent his voice to a series of Budweiser ads beginning in 2005.

Clooney was named one of Time magazine's 100 Most Influential People in the World in 2007, 2008, and 2009.[citation needed]

South Park creators Matt Stone and Trey Parker lampooned Clooney, among other stars, in their feature film *Team America: World Police*. Clooney later said that he would have been offended if he *hadn't* been made fun of in the film. He was also mentioned in the *South Park* episode "Smug Alert!", which mocks his acceptance speech at the 78th Academy Awards.

Political views

Clooney is a self-described political liberal.[citation needed] In 2003, he opposed the Iraq war, saying: "You can't beat your enemy anymore through wars; instead you create an entire generation of people seeking revenge.... Our opponents are going to resort to car bombs and suicide attacks because they have no other way to win.... I believe (Rumsfeld) thinks this is a war that can be won, but there is no such thing anymore. We can't beat anyone anymore."

In February 2003, syndicated columnist Liz Smith reported that while speaking at a National Board of Review event, Clooney had made the following remarks: "Charlton Heston announced again today that he is suffering from Alzheimer's." Clooney later said, "It was a joke,... They got the quote wrong. What I said was 'The head of the NRA announced today ...' (Filmmaker) Michael Moore had just gotten an award. Anyway, Charlton Heston shows up with guns over his head after a school shooting and then says in the documentary it's because of ethnic diversity that we have problems with violence in America. I think he's going to have to take whatever hits he gets. It was just a joke. That was someone else trying to make a bigger story." When asked if the actor went too far with his remarks, Clooney responded by saying, "I don't care. Charlton Heston is the head of the National Rifle Association; he deserves whatever anyone says about him." Heston himself commented, "It just goes to show that sometimes class does skip a generation," referring to Clooney's aunt, Rosemary Clooney. Heston further commented on the Clooney joke: "I don't know the man — never met him, never even spoken to him, but I feel sorry for George Clooney — one day he may get Alzheimer's disease. I served my country in World War II. I survived that — I guess I can survive some bad words from this fellow". Clooney said he subsequently apologized to Heston in a letter, and that he received a positive response from Heston's wife.

On January 16, 2006, during his acceptance speech for the Golden Globe Award for Best Performance by an Actor in a Supporting Role for *Syriana*, Clooney paused to sarcastically thank disgraced lobbyist Jack Abramoff before adding, "Who would name their kid Jack with the word 'off' at the end of your last name? No wonder that guy is screwed up!"

Clooney supported then-Senator Barack Obama's campaign in the 2008 presidential election.

About the possibility of him ever running for office, Clooney has said: "Run for office? No. I've slept with too many women, I've done too many drugs, and I've been to too many parties."

Personal life

Clooney was married to Talia Balsam from 1989 to 1993. Since then, Clooney has said that he will never marry again. After meeting on the set of a Martini advert in 2000, he had a five-year on/off relationship with British model Lisa Snowdon. In 2007, he started dating Sarah Larson and the couple broke up in May 2008. Since 2009, Clooney has been in a relationship with Elisabetta Canalis.

Clooney's main home is in Los Angeles. He purchased the 7354 square feet (683.2 m^2) house in 1995 through his George Guifoyle Trust. His villa in Italy is situated in the village of Laglio, situated on Lake Como near the former residence of famous Italian author Ada Negri

On September 21, 2007, Clooney and then-girlfriend Larson were injured in a motorcycle accident in Weehawken, New Jersey. Clooney's motorcycle was hit by a car. The driver of the car reported that Clooney attempted to pass on the right, while Clooney stated that the driver signaled left and then decided to make an abrupt right turn and clipped the motorcycle. He was treated and released from the Palisades Medical Center in North Bergen, New Jersey. On October 9, 2007, more than two dozen hospital staff members were suspended without pay for looking at Clooney's medical records in violation of federal law. Clooney himself quickly issued a statement on the hospital records matter, saying no one should be punished. He said "This is the first I've heard of it. And while I very much believe in a patient's right to privacy, I would hope that this could be settled without suspending medical workers."

Clooney owned a 280-pound Vietnamese black-bristled pot-bellied pig named Max which lived with him for eighteen years until its death in December 2006. He also owned two bulldogs, named Bud and Lou after the famous comedy team Abbott and Costello. Both dogs have died; one from a rattlesnake bite.

Awards and honors

Main article: List of awards and nominations received by George Clooney

Filmography

Actor

Year	Production	Film/TV	Role	Notes
1984–85	E/R	TV	Mark "Ace" Kolmar	
1985	Street Hawk	TV	Kevin Stark	
1985–86	The Facts of Life	TV	George Burnett	
1987	Return to Horror High	Film	Oliver	
	Grizzly II: The Predator	Film		Uncredited
	Combat Academy	Film	Maj. Biff Woods	
	Murder, She Wrote	TV	Kip Howard	Episode: "No Laughing Murder"
	The Golden Girls	TV	Detective Bobby Hopkins	Episode: "To Catch a Neighbor"
1988	Return of the Killer Tomatoes	Film	Matt Stevens	
1988–91	Roseanne	TV	Booker Brooks	11 episodes
1990	Red Surf	Film	Remar	
1992	Unbecoming Age	Film	Mac	
1993	The Harvest	Film	Lip Synching Transvestite	
1993–94	Sisters	TV	Detective James Falconer	
1994–99, 2009	ER	TV	Dr. Doug Ross	107 episodes Nominated — Emmy Award for Outstanding Lead Actor - Drama Series, 1995, 1996 Nominated — Golden Globe Award for Best Actor – Television Series Drama, 1995, 1996, 1997
1995	Friends	TV	Dr. Michael Mitchell	Episode: "The One with Two Parts, Part Two"
1996	From Dusk till Dawn	Film	Seth Gecko	MTV Movie Award for Best Breakthrough Performance Saturn Award for Best Actor
	One Fine Day	Film	Jack Taylor	
	Curdled	Film	Seth Gecko	Uncredited; only photo shown

1997	Full-Tilt Boogie	TV	Himself	Documentary
	The Peacemaker	Film	Thomas Devoe	
	Batman & Robin	Film	Bruce Wayne/Batman	
	South Park	TV	Sparky the Dog	Voice only; episode: "Big Gay Al's Big Gay Boat Ride"
1998	The Thin Red Line	Film	Captain Bosche	
	Out of Sight	Film	Jack Foley	
	Waiting for Woody	Film	Himself	Comedic short
1999	Three Kings	Film	Major Archie Gates	
	The Book That Wrote Itself	Film	Himself	
	South Park: Bigger, Longer & Uncut	Film	Doctor Gouache	Voice only
	The Limey	Film		Archive footage, uncredited
2000	The Perfect Storm	Film	Billy 'Skip' Tyne	
	Fail Safe	TV	Col. Jack Grady	
	O Brother, Where Art Thou?	Film	Ulysses Everett McGill	Golden Globe Award for Best Actor – Motion Picture Musical or Comedy Nominated — Empire Award for Best Actor Nominated — Satellite Award for Best Actor - Motion Picture Musical or Comedy
2001	Ocean's Eleven	Film	Danny Ocean	Nominated — MTV Movie Award for Best Dressed Nominated — Phoenix Film Critics Society Award for Best Cast
	Spy Kids	Film	Devlin	
2002	Confessions of a Dangerous Mind	Film	CIA Officer Jim Byrd	Also director
	Solaris	Film	Chris Kelvin	Nominated — Saturn Award for Best Actor
	Welcome to Collinwood	Film	Jerzy	Also producer
	Starbuck Holger Meins	Film		Documentary

2003	*Intolerable Cruelty*	Film	Miles Massey	
	Spy Kids 3-D: Game Over	Film	Devlin	
2004	*Ocean's Twelve*	Film	Danny Ocean	Nominated — Broadcast Film Critics Association Award for Best Cast
2005	*Good Night, and Good Luck*	Film	Fred Friendly	also director Golden Osella for Best Screenplay Satellite Award for Best Original Screenplay Nominated — Academy Award for Writing (Original Screenplay) Nominated — BAFTA Award for Best Original Screenplay Nominated — BAFTA Award for Best Actor in a Supporting Role Nominated — BFCA Critics' Choice Award for Best Writer Nominated — Chicago Film Critics Association Award for Best Original Screenplay Nominated — Chicago Film Critics Association Award for Best Director Nominated — Chlotrudis Award for Best Director Nominated — Golden Globe Award for Best Screenplay Nominated — Gotham Award for Best Cast Nominated — Screen Actors Guild Award for Outstanding Performance by a Cast in a Motion Picture Nominated — Washington D.C. Area Film Critics Association Award for Best Screenplay Nominated — Writers Guild of America Award for Best Original Screenplay
	Syriana	Film	Bob Barnes	Academy Award for Best Supporting Actor Golden Globe Award for Best Supporting Actor – Motion Picture Nominated — BAFTA Award for Best Actor in a Supporting Role Nominated — Broadcast Film Critics Association Award for Best Supporting Actor Nominated — Screen Actors Guild Award for Outstanding Performance by a Male Actor in a Supporting Role
2006	*The Good German*	Film	Jake Geismar	

2007	*Michael Clayton*	Film	Michael Clayton	National Board of Review Award for Best Actor San Francisco Film Critics Circle Award for Best Actor San Francisco Film Critics Circle Award for Best Screenplay Washington D.C. Area Film Critics Association Award for Best Actor Nominated — Academy Award for Best Actor Nominated — BAFTA Award for Best Actor in a Leading Role Nominated — Broadcast Film Critics Association Award for Best Actor Nominated — Chicago Film Critics Association Award for Best Actor Nominated — Golden Globe Award for Best Actor - Motion Picture Drama Nominated — London Film Critics Circle Award for Best Actor Nominated — Online Film Critics Society Award for Best Actor Nominated — Screen Actors Guild Award for Outstanding Performance by a Male Actor in a Leading Role
	Darfur Now	Film	Himself	
	Ocean's Thirteen	Film	Danny Ocean	
2008	*Leatherheads*	Film	Jimmy "Dodge" Connelly	Co-writer Also director
	Burn After Reading	Film	Harry Pfarrer	

2009	*Fantastic Mr. Fox*	Film	Mr. Fox	Voice only New York Film Critics Circle Award for Best Actor and *Up in the Air*
	The Men Who Stare At Goats	Film	Lyn Cassady	
	Up in the Air	Film	Ryan Bingham	Dallas-Fort Worth Film Critics Association Award for Best Actor Florida Film Critics Circle Award for Best Actor Houston Film Critics Society Award for Best Actor National Board of Review Award for Best Actor tied with Morgan Freeman for *Invictus* New York Film Critics Circle Award for Best Actor and *Fantastic Mr. Fox* Phoenix Film Critics Society Award for Best Actor Southeastern Film Critics Association Award for Best Actor Washington D.C. Area Film Critics Association for Best Actor Nominated — Academy Award for Best Actor Nominated — Broadcast Film Critics Association Award for Best Actor Nominated — Chicago Film Critics Association Award for Best Actor Nominated — Detroit Film Critics Society Award for Best Actor Nominated — Golden Globe Award for Best Actor – Motion Picture Drama Nominated — San Diego Film Critics Society Award for Best Actor Nominated — Satellite Award for Best Actor - Motion Picture Musical or Comedy Nominated — Screen Actors Guild Award for Outstanding Performance by a Male Actor in a Leading Role Nominated — Toronto Film Critics Association Award for Best Actor
2010	*The American*	Film	Jack	
2011	*The Descendants*	Film		*Filming*
2012	*Suburbicon*	Film		also director

Director

Year	Title	Notes
2002	*Confessions of a Dangerous Mind*	Nominated — Golden Bear Nominated — Chicago Film Critics Association for Most Promising New Director
2005	*Good Night, and Good Luck*	Film Critics Circle of Australia Award for Best Foreign Film Kansas City Film Critics Circle Award for Best Original Screenplay Online Film Critics Society Award for Best Original Screenplay Pasinetti Award for Best Film Nominated — Academy Award for Best Director Nominated — BAFTA Award for Best Direction Nominated — Bodil Award for Best American Film Nominated — Broadcast Film Critics Association Award for Best Director Nominated — David di Donatello for Best Foreign Film Nominated — Directors Guild of America Award for Best Director Nominated — Empire Award for Best Director Nominated — Golden Lion Nominated — Golden Globe Award for Best Director – Motion Picture Nominated — Independent Spirit Award for Best Director Nominated — Online Film Critics Society Award for Best Director Nominated — Satellite Award for Best Director Nominated — Washington D.C. Area Film Critics Association Award for Best Director
	Unscripted	5 episodes
2008	*Leatherheads*	
2012	*Suburbicon*	Announced

Producer

Year	Title	Notes
1999	*Kilroy*	(TV) also writer
2000	*Fail Safe*	Executive producer
2001	*Rock Star*	Executive producer
2002	*Insomnia*	Executive producer
	Welcome to Collinwood	Executive producer
	Far from Heaven	Executive producer
2003	*K Street*	Executive producer, 10 episodes

Year	Title	Notes
2004	*Criminal*	
2005	*The Jacket*	
	Unscripted	10 episodes
	The Big Empty	Executive producer
	Syriana	Executive producer
	Rumor Has It...	Executive producer
2006	*A Scanner Darkly*	Executive producer
	Pu-239	Executive producer
2007	*Michael Clayton*	Executive producer
	Sand and Sorrow	Executive producer Documentary
	Wind Chill	Executive producer
2008	*Leatherheads*	
2009	*The Informant!*	Executive producer
	Playground	Executive producer
	The Men Who Stare At Goats	
2010	*Hope for Haiti Now*	Producer

External links

- George Clooney [1] at the Internet Movie Database
- George Clooney [2] at People.com
- George Clooney [3] at TV.com
- George Clooney [4] on Moviefone
- NPR interview 10/2005 [5]
- Text, Audio, and Video of Speech to the United Nations Security Council on Darfur [6]
- George Clooney Public Service Announcement [7]
- George Clooney calls for unity among actors [8]
- Not On Our Watch: Official site for charity founded by George Clooney, Brad Pitt, Matt Damon, Don Cheadle, Jerry Weintraub, David Pressman [9]

1. REDIRECT Template:Navboxes

Back to the Basics

Batman Begins

Batman Begins	
Theatrical release poster	
Directed by	Christopher Nolan
Produced by	Emma Thomas Larry J. Franco Charles Roven
Screenplay by	David S. Goyer Christopher Nolan
Story by	David S. Goyer Bob Kane (comic book) Bill Finger (comic book)
Starring	Christian Bale Michael Caine Liam Neeson Katie Holmes Gary Oldman Cillian Murphy Morgan Freeman
Music by	Hans Zimmer James Newton Howard
Cinematography	Wally Pfister
Editing by	Lee Smith
Studio	DC Comics Legendary Pictures Syncopy Films
Distributed by	Warner Bros.
Release date(s)	June 10, 2005 (Russia) June 15, 2005
Running time	139 minutes
Country	United States

Language	English
Budget	$150 million
Gross revenue	$372,710,015
Followed by	*The Dark Knight*

Batman Begins is a 2005 superhero film based on the fictional DC Comics character Batman, directed by Christopher Nolan. It stars Christian Bale as Batman, along with Michael Caine, Gary Oldman, Liam Neeson, Katie Holmes, Cillian Murphy, Morgan Freeman, Ken Watanabe, Tom Wilkinson, and Rutger Hauer. The film reboots the *Batman* film series, telling the origin story of the character and begins with Bruce Wayne's initial fear of bats, the death of his parents, and his journey to becoming Batman. It draws inspiration from classic comic book storylines such as *The Man Who Falls*, *Batman: Year One*, and *Batman: The Long Halloween*.

After a series of unsuccessful projects to resurrect Batman on screen following the 1997 critical failure of *Batman & Robin*, Nolan and David S. Goyer began work on the film in early 2003 and aimed for a darker and more realistic tone, with humanity and realism being the basis of the film. The goal was to get the audience to care for both Batman and Bruce Wayne. The film, which was primarily shot in England and Chicago, relied on traditional stunts and miniatures—computer-generated imagery was used minimally. A new Batmobile (called the Tumbler) and a more mobile Batsuit were both created specifically for the film.

Batman Begins was critically and commercially successful. The film opened on June 15, 2005 in the United States and Canada in 3,858 theaters. It grossed $48 million in its opening weekend, eventually grossing over $372 million worldwide. The film received an 84% overall approval rating from Rotten Tomatoes. Critics noted that fear was a common theme throughout the film, and remarked that it had a darker tone compared to previous *Batman* films. A sequel titled *The Dark Knight* was released in July 2008 and also saw the return of both Nolan and Bale to the franchise.

Plot

A young Bruce Wayne falls down a well and is attacked by bats. Bruce then awakens from this nightmare of his past and is revealed to be a prisoner in Bhutan. He is approached by Henri Ducard, who speaks for Ra's al Ghul, leader of the League of Shadows, and invites him to train with the elite vigilante group. The narrative returns to Bruce's childhood, to the fateful night he witnessed his parents' murder by a mugger named Joe Chill. Chill is later arrested and Bruce is taken home and raised by the family butler Alfred Pennyworth.

Years later, Bruce returns to Gotham City from Princeton University, intent on killing Chill, whose prison sentence is being suspended in exchange for testifying against crime boss Carmine Falcone. Before he can act, however, one of Falcone's assassins kills Chill. Rachel Dawes, Bruce's childhood friend and now an assistant district attorney, is disgusted with Bruce's intent, telling him his father would be ashamed of him. That night, Bruce confronts Falcone, who tells the young man that his criminal empire is invincible because it runs on fear. Inspired, Bruce decides to travel the world for several years, learning the various ways of the criminal underworld, before himself becoming a criminal and being arrested. After Bruce's training in the League of Shadows, Ra's and Ducard tell Bruce his purpose: He must lead the League to destroy Gotham, which they believe is corrupt beyond saving. Bruce refuses to become a murderer and battles Ra's, burning the temple in the process, before making his escape. Ra's is killed by falling debris, but Bruce saves an unconscious Ducard and returns to Gotham.

Falcone now dominates the city. Bruce enlists the help of Sgt. Jim Gordon, one of the city's few honest police officers, and befriends Lucius Fox, a former board member of Wayne Enterprises. Fox helps Bruce acquire a prototype armored car and an experimental armored suit. With Alfred, Bruce finds another entrance to the cave under the well and creates a workshop, modifying his equipment to take up the identity of Batman. On his first night out as a vigilante, he intercepts a drug shipment, captures Falcone and provides Rachel with the evidence to indict him. Falcone and his men are transferred to Arkham Asylum with the help of the hospital's corrupt administrator, Dr. Jonathan Crane, who has been paying off Falcone to ship a toxic hallucinogenic into Gotham City; Crane uses the toxin in his experiments, using his patients as guinea pigs. When Falcone demands a bigger share, Crane gasses Falcone with the same toxin, literally driving him insane with fear. While investigating the drugs, Batman encounters Crane, who also sprays him with the fear toxin. Alfred rescues him, using an anti-toxin developed by Fox. Crane later summons Rachel to Arkham and shows her that the toxin has been introduced into Gotham's water supply from Arkham for weeks, and then infects her. Batman doses Crane with the toxin, saves Rachel, and then takes her to his cave giving her vials for Gordon: One for inoculating himself and the other for mass production.

At Bruce's birthday celebration at Wayne Manor, he is confronted by Ducard, who reveals himself to be the real Ra's al Ghul, and has now arrived in Gotham personally to destroy the city; he had conspired with Crane to poison Gotham's water supply with the toxin, vaporizing it with a stolen device from Wayne Enterprises. After Bruce pretends to be drunk to get everyone to leave, he and Ra's fight. Ra's' men burn down the mansion, release all the inmates at Arkham, and vaporize the hallucinogen into the atmosphere. Although Wayne Manor is destroyed, Bruce escapes the inferno with help from Alfred. Rachel delivers the antidote to Gordon and wards off Crane, now calling himself Scarecrow, with a taser. Batman reveals his identity to Rachel and then has Gordon drive the Batmobile to Wayne Tower, the central hub of the Gotham elevated rail system. Ra's boards the train; his objective is to reach Wayne Tower with the vaporizer as it is also a major water hub. As Batman confronts Ra's on the train, Gordon destroys the elevated tracks. Batman jams the controls and escapes the train as it crashes, leaving Ra's to die.

Following the battle, Batman becomes a public hero and Bruce gains control of his company; he fires the former CEO, William Earle, and replaces him with Lucius Fox. However, he loses Rachel, who cannot bring herself to love both Bruce and Batman. Gordon, now a Lieutenant, shows Batman the Bat-Signal and mentions a new criminal who leaves Joker playing cards at crime scenes. Batman promises to investigate, and disappears into the night.

Cast

- Christian Bale as Bruce Wayne / Batman: Wayne is a billionaire industrialist whose parents were killed by a mugger when he was eight years old. Traveling the world for several years to seek the means to fight injustice, he returns to Gotham. At night, Bruce becomes Batman, Gotham City's vigilante protector. Bale was cast on September 11, 2003, having expressed interest in playing Batman since Darren Aronofsky was planning his own film adaptation. Some of the early candidates for the Batman/Bruce Wayne role were Billy Crudup, Jake Gyllenhaal, Hugh Dancy, Joshua Jackson, Eion Bailey, and Cillian Murphy. Bale felt the previous films underused Batman's character, overplaying the villains instead. To best pose as Batman, Bale studied graphic novels and illustrations of the superhero. David Boreanaz was the first choice for the role before Bale.

Director Nolan said of Bale, "He has exactly the balance of darkness and light that we were looking for." Goyer stated that while some actors could play a great Bruce Wayne or a great Batman, Bale could portray both radically different personalities. Bale described the part as playing four characters: the raging Batman persona; the shallow playboy façade Bruce uses to ward off suspicion; the vengeful young man; and the older, angrier Bruce who is discovering his purpose in life. Bale's dislike of his costume, which heated up regularly, helped him get into a necessarily foul mood. He said, "Batman's meant to be fierce, and you become a beast in that suit, as Batman should be — not a man in a suit, but a different creature."

Since he had lost a great deal of weight in preparation for his role in *The Machinist*, Bale hired a personal trainer to help him gain 100 pounds (45 kg) in the span of only a couple of months to help him physically prepare for the role. He first went well over the weight required and created concern over whether he would look right for the part. Bale recognized that his large physique was not appropriate for Batman, who relies on speed and strategy. He lost the excess weight by the time filming began. The role of Bruce Wayne at age eight was portrayed by Gus Lewis.

- Michael Caine as Alfred Pennyworth: The trusted butler to Bruce Wayne's parents, who continues his loyal service to their son after their deaths. He is Bruce Wayne's closest confidant. Nolan felt Caine would effectively portray the foster father element of the character. Although Alfred's family is depicted in the film as having served the Wayne family for generations, Caine created his own backstory, in that before becoming Wayne's butler, Alfred served in the Special Air Service. After being wounded, he was invited to the position of the Wayne family butler by Thomas Wayne because, "He wanted a butler, but someone a bit tougher than that, you know?"

- Liam Neeson as Henri Ducard: In reality Ra's al Ghul in disguise and the main antagonist of the film, Ducard trains Bruce in ninjutsu, a form of martial arts. Writer David Goyer said he felt Ra's was the most complex of all the Batman villains, comparing him to Osama bin Laden; "He's not crazy in the way that all the other Batman villains are. He's not bent on revenge; he's actually trying to heal the world. He's just doing it by very draconian means." Neeson is commonly cast as a mentor, so the revelation that his character was the main villain was intended to shock viewers.

- Katie Holmes as Rachel Dawes: Bruce's childhood friend who serves as Gotham City's assistant district attorney, fighting against the corruption in the city. Nolan found a "tremendous warmth and great emotional appeal" in Holmes, and also felt "she has a maturity beyond her years that comes across in the film and is essential to the idea that Rachel is something of a moral conscience for Bruce". Sarah Michelle Gellar and Rachel McAdams were in the running for the role. Emma Lockhart portrays the young Rachel Dawes.

- Gary Oldman as Sgt. James Gordon: One of the few uncorrupted Gotham City police officers. He was the officer on duty the night of the murder of Bruce Wayne's parents. In this way, he shares a special bond with the adult Bruce and thus with Batman. Nolan originally wanted to cast Oldman as a villain, but when Chris Cooper turned down the role of Gordon to spend time with his family he decided that it would be refreshing for Oldman to play the role instead. "I embody the themes of the movie which are the values of family, courage and compassion and a sense of right and wrong, good and bad and justice," Oldman said of his character. Oldman filmed most of his scenes in Britain. Goyer said Oldman heavily resembled Gordon as drawn by David Mazzucchelli in *Batman: Year One*.

- Cillian Murphy as Dr. Jonathan Crane / The Scarecrow: A psychopharmacologist who works at Arkham Asylum and has developed fear-inducing toxins. He takes on the persona of the Scarecrow to use during his experiments, in which he uses his patients as human guinea pigs for his toxins. He is the primary antagonist and works with Ra's al Ghul and Carmine Falcone. Nolan decided against Irish actor Murphy for Batman, before casting him as Scarecrow. Murphy read numerous comics featuring the Scarecrow, and discussed making the character look less theatrical with Nolan. Murphy explained, "I wanted to avoid the Worzel Gummidge look, because he's not a very physically imposing man — he's more interested in the manipulation of the mind and what that can do."

- Tom Wilkinson as Carmine Falcone: The ruler of the Gotham City underworld. He had shared a prison cell with Joe Chill after Joe murdered Wayne's parents. He had Chill murdered when he decided to testify against Falcone. He goes into business with Dr. Jonathan Crane and Ra's al Ghul by smuggling a fear toxin through a shipment and putting it in the city's water supply.

- Morgan Freeman as Lucius Fox: A high-ranking Wayne Enterprises employee who was demoted to working in the company's Applied Science Division, where he conducts advanced studies in biochemistry and mechanical engineering. Fox supplies Bruce with much of the gear necessary to carry out Batman's mission and is promoted to CEO when Bruce repossesses the company by the end of the film. Freeman was Goyer's first and only choice for the role.

Other cast members include Rutger Hauer as William Earle, the CEO of Wayne Enterprises who takes the company public in the long-term absence of Bruce Wayne; Mark Boone Junior as Gordon's corrupt partner Detective Arnold Flass; Ken Watanabe as Ra's al Ghul's decoy; Larry Holden as district attorney Finch; Colin McFarlane as Police commissioner Gillian B. Loeb; Linus Roache and Sara Stewart as Thomas and Martha Wayne, Bruce's parents; Richard Brake as Joe Chill, the Waynes' killer; Gerard Murphy as the corrupt High Court Judge Faden; Tim Booth as Victor Zsasz; Rade Šerbedžija as a homeless man, who is the last person to meet Bruce when he leaves Gotham, and the first civilian to see Batman, and Andrew Pleavin as a uniformed policeman. Actors John Foo and Mark Strange appear as members of the League of Shadows Warriors.

Production

Development

Further information: Batman in film#Proposals for fifth film

In January 2003, Warner Bros. hired *Memento* director Christopher Nolan to direct an untitled *Batman* film, and David S. Goyer signed on to write the script two months later. Nolan stated his intention to reinvent the film franchise of Batman by "doing the origins story of the character, which is a story that's never been told before". Nolan said that humanity and realism would be the basis of the origin film, and that "the world of Batman is that of grounded reality. [It] will be a recognizable, contemporary reality against which an extraordinary heroic figure arises." Goyer said that the goal of the film was to get the audience to care for both Batman and Bruce Wayne. Nolan felt the previous films were exercises in style rather than drama, and described his inspiration as being Richard Donner's 1978 film *Superman*, in its focus on depicting the character's growth. Also similar to *Superman*, Nolan wanted an all-star supporting cast for *Batman Begins* to lend a more epic feel and credibility to the story.

Nolan's personal "jumping off point" of inspiration was "Batman: The Man Who Falls", a short story by Denny O'Neil and Dick Giordano about Bruce's travels throughout the world. The early scene in *Batman Begins* of young Bruce Wayne falling into a well was adapted from "The Man Who Falls". *Batman: The Long Halloween*, written by Jeph Loeb and drawn by Tim Sale, influenced Goyer in writing the screenplay, with the villain Carmine Falcone as one of many elements which were drawn from *Halloween*'s "sober, serious approach". The writers considered having Harvey Dent in the film, but replaced him with the new character Rachel Dawes when they realized they "couldn't do him justice". The character was later portrayed by Aaron Eckhart in the 2008 sequel *The Dark Knight*. The sequel to *Halloween*, *Batman: Dark Victory*, also served as an influence. Goyer used the vacancy of Bruce Wayne's multi-year absence presented in *Batman: Year One* to help set up some of the film's events in the transpiring years. In addition, the film's Sergeant James Gordon was based on his comic book incarnation as seen in *Year One*. The writers of *Batman Begins* also used Frank Miller's *Year One* plot device, which was about a corrupt police force that led to Gordon and Gotham City's need for Batman.

A common idea in the comics is that Bruce saw a Zorro film with his parents before they were murdered. Nolan explained that by ignoring that idea — which he stated is not found in Batman's first appearances — it emphasized the importance of bats to Bruce and that becoming a superhero is a wholly original idea on his part. It is for this reason Nolan believes other DC characters do not exist in the universe of his film; otherwise, Wayne's reasons for taking up costumed vigilantism would have been very different.

Filming

As with all his films, Nolan refused a second unit to keep his vision consistent. Filming began in March 2004 in the Vatnajökull glacier in Iceland (standing in for Bhutan). The crew built a village and the front doors to Ra's temple, as well as a road to access the remote area. The weather was problematic, with 75 miles per hour (121 km/h) winds, rain, and a lack of snow. A shot Wally Pfister had planned with a crane had to be done with a handheld camera.

In seeking inspiration from *Superman* and other blockbuster films of the late 1970s and early 1980s, Nolan based most of the production in England, specifically Shepperton Studios. A Batcave set was built there and measured 250 feet (76 m) long, 120 feet (37 m) wide, and 40 feet (12 m) high. Production designer Nathan Crowley installed twelve pumps to create a waterfall with 12000 imperial gallons (55000 l; 14000 US gal), and built rocks using molds of real caves. In January 2004, an airship hangar at Cardington, Bedfordshire was rented by Warner Bros. for filming in April 2004. There, the Narrows and the feet of the monorails filled the 900 feet (270 m) long stage.

Mentmore Towers was chosen from twenty different locations for Wayne Manor, as Nolan and Crowley liked its white floors, which gave the impression of the manor as a memorial to Wayne's parents. The building chosen to represent Arkham Asylum was the National Institute for Medical Research building in Mill Hill, northwest London, England. The St. Pancras railway station and the Abbey Mills Pumping Stations were used for Arkham's interiors. The University College London was used for courtrooms. Some scenes, including the Batmobile pursuit, were filmed in Chicago at locations such as Lower Wacker Drive and 35 East Wacker. Authorities agreed to raise Franklin Street Bridge for a scene where access to the Narrows is closed.

Despite the film's darkness, Nolan wanted to make the film appeal to a wide age range. "Not the youngest kids obviously, I think what we've done is probably a bit intense for them but I certainly didn't want to exclude the sort of ten to 12-year olds, because as a kid I would have loved to have seen a movie like this." Because of this, nothing gory or bloody was filmed.

Design

Nolan used the 1982 cult science fiction film *Blade Runner* as a source of inspiration for *Batman Begins*. He screened *Blade Runner* to cinematographer Wally Pfister and two others to show the attitude and style that he wanted to draw from the film. Nolan described the film's world as "an interesting lesson on the technique of exploring and describing a credible universe that doesn't appear to have any boundaries", a lesson that he applied to the production of *Batman Begins*.

Nolan worked with production designer Nathan Crowley to create the look of Gotham City. Crowley built a model of the city that filled Nolan's garage. Crowley and Nolan designed it as a large, modern metropolitan area that would reflect the various periods of architecture that the city had gone through. Elements were drawn from New York City, Chicago, and Tokyo; the latter for its elevated freeways and monorails. The Narrows was based on the slummish nature of the (now demolished) walled city of Kowloon in Hong Kong.

Batmobile

See also: Batmobile

Crowley started the process of designing the Tumbler for the film by model bashing. Crowley used the nose cone of a P-38 Lightning model to serve as the chassis for the Tumbler's turbine engine. Six models of the Tumbler were built to 1:12 scale in the course of four months. Following the scale model creation, a crew of over 30 people, including Crowley and engineers Chris Culvert and Annie Smith, carved a full-size replica of the Tumbler out of a large block of Styrofoam in two months.

The Tumbler, the Batmobile used in *Batman Begins*

The Styrofoam model was used to create a steel "test frame", which had to stand up to several standards: have a speed of over 100 miles per hour (160 km/h), go from 0 to 60 miles per hour (97 km/h) in 5 seconds, possess a steering system to make sharp turns at city corners, and withstand a self-propelled launch of up to 30 feet (9.1 m). On the first jump test, the Tumbler's front end collapsed and had to be completely rebuilt. The basic configuration of the newly designed Tumbler included a 8.7-liter Chevy V8 engine, a truck axle for the rear axle, front tires by Hoosier (which are actually dirt racing tires used on the right rear of open wheel sprint cars), rear 4x4 mud tires by Interco., and the suspension system of Baja racing trucks. The design and development process took nine months and cost several million dollars.

The rear of the Tumbler, showing the flaps and engine

With the design process complete, four street-ready race cars were constructed, with each vehicle possessing 65 panels and costing $250,000 to build. Two of the four cars were specialized versions. One version was the flap version, which had hydraulics and flaps to detail the close-up shots where the vehicle propelled itself through the air. The other version was the jet version, in which an actual jet engine was mounted onto the vehicle, fueled by six propane tanks. Due to the poor visibility inside the vehicle by the driver, monitors were connected to cameras on the vehicle body. The professional drivers for the Tumblers practiced driving the vehicles for six months before they drove on the streets of Chicago for the film's scenes.

The interior of the Tumbler was an immobile studio set and not actually the interior of a street-capable Tumbler. The cockpit was over-sized to fit cameras for scenes filmed in the Tumbler interior. In addition, another version of the Tumbler was a miniature model that was 1:5 scale of the actual Tumbler. This miniature model had an electric motor and was used to show the Tumbler flying across ravines and between buildings. However, the actual Tumbler was used for the waterfall sequence.

Batsuit

The filmmakers intended to create a very mobile Batsuit that would allow the wearer to move easily to fight and crouch. Previous film incarnations of the Batsuit had been stiff and especially restricted full head movement. Costume designer Lindy Hemming and her crew worked on the Batsuit at an FX workshop codenamed "Cape Town", a secured compound located at Shepperton Studios in London. The Batsuit's basic design was a neoprene undersuit, which was shaped by attaching molded cream latex sections. Christian Bale was molded and sculpted prior to his physical training so the team could work on a full body cast. To avoid imperfections picked up by sculpting with clay, plastiline was used to smooth the surface. In addition, the team brewed different mixtures of foam to find the mixture that would be the most flexible, light, durable, and black. The latter presented a problem, since the process to make the foam black reduced the foam's durability.

For the cape, director Christopher Nolan wanted to have a "flowing cloak... that blows and flows as in so many great graphic novels". Hemming's team created the cape out of their own version of parachute nylon that had electrostatic flocking, a process shared with the team by the British Ministry of Defence. The process was used by the London police force to minimize night vision detection. The cape was topped by a cowl, which was designed by Nolan, Hemming, and costume effects supervisor Graham Churchyard. The cowl was created to be thin enough to allow motion but thick enough to avoid wrinkling when Bale turned his head in the Batsuit. Churchyard explained the cowl had been designed to show "a man who has angst", so his character would be revealed through the mask.

Special effects

For *Batman Begins*, Nolan preferred using traditional stuntwork over computer generated imagery. Scale models were used to represent the Narrows and Ra's al Ghul's temple. There were, however, several establishing shots that were CG composite images; that is, an image composed of multiple images. Examples include Gotham's skyline, exterior shots of Wayne Tower, and some of the exterior monorail shots. The climactic monorail sequence mixed live action footage, model work, and CGI.

The bats were entirely digital (except in shots containing only one or two bats), as it was decided directing larger amounts of real bats on set would be problematic. Dead bats were scanned to create digital models. Locations and sets were recreated on the computer so the flying bats would not be superfluous once incorporated into the finished film.

Soundtrack

See also: Batman Begins soundtrack

The score for *Batman Begins* was composed by Hans Zimmer and James Newton Howard. Nolan originally invited Zimmer to compose the music, and Zimmer asked Nolan if he could invite Howard to compose as well, as they had always planned a collaboration. The two composers collaborated on separate themes for the "split personality" of Bruce Wayne and his alter ego, Batman. Zimmer and Howard began composing in Los Angeles and moved to London where they stayed for twelve weeks to complete most of their writing. Zimmer and Howard sought inspiration for shaping the score by visiting the *Batman Begins* sets.

Zimmer wanted to avoid writing music that had been done in earlier Batman films, so the score became an amalgamation of orchestra and electronic music. The film's ninety-piece orchestra was developed from members of various London orchestras, and Zimmer chose to use more than the normal number of cellos. Zimmer enlisted a boy soprano to help reflect the music in some of film's scenes where Bruce Wayne's parents tragic memories are involved. "He's singing a fairly pretty tune and then he gets stuck, it's like froze, arrested development," said Zimmer. He also attempted to add human dimension to Batman, whose behavior would typically be seen as "psychotic", through the music. Both composers collaborated to create 2 hours and 20 minutes worth of music for the film. Zimmer composed the action sequences, while Howard focused on the film's drama.

Themes

Comic book writer and author Danny Fingeroth argues that a strong theme in the film is Bruce's search for a father figure, saying "[Alfred] is the good father that Bruce comes to depend on. Bruce's real father died before they could establish an adult relationship, and Liam Neeson's Ducard is stern and demanding, didactic and challenging, but not a father figure with any sympathy. If Bruce is anyone's son, it is Alfred's. [Morgan] Freeman's Lucius is cool and imperturbable, another steady anchor in

Bruce's life." Blogger Mark Fisher states that Bruce's search for justice requires him to learn from a proper father figure, with Thomas Wayne and Ra's al Ghul being the two counterpoints. Alfred provides a maternal figure of unconditional love, despite the overall lack of focus on a mother figure in Bruce's life.

Fingeroth also argues that a major theme in the film is fear, which supports the story of Bruce Wayne becoming a hero. Director Christopher Nolan stated that the idea behind the film was "a person who would confront his innermost fear and then attempt to become it". Fingeroth referred to this film's depiction as "the man with fear—but who rises above it". The theme of fear is further personified by the choice of antagonist, the Scarecrow. The film depicts how fear can affect all creatures regardless of might. Allusions to fear are seen throughout, from Bruce's conquering of his demons, to becoming Batman, to the Scarecrow and his deadly fear toxin. The macabre, distorted images presented in the Scarecrow's toxin-induced hallucinations also express the idea of terror to an extreme.

Critic Brian Orndorf considered *Batman Begins* "fierce" and "demonstrative in brood", giving the film an abundance of gravitas and energy. It strays away from the lighter fare of Joel Schumacher's 1997 Batman film, *Batman & Robin*, which contained camp one-liners throughout. The theme of fear is intensified with the help of the musical score by Zimmer and Howard, which also "eschews traditional heroic themes". Also contrary to previous Batman films, a psychological investigation of Bruce Wayne's split personality in the bat suit is only lightly touched upon. Orndorf noted that Bruce is a "character constantly striving to do the right thing, not worn down by incessant reexamination".

Release

Reception

The film received positive reviews from critics. Based on 257 reviews collected by Rotten Tomatoes, *Batman Begins* currently garners an 84% "fresh" rating. The film's reception was more ambivalent within the 43 reviews in Rotten Tomatoes' "Top Critics" subset, reaching a 60% positive consensus. By comparison, Metacritic calculated an average score of 70 from the 41 reviews it collected.

James Berardinelli applauded Nolan and Goyer's work creating more understanding into "who [Batman] is and what motivates him", something Berardinelli felt Tim Burton's film lacked; at the same time, Berardinelli felt the romantic aspect between Bale and Holmes did not work because the actors lacked the chemistry Christopher Reeve and Margot Kidder (*Superman*), or Tobey Maguire and Kirsten Dunst (*Spider-Man*) shared in their respective roles. According to *Total Film*, Nolan manages to create such strong characters and story that the third-act action sequences cannot compare to " the frisson of two people talking", and Katie Holmes and Christian Bale's romantic subplot has a spark "refreshingly free of Peter Parker/Mary Jane-style whining".

Los Angeles Times' Kenneth Turan, who felt the film began slowly, stated that the "story, psychology and reality, not special effects", assisted the darkness behind Batman's arsenal; he noted that Neeson and Holmes, unlike Bale's ability to "feel his role in his bones", do not appear to fit their respective characters in "being both comic-book archetypes and real people". *The New Yorker*'s David Denby did not share Berardinelli and Turan's opinion. He was unimpressed with the film, when comparing it to the two Tim Burton films, and that Christian Bale's presence was hindered by the "dull earnestness of the screenplay", the final climax was "cheesy and unexciting", and that Nolan had resorted to imitating the "fakery" used by other filmmakers when filming action sequences.

Michael Wilmington of the *Chicago Tribune* believed Nolan and Miller managed to "comfortably mix the tormented drama and revenge motifs with light hearted gags and comic book allusions", and that Nolan takes the series out of the "slam-bang Hollywood jokefests" the franchise had drifted into. Comic book scribe and editor Dennis O'Neil stated that he "felt the filmmakers really understood the character they were translating", citing this film as the best of the live-action Batman films. In contrast, J.R. Jones, from the *Chicago Reader*, criticized the script, and Nolan and David Goyer for not living up to the "hype about exploring Batman's damaged psyche". Roger Ebert, who gave mixed reviews to the previous films, wrote this was "the Batman movie I've been waiting for; more correctly, this is the movie I did not realize I was waiting for". Giving it four out of four stars, he commended the realistic portrayals of the Batman arsenal — the Batsuit, Batcave, Batmobile, and the Batsignal — as well as the focus on "the story and character" with less stress on "high-tech action".

Like Berardinelli, *USA Today*'s Mike Clark thought Bale performed the role of Batman as well as he did Patrick Bateman in *American Psycho*, but that the relationship between Bruce Wayne and Rachel Dawes was "frustratingly underdeveloped". Kyle Smith thought Bale exhibited "both the menace and the wit he showed in his brilliant turn in *American Psycho*", and that the film works so well because of the realism, stating, "Batman starts stripping away each layer of Gotham crime only to discover a sicker and more monstrous evil beneath, his rancid city simultaneously invokes early '90s New York, when criminals frolicked to the tune of five murders a day; *Serpico* New York, when cops were for sale; and today, when psychos seek to kill us all at once rather than one by one." In contrast, Salon.com's Stephanie Zacharek felt Nolan did not deliver the emotional depth expected of "one of the most soulful and tortured superheroes of all"; she thought Bale, unlike Michael Keaton who she compared him to, failed to connect with the audience underneath the mask, but that Gary Oldman succeeds in "emotional complexity" where the rest of the movie fails. However, Tim Burton felt Nolan "captured the real spirit that these kind of movies are supposed to have nowadays. When I did *Batman* twenty years ago, in 1988 or something, it was a different time in comic book movies. You couldn't go into that dark side of comics yet. The last couple of years that has become acceptable and Nolan certainly got more to the root of what the Batman comics are about."

Box office

Batman Begins opened on June 15, 2005 in the United States and Canada in 3,858 theaters, including 55 IMAX theaters. The film ranked at the top in its opening weekend, accumulating $48,745,440, which was seen as "strong but unimpressive by today's instantaneous blockbuster standards". The film's five-day gross was $72.9 million, beating *Batman Forever* (1995) as the franchise high. *Batman Begins* also broke the five-day opening record in the 55 IMAX theaters, grossing $3.16 million. Polled moviegoers rated the film with an A, and according to the studio's surveys, *Batman Begins* was considered the best of all the *Batman* films. The audience's demographic was 57 percent male and 54 percent people over the age of 25.

The film held its top spot for another weekend, accumulating $27,589,389 in a 43 percent drop from its first weekend. *Batman Begins* went on to gross $205,343,774 domestically and had a worldwide total of $372,710,015. It is the third-highest grossing Batman film to date, behind Tim Burton's *Batman*, which grossed $411,348,924 worldwide and *The Dark Knight* which has grossed over $1 billion. In comparison to the previous Batman films, *Batman Begins* averaged $12,634 per theater. It was released in more theaters, but sold fewer tickets then the other previous Batman movies, with the exception of *Batman & Robin*. *Batman Begins* was the eighth-highest grossing film of 2005 in the US.

Home media

The DVD of *Batman Begins* was released on October 18, 2005 in both single disc and two-disc deluxe editions. In addition to the film, the deluxe edition contained featurettes and other bonus materials. The edition contained a small paperback booklet, the first *Batman* story *Detective Comics* #27, as well as *Batman: The Man Who Falls* and an excerpt from *Batman: The Long Halloween*. *Batman Begins* achieved first place in national sales and rental charts in October 2005, becoming the top-selling DVD in the fourth quarter of 2005. The DVD grossed $11.36 million in rental revenue. The DVD held its position at the top of the sales chart for a second week, but fell to second place behind *Bewitched* on video rental charts.

Batman Begins was released on HD DVD on October 10, 2006. A *Limited Edition Giftset* of the film was released on DVD and Blu-ray on July 8, 2008, to coincide with *The Dark Knight* which hit theaters July 18, 2008. Due to the successful box office performance of *The Dark Knight*, the *Batman Begins* DVD has seen an increase in both sales and rentals. The film grossed $125,000,000 in DVD sales, bringing its total film gross to $496,853,783.

Tie-in products

Three novels, *Dead White*, *Inferno*, and *Fear Itself*, based on the film's version of Batman were released. All of them took place after the events of the film. In addition, a novelization written by Denny O'Neil, and a video game were released.

Accolades

Wally Pfister was nominated for Best Cinematography at the 78th Academy Awards, receiving the film's only Oscar nomination. The film received three nominations at the 59th BAFTA Awards. Just months after its release, *Batman Begins* was voted by *Empire* readers as the 36th greatest film of all time. In 2006, the American Society of Composers, Authors and Publishers honored James Newton Howard, Hans Zimmer, and Ramin Djawadi with an ASCAP award for composing a film that became one of the top grossing films of 2005. The film was awarded three Saturn Awards in 2006 as well: Best Fantasy Film, Best Actor for Christian Bale, and Best Writing for Nolan and Goyer. Christian Bale would go on to win an MTV Movie Award for Best Hero. However, Katie Holmes's performance was not well received, and she was nominated for a Razzie Award for Worst Supporting Actress. *Batman Begins* won the fan-based *Total Film* award for Best Film.

Impact

Shawn Adler of *MTV* stated *Batman Begins* heralded a trend of darker genre films, that either retold back-stories or rebooted them altogether. Examples he cited were *Casino Royale*, as well as the in-development *RoboCop*, *Red Sonja*, and *He-Man*. Filmmakers, screenwriters and producers who have mentioned the film to describe their projects include: Jon Favreau and *Iron Man*, Edward Norton and *The Incredible Hulk*, McG and *Terminator Salvation* (which also stars Bale), Damon Lindelof and *Star Trek*, Robert Downey, Jr. and *Sherlock Holmes*, Lorenzo di Bonaventura and *G.I. Joe: The Rise of Cobra*, and Hugh Jackman and *X-Men Origins: Wolverine*.

External links

- Official website [1]
- *Batman Begins* [2] at the Internet Movie Database
- *Batman Begins* [3] at Allmovie
- *Batman Begins* [4] at Rotten Tomatoes
- *Batman Begins* [5] at Box Office Mojo
- *Batman Begins* [6] hype at Superhero Hype!
- Batman Begins [7] at the Open Directory Project
- Official production notes [8]
- Scene-by-scene annotations of *Batman Begins* [9]
- Comic Vs. Film analysis [10] at IGN

- Film analysis [11] at IGN

The Dark Knight (film)

The Dark Knight	
Theatrical release poster	
Directed by	Christopher Nolan
Produced by	Christopher Nolan Charles Roven Emma Thomas
Screenplay by	Christopher Nolan Jonathan Nolan
Story by	David S. Goyer Christopher Nolan *Comic book*: Bob Kane Bill Finger
Starring	Christian Bale Michael Caine Heath Ledger Gary Oldman Aaron Eckhart Maggie Gyllenhaal Morgan Freeman
Music by	Hans Zimmer James Newton Howard
Cinematography	Wally Pfister
Editing by	Lee Smith
Studio	Legendary Pictures Syncopy Films
Distributed by	Warner Bros.
Release date(s)	July 14, 2008 (New York City) July 18, 2008
Running time	152 minutes
Country	United States
Language	English

The Dark Knight (film)

Budget	$185 million
Gross revenue	$1,001,921,825
Preceded by	*Batman Begins*

The Dark Knight is a 2008 superhero film directed and co-written by Christopher Nolan. Based on the DC Comics character Batman, the film is part of Nolan's *Batman* film series and a sequel to 2005's *Batman Begins*. Christian Bale reprises the lead role. The film follows Bruce Wayne/Batman (Bale), District Attorney Harvey Dent (Aaron Eckhart), Assistant D.A. Rachel Dawes (Maggie Gyllenhaal), and Police Commissioner James Gordon (Gary Oldman) and their struggles and journey in combating the new rising threat of a criminal who goes by the name of the "Joker" (Heath Ledger).

Nolan's inspiration for the film was the Joker's comic book debut in 1940, and the 1996 series *The Long Halloween*, which retold Two-Face's origin. *The Dark Knight* was filmed primarily in Chicago, as well as in several other locations in the United States, the United Kingdom, and Hong Kong. Nolan used an IMAX camera to film some sequences, including the Joker's first appearance in the film.

On January 22, 2008, after he had completed filming *The Dark Knight*, Heath Ledger died from a toxic combination of prescription drugs, leading to intense attention from the press and moviegoing public. Warner Bros. had initially created a viral marketing campaign for *The Dark Knight*, developing promotional websites and trailers highlighting screen shots of Ledger as the Joker, but after Ledger's death, the studio refocused its promotional campaign.

The Dark Knight was released on July 16, 2008 in Australia, on July 18, 2008 in North America, and on July 24, 2008 in the United Kingdom. Critically acclaimed, it set numerous records during its theatrical run and is currently one of only three films to have earned more than $500 million at the North American box office. With over $1 billion in revenue worldwide, it is the seventh highest-grossing film of all time (unadjusted for inflation). The film received eight Academy Award nominations and won for Best Sound Editing and Best Supporting Actor for Ledger's performance.

Plot

In Gotham City, the Joker and his accomplices rob a mob bank. Batman and Lieutenant James Gordon decide to include new district attorney Harvey Dent, who is dating Rachel Dawes, in their plan to eradicate the mob. Bruce later meets Harvey and offers him a fundraiser after realizing his sincerity. Mob bosses Sal Maroni, Gambol, and the Chechen meet with other criminals to discuss the new pressure on their crime operations. Lau, a Chinese mafia accountant, informs them that he has hidden their money and fled to Hong Kong in an attempt to preempt Gordon's plan to seize their funds and hide from Dent's jurisdiction. The Joker appears, warning that Batman will come after Lau, and instead offers to kill Batman for half of the funds. They flatly refuse and Gambol places a bounty on the Joker's head. Not long after, the Joker kills Gambol and takes control of his men.

The Dark Knight (film)

In Hong Kong, Batman captures Lau with a skyhook and delivers him to the Gotham City police where Lau agrees to testify, letting Dent and Gordon arrest the mob. In retaliation the Joker issues an ultimatum to Gotham that people will die each day unless Batman reveals his identity, resulting in the deaths of Commissioner Gillian B. Loeb and the judge presiding over the mob trials. Gordon foils Joker's assassination attempt on the mayor and is apparently killed. As a result, Bruce plans to reveal his persona, but Harvey instead reveals himself as Batman to protect the truth and is taken into protective custody. Escorted across the city, Harvey is pursued by the Joker while Batman rushes to aid. Gordon, who faked his death to lure the Joker, arrests him with Batman's help and is promoted to Commissioner. However, Harvey goes missing and the Joker reveals that he, along with Rachel, have been taken to separate buildings on opposite sides of town which will explode at the same time. Batman goes after Rachel whilst Gordon and the police go for Harvey. At the same time the Joker escapes custody with Lau using a smuggled bomb. Batman instead finds Harvey and rescues him though he pressures him to go for Rachel. The buildings explode; Rachel dies while half of Harvey's face is burnt in his escape, leaving him traumatized and vengeful.

After killing Lau and the Chechen, the Joker threatens to destroy a hospital if Coleman Reese, an accountant at Wayne Enterprises who discovers Batman's identity, is not dead within an hour. Bruce saves Reese, whilst the Joker visits Harvey in the hospital and convinces him to go on a personal vendetta against those who played a part in Rachel's death. Now Two-Face, Harvey judges Joker by the toss of a coin and spares him. The Joker blows up the hospital and leaves with a bus of hostages, whilst Two-Face confronts and kills Maroni and others. That night, as civilians are evacuated from the city, the Joker has two ferries rigged with explosives, offering both civilian and prisoner passenger groups to destroy the other ferry to live. Batman stops Gordon's SWAT teams from taking out the Joker, in order to protect the hostages and to capture the Joker himself. The ferry passengers refuse to kill one another and the Joker is captured, but not before explaining his complex relationship with Batman and revealing what he has done to Harvey; stating that while Batman is truly incorruptible, Harvey was not.

At the remains of the building where Rachel died, Batman finds Two-Face holding Gordon and his family at gunpoint. Two-Face judges the fate of Batman, himself, and Gordon's son with three coin tosses. As the result of the first two flips, he shoots Batman in the abdomen and spares himself. Flipping the coin to determine the boy's fate, Two-Face is tackled over the side by a wounded Batman, resulting in Two-Face's death. Knowing that the citizens of Gotham will lose hope and all morale if Harvey's rampage becomes known, Gordon is convinced by Batman to hold Batman publicly responsible for the murders. The police swarm the building, and a manhunt for Batman ensues. Gordon later delivers the eulogy at Harvey's funeral and smashes the Bat-Signal.

Cast

- Christian Bale as Bruce Wayne / Batman, a billionaire dedicated to protecting Gotham City from the criminal underworld by night. Bale said he was confident in his choice to return in the role because of the positive response to his portrayal in *Batman Begins*. He continued training in the Keysi Fighting Method and performed many of his own stunts, but did not gain as much muscle as in the previous film because the new Batsuit allowed him to move with greater agility. Bale described Batman's dilemma as whether "[his crusade is] something that has an end. Can he quit and have an ordinary life? The kind of manic intensity someone has to have to maintain the passion and the anger that they felt as a child, takes an effort after a while, to keep doing that. At some point, you have to exorcise your demons." He added, "Now you have not just a young man in pain attempting to find some kind of an answer, you have somebody who actually has power, who is burdened by that power, and is having to recognize the difference between attaining that power and holding on to it." Bale felt Batman's personality had been strongly established in the first film, so it was unlikely his character would be overshadowed by the villains, stating: "I have no problem with competing with someone else. And that's going to make a better movie."

Cast and crew of *The Dark Knight* at the European premiere in London. From left to right: Director Christopher Nolan, producers Emma Thomas and Charles Roven, actors Monique Gabriela Curnen, Michael Caine, Aaron Eckhart, Maggie Gyllenhaal and Christian Bale.

- Michael Caine as Alfred Pennyworth, Bruce's trusted butler and adviser. His supply of useful advice to Bruce and his likeness as a fatherly figure has led to him being labeled "Batman's batman."

- Heath Ledger as The Joker. Before Ledger was confirmed to play the Joker in July 2006, Paul Bettany, Lachy Hulme, Adrien Brody, Steve Carell, and Robin Williams publicly expressed interest in the role. Yet Nolan had wanted to work with Ledger on a number of projects in the past (though he had been unable to do so), and was agreeable to Ledger's chaotic interpretation of the character. When Ledger saw *Batman Begins*, he had realized a way to make the character work consistent with the film's tone: he described his Joker as a "psychopathic, mass murdering, schizophrenic clown with zero empathy."

To prepare for the role, Ledger lived alone in a hotel room for a month, formulating the character's posture, voice, and personality, and kept a diary, in which he recorded the Joker's thoughts and feelings. While he initially found it difficult, Ledger eventually generated a voice unlike Jack Nicholson's character in Tim Burton's 1989 *Batman* film. He was also given *Batman: The Killing Joke* and *Arkham Asylum: A Serious House on Serious Earth,* which he "really tried to read and put it down." Ledger also cited *A Clockwork Orange* and Sid Vicious as "a very early starting point for

Christian [Bale] and I. But we kind of flew far away from that pretty quickly and into another world altogether." "There's a bit of everything in him. There's nothing that consistent," Ledger said, and added, "There are a few more surprises to him." Ledger was allowed to shoot and mostly direct the videos the Joker sends out as warnings. Each take Ledger made was different from the last. Nolan was impressed enough with the first video shoot that he chose to not be present when Ledger shot the video with a kidnapped reporter (Anthony Michael Hall).

On January 22, 2008, after he had completed filming *The Dark Knight*, Ledger died of an accidental prescription drug overdose, leading to intense press attention and memorial tributes. "It was tremendously emotional, right when he passed, having to go back in and look at him every day [during editing]," Nolan recalled. "But the truth is, I feel very lucky to have something productive to do, to have a performance that he was very, very proud of, and that he had entrusted to me to finish." All of Ledger's scenes appear as he completed them in the filming; in editing the film, Nolan added no "digital effects" to alter Ledger's actual performance posthumously. Nolan has dedicated the film in part to Ledger's memory.

- Gary Oldman as James Gordon, a lieutenant in the Gotham City Police Department and one of the few police officers who is not corrupt. He forms a tenuous, unofficial alliance with Batman and Harvey. When the Joker assassinates Police Commissioner Loeb, Mayor Garcia gives Gordon the position. Oldman described his character as "incorruptible, virtuous, strong, heroic, but understated." Nolan explained that "*The Long Halloween* has a great, triangular relationship between Harvey Dent and Gordon and Batman, and that's something we very much drew from." Oldman added that "Gordon has a great deal of admiration for him at the end, but [Batman] is more than ever now the dark knight, the outsider. I'm intrigued now to see: If there is a third one, what he's going to do?" On the possibility of another sequel, he said that "returning to [the role] is not dependent on whether the role was bigger than the one before."

- Aaron Eckhart as Harvey Dent / Two-Face, the district attorney who is hailed as Gotham's "White Knight." Harvey's battle with the Joker transforms Harvey into a murderous, disfigured vigilante called "Two-Face." Wayne sees Dent as his heir, recognizing that Batman will be a lifelong mission, and heightening the tragedy of Dent's downfall. Nolan and David S. Goyer had originally considered using Dent in *Batman Begins*, but they replaced him with the new character Rachel Dawes when they realized they "couldn't do him justice." Before Eckhart was cast in February 2007, Liev Schreiber, Josh Lucas, and Ryan Phillippe had expressed interest in the role, while Mark Ruffalo auditioned. Hugh Jackman was also considered for the part of Harvey. Nolan chose Eckhart, whom he had considered for the lead role in *Memento*, citing his "extraordinary" ability as an actor, his embodiment of "that kind of chiselled, American hero quality" projected by Robert Redford, and his subtextual "edge."

Eckhart was "interested in good guys gone wrong," and had played corrupt men in films such as *The Black Dahlia*, *Thank You for Smoking*, and *In the Company of Men*. Whereas Two-Face is an evil villain in the comics, Nolan chose to portray him as a twisted vigilante to emphasize his role as Batman's counterpart. Eckhart explained, "[He] is still true to himself. He's a crime fighter, he's not killing good people. He's not a bad guy, not purely." For Dent, Eckhart "kept on thinking about the Kennedys," particularly Robert F. Kennedy, who was "idealistic, held a grudge and took on the Mob." He had his hair lightened and styled to make him appear more dashing. Nolan told Eckhart to not make Two-Face "jokey with slurping sounds or ticks."

- Maggie Gyllenhaal as Rachel Dawes, the Gotham assistant district attorney and Wayne's childhood friend. Before the events of the film, she told Wayne that if he ever decided to stop being Batman, they would be together. She is one of the few people to know Batman's identity. Gyllenhaal took over the role from Katie Holmes, who played it in *Batman Begins*. In August 2005, Holmes was reportedly planning to reprise the role, but she eventually turned it down to do *Mad Money* with Diane Keaton and Queen Latifah. By March 2007, Gyllenhaal was in "final talks" for the part. Gyllenhaal has acknowledged her character is a damsel in distress to an extent, but says Nolan sought ways to empower her character, so "Rachel's really clear about what's important to her and unwilling to compromise her morals, which made a nice change" from the many conflicted characters whom she has previously portrayed.
- Morgan Freeman as Lucius Fox, the recently-promoted chief executive officer of Wayne Enterprises who, now fully aware of his employer's double life, serves more directly as Bruce's armorer in addition to his corporate duties.
- Ng Chin Han as Lau, the accountant who handles the money for the mobs.
- Eric Roberts as Sal Maroni, a gangster who has taken over Carmine Falcone's mob. Bob Hoskins and James Gandolfini auditioned for the role.
- Colin McFarlane as Gillian B. Loeb, the Police Commissioner of Gotham until his murder at the hands of the Joker.

The film's Gotham officials and authorities include Nestor Carbonell as Mayor Anthony Garcia, Keith Szarabajka as Detective Gerard Stephens, Monique Gabriela Curnen as Anna Ramirez, and Ron Dean as Detective Michael Wuertz. While Stephens is an honest and good cop, the latter two are two corrupt officers who betray Harvey Dent and Rachel Dawes to the Joker. The film also cast Anthony Michael Hall as Gotham Cable News reporter Mike Engel, Nydia Rodriguez Terracina as Judge Janet Surrillo, Joshua Harto as Coleman Reese, Melinda McGraw and Nathan Gamble as Gordon's wife and son, and Tom "Tiny" Lister, Jr. as a prison inmate on one of the bomb-rigged ferries. The film's criminals include Michael Jai White as gang leader Gambol and Ritchie Coster as the Chechen. William Fichtner features as the Gotham National Bank manager. David Banner originally auditioned for the role of Gambol. Cillian Murphy returns in a cameo as Jonathan Crane / Scarecrow, who is captured early on in the film by Batman.

Musician Dwight Yoakam was approached for the roles of either the manager or a corrupt cop, but he chose to focus on his album *Dwight Sings Buck*. Another cameo was made by United States Senator

Patrick Leahy, a Batman fan who was previously an extra in the 1997 *Batman & Robin* and also was a guest voice actor on *Batman: The Animated Series*. Leahy cameos as a guest who defies the Joker at a fundraiser thrown by Bruce Wayne. Matt Skiba, lead singer of Chicago punk band Alkaline Trio made a small appearance in the movie.

Production

Development

As we looked through the comics, there was this fascinating idea that Batman's presence in Gotham actually attracts criminals to Gotham, [it] attracts lunacy. When you're dealing with questionable notions like people taking the law into their own hands, you have to really ask, where does that lead? That's what makes the character so dark, because he expresses a vengeful desire.

Nolan on the theme of escalation

Before the release of *Batman Begins*, screenwriter David S. Goyer wrote a treatment for two sequels which introduced the Joker and Harvey Dent. His original intent was for the Joker to scar Dent during the Joker's trial in the third film, turning Dent into Two-Face. Goyer, who penned the first draft of the film, cited the DC Comics 13-issue comic book limited series *Batman: The Long Halloween* as the major influence on his storyline. While initially uncertain of whether or not he would return to direct the sequel, Nolan did want to reinterpret the Joker on screen. On July 31, 2006, Warner Bros. officially announced initiation of production for the sequel to *Batman Begins* titled *The Dark Knight*; it is the first live-action *Batman* film without the word "Batman" in its title, which Bale noted as signaling that "this take on Batman of mine and Chris' is very different from any of the others."

After much research, Nolan's brother and co-writer, Jonathan, suggested the Joker's first two appearances, published in the first issue of *Batman* (1940), as the crucial influences. Jerry Robinson, one of the Joker's co-creators, was consulted on the character's portrayal. Nolan decided to avoid divulging an in-depth origin story for the Joker, and instead portray his rise to power so as to not diminish the threat he poses, explaining to MTV News, "the Joker we meet in *The Dark Knight* is fully formed...To me, the Joker is an absolute. There are no shades of gray to him – maybe shades of purple. He's unbelievably dark. He bursts in just as he did in the comics." Nolan reiterated to IGN, "We never wanted to do an origin story for the Joker in this film," because "the arc of the story is much more Harvey Dent's; the Joker is presented as an absolute. It's a very thrilling element in the film, and a very important element, but we wanted to deal with the rise of the Joker, not the origin of the Joker." Nolan suggested *Batman: The Killing Joke* influenced a section of the Joker's dialogue in the film, in which he says that anyone can become like him given the right circumstances.

Nolan also cited *Heat* as "sort of an inspiration" for his aim "to tell a very large, city story or the story of a city": "If you want to take on Gotham, you want to give Gotham a kind of weight and breadth and depth in there. So you wind up dealing with the political figures, the media figures. That's part of the whole fabric of how a city is bound together."

According to Nolan, an important theme of the sequel is "escalation," extending the ending of *Batman Begins*, noting "things having to get worse before they get better." While indicating *The Dark Knight* would continue the themes of *Batman Begins*, including justice vs. revenge and Bruce Wayne's issues with his father, Nolan emphasized the sequel would also portray Wayne more as a detective, an aspect of his character not fully developed in *Batman Begins*. Nolan described the friendly rivalry between Bruce Wayne and Harvey Dent as the "backbone" of the film. He also chose to compress the overall storyline, allowing Dent to become Two-Face in *The Dark Knight*, thus giving the film an emotional arc the unsympathetic Joker could not offer. Nolan acknowledged the title was not only a reference to Batman, but also the fallen "white knight" Harvey Dent.

Filming

While scouting for shooting locations in October 2006, location manager Robin Higgs visited Liverpool, concentrating mainly along the city's waterfront. Other candidates included Yorkshire, Glasgow, and parts of London. In August 2006, one of the film's producers, Charles Roven, stated that its principal photography would begin in March 2007, but filming was pushed back to April. For its release in IMAX theaters, Nolan shot four major sequences in that format, including the Joker's introduction, and said that he wished that it were possible to shoot the entire film in IMAX: "if you could take an IMAX camera to Mount Everest or outer space, you could use it in a feature movie." For fifteen years Nolan had wanted to shoot in the IMAX format, and he also used it for "quiet scenes which pictorially we thought would be interesting."

Warner Bros. chose to film in Chicago for thirteen weeks, because Nolan had a "truly remarkable experience" filming part of *Batman Begins* there. Instead of using the Chicago Board of Trade Building as the location for the headquarters of Wayne Enterprises, as *Batman Begins* did, *The Dark Knight* used the Richard J. Daley Center. While filming in Chicago, the film was given the false title *Rory's First Kiss* to lower the visibility of production, but the local media eventually uncovered the ruse. Richard Roeper of the *Chicago Sun-Times* commented on the absurdity of the technique, "Is there a Bat-fan in the world that doesn't know *Rory's First Kiss* is actually *The Dark Knight*, which has been filming in Chicago for weeks?" Production of *The Dark Knight* in Chicago generated $45 million in the city's economy and created thousands of jobs. For the film's prologue involving the Joker, the crew shot in Chicago from April 18, 2007 to April 24, 2007. They returned to shoot from June 9, 2007 to early September. Shooting locations included Navy Pier, 330 North Wabash, James R. Thompson Center, LaSalle Street, The Berghoff, Millennium Station, Hotel 71, the old Brach's factory, the old Van Buren Street Post Office, and Wacker Drive. Pinewood Studios, near London, was the primary studio space used for the production. Marina City was in the background throughout the movie.

While planning a stunt with the Batmobile in a special effects facility near Chertsey, England in September 2007, technician Conway Wickliffe was killed when his car crashed. The film is dedicated to both Ledger and Wickliffe. The following month in London at the defunct Battersea Power Station, a rigged 200-foot fireball was filmed, reportedly for an opening sequence, prompting calls from local residents who feared a terrorist attack on the station. A similar incident occurred during the filming in Chicago, when an abandoned Brach's candy factory (which was Gotham Hospital in the film) was demolished.

Filming took place in Hong Kong from November 6 to November 11, 2007, at various locations in the CBD, including International Finance Centre, Hong Kong's tallest building. The city's walled city of Kowloon influenced the Narrows in *Batman Begins*. The shoot hired helicopters and C-130 aircraft. Officials expressed concern over possible noise pollution and traffic. In response, letters sent to the city's residents promised that the sound level would approximate noise decibels made by buses. Environmentalists also criticized the filmmakers' request to tenants of the waterfront skyscrapers to keep their lights on all night to enhance the cinematography, describing it as a waste of energy. Cinematographer Wally Pfister found the city officials a "nightmare," and ultimately Nolan had to create Batman's jump from a skyscraper digitally.

Design

Costume designer Lindy Hemming described the Joker's look as reflecting his personality – that "he doesn't care about himself at all"; she avoided designing him as a vagrant but still made him appear to be "scruffier, grungier," so that "when you see him move, he's slightly twitchier or edgy." Nolan noted, "We gave a Francis Bacon spin to [his face]. This corruption, this decay in the texture of the look itself. It's grubby. You can almost imagine what he smells like." In creating the "anarchical" look of the Joker, Hemming drew inspiration from such countercultural pop culture artists as Pete Doherty, Iggy Pop, and Johnny Rotten. Ledger described his "clown" mask, made up of three pieces of stamped silicone, as a "new technology," taking much less time for the make-up artists to apply than more-conventional prosthetics usually requires – the process took them only an hour – and said that he felt he was barely wearing any make-up. Hemming and Ledger's notable Joker design has had an impact in popular and political culture in the form of the Barack Obama "Joker" poster, and has since become a meme in its own right.

Designers improved on the design of the Batsuit from *Batman Begins*, adding wide elastic banding to help bind the costume to Bale, and suggest more sophisticated technology. It was constructed from 200 individual pieces of rubber, fiberglass, metallic mesh, and nylon. The new cowl was modeled after a motorcycle helmet and separated from the neck piece, allowing Bale to turn his head left and right and nod up and down. The cowl is equipped to show white lenses over the eyes when the character turns on his sonar detection, which gives Batman the white eyed look from the comics and animation. The gauntlets have retractable razors which can be fired. Though the new costume is eight pounds heavier, Bale found it more comfortable and less hot to wear. The original suit was also worn during part of the film, where Batman employs hydraulic assistance on the gauntlets to bend a gun barrel and cut through steel. Bruce Wayne drives a Lamborghini Murciélago in the film. 'Murciélago' means 'bat' in Spanish.

The depiction of Gotham City is less gritty than in *Batman Begins*. "I've tried to unclutter the Gotham we created on the last film," said Crowley. "Gotham is in chaos. We keep blowing up stuff, so we can keep our images clean."

Effects

A view of the "Batpod" on display in Los Angeles

The film introduces the Batpod, which is a recreation of the Batcycle. Production designer Nathan Crowley, who designed the Tumbler for *Batman Begins*, designed six models (built by special effects supervisor Chris Corbould) for use in the film's production, because of necessary crash scenes and possible accidents. Crowley built a prototype in Nolan's garage, before six months of safety tests were conducted. The Batpod is steered by shoulder instead of hand, and the rider's arms are protected by sleeve-like shields. The bike has 508-millimeter (20-inch) front and rear tires, and is made to appear as if it is armed with grappling hooks, cannons, and machine guns. The engines are located in the hubs of the wheels, which are set 3 1/2 feet (1067 mm) apart on either side of the tank. The rider lies belly down on the tank, which can move up and down to dodge any incoming gunfire that Batman may encounter. Stuntman Jean-Pierre Goy doubled for Christian Bale during the riding sequences in *The Dark Knight*.

Nolan designed Two-Face's appearance in the film as one of the least disturbing, explaining, "When we looked at less extreme versions of it, they were too real and more horrifying. When you look at a film like *Pirates of the Caribbean* – something like that, there's something about a very fanciful, very detailed visual effect, that I think is more powerful and less repulsive." Framestore created 120 computer-generated shots of Two-Face's scarred visage. Nolan felt using make-up would look unrealistic, as it adds to the face, unlike real burn victims. Framestore acknowledged they rearranged the positions of bones, muscles and joints to make the character look more dramatic. For each shot, three 720-pixel HD cameras were set up at different angles on set to fully capture Aaron Eckhart's performance. Eckhart wore markers on his face and a prosthetic skullcap, which acted as a lighting reference. A few shots of the skullcap were kept in the film. Framestore also integrated shots of Bale and Eckhart into that of the exploding building where Dent is burned. It was difficult simulating fire on Eckhart because only having half of something being burned is inherently unrealistic.

Music

See also: The Dark Knight (soundtrack)

Batman Begins composers Hans Zimmer and James Newton Howard returned to score the sequel. Composition began before shooting, and during filming Nolan received an iPod with ten hours of recordings. Their nine-minute suite for the Joker, "Why So Serious?," is based around two notes. Zimmer compared its style to that of Kraftwerk, a band from his native Germany, as well as bands like The Damned. When Ledger died, Zimmer felt like scrapping and composing a new theme, but decided that he could not be sentimental and compromise the "evil [performance] projects." Howard composed Dent's "elegant and beautiful" themes, which are brass-focused.

Marketing

In May 2007, 42 Entertainment began a viral marketing campaign utilizing the film's "Why So Serious?" tagline with the launch of a website featuring the fictional political campaign of Harvey Dent, with the caption, "I Believe in Harvey Dent." The site aimed to interest fans by having them try to earn what they wanted to see and, on behalf of Warner Bros., 42 Entertainment also established a "vandalized" version of *I Believe in Harvey Dent*, called "I believe in Harvey Dent too," where e-mails sent by fans slowly removed pixels, revealing the first official image of the Joker; it was ultimately replaced with many "Haha"s and a hidden message that said "see you in December."

During the 2007 San Diego Comic-Con International, 42 Entertainment launched WhySoSerious.com, sending fans on a scavenger hunt to unlock a teaser trailer and a new photo of the Joker. On October 31, 2007, the film's website morphed into another scavenger hunt with hidden messages, instructing fans to uncover clues at certain locations in major cities throughout the United States, and to take photographs of their discoveries. The clues combined to reveal a new photograph of the Joker and an audio clip of him from the film saying "And tonight, you're gonna break your one rule." Completing the scavenger hunt also led to another website called Rory's Death Kiss (referencing the false working title of *Rory's First Kiss*), where fans could submit photographs of themselves costumed as the Joker. Those who sent photos were mailed a copy of a fictional newspaper called *The Gotham Times*, whose electronic version led to the discovery of numerous other websites.

The Dark Knight's opening sequence, (showing a bank raid by the Joker) and closing montage of other scenes from the film, was screened with selected IMAX screenings of *I Am Legend*, which was released on December 14, 2007. A theatrical teaser was also released with non-IMAX showings of *I Am Legend*, and also on the official website. The sequence was released on the Blu-ray Disc edition of *Batman Begins* on July 8, 2008. Also on July 8, 2008, the studio released *Batman: Gotham Knight*, a direct-to-DVD animated film, set between *Batman Begins* and *The Dark Knight* and featuring six original stories, directed by Bruce Timm, co-creator and producer of *Batman: The Animated Series*, and starring veteran Batman voice actor Kevin Conroy. Each of these segments, written by Josh Olson, David S. Goyer, Brian Azzarello, Greg Rucka, Jordan Goldberg, and Alan Burnett, presents its own distinctive artistic style, paralleling numerous artists collaborating in the same DC Universe.

After the death of Heath Ledger on January 22, 2008, Warner Bros. adjusted its promotional focus on the Joker, revising some of its websites dedicated to promoting the film and posting a memorial tribute to Ledger on the film's official website and overlaying a black memorial ribbon on the photo collage in *WhySoSerious.com*. On February 29, 2008, *I Believe in Harvey Dent* was updated to enable fans to send their e-mail addresses and phone numbers. In March 2008, Harvey Dent's fictional campaign informed fans that actual campaign buses nicknamed "Dentmobiles" would tour various cities to promote Dent's candidacy for district attorney.

Toyota Formula One racing car featuring the Batman insignia, at the 2008 British Grand Prix

On May 15, 2008, Six Flags Great America and Six Flags Great Adventure theme parks opened *The Dark Knight* roller coaster, which cost US$7.5 million to develop and which simulates being stalked by the Joker. Mattel produced toys and games for *The Dark Knight*, action figures, role play costumes, board games, puzzles, and a special-edition UNO card game, which began commercial distribution in June 2008.

Warner Bros. devoted six months to an anti-piracy strategy that involved tracking the people who had a pre-release copy of the film at any one time. Shipping and delivery schedules were also staggered and spot checks were carried out both domestically and overseas to ensure illegal copying of the film was not taking place in cinemas. A pirated copy was released on the Web approximately 38 hours after the film's release. BitTorrent search engine The Pirate Bay taunted the movie industry over its ability to provide the movie free, replacing its logo with a taunting message.

Release

Warner Bros. held the world premiere for *The Dark Knight* in New York City on July 14, 2008, screening in an IMAX theater with the film's composers James Newton Howard and Hans Zimmer playing a part of the film score live. Leading up to *The Dark Knight*'s commercial release, the film had drawn "overwhelmingly positive early reviews and buzz on Heath Ledger's turn as the Joker." *The Dark Knight* was commercially released on July 16, 2008 in Australia, grossing almost $2.3 million in its first day.

In the United States and Canada, *The Dark Knight* was distributed to 4,366 theaters, breaking the previous record for the highest number of theaters held by *Pirates of the Caribbean: At World's End* in 2007. The number of theaters also included 94 IMAX theaters, with the film estimated to be played on 9,200 screens in the United States and Canada. Online, ticketing services sold enormous numbers of tickets for approximately 3,000 midnight showtimes as well as unusually early showtimes for the film's opening day. All IMAX theaters showing *The Dark Knight* were sold out for the opening weekend.

Reception

Based on 275 reviews collected by Rotten Tomatoes, the film received a 93% approval rating from critics, with an average score of 8.4/10. Among Rotten Tomatoes' *Top Critics*, which consists of popular and notable critics from the top newspapers, websites, television, and radio programs, the film holds an overall approval rating of 91%. By comparison, Metacritic, which assigns a normalized rating out of 100 top reviews from mainstream critics, calculated an average score of 82, based on 39 reviews. CinemaScore polls reported that the average grade cinemagoers gave the film was "A" on an A+ to F scale, and that audiences skewed slightly male and older.

Roger Ebert of the *Chicago Sun-Times* describes *The Dark Knight* as a "haunted film that leaps beyond its origins and becomes an engrossing tragedy." He praises the performances, direction, and writing, and says the film "redefine[s] the possibilities of the comic-book movie." Ebert states that the "key performance" is by Heath Ledger, and pondered whether he would become the first posthumous Academy Award-winning actor since Peter Finch in 1976. Ledger ultimately won the Oscar. He named it one of his twenty favorite films of 2008. Peter Travers of *Rolling Stone* writes that the film is deeper than its predecessor, with a "deft" script that refuses to scrutinize the Joker with popular psychology, instead pulling the viewer in with an examination of Bruce Wayne's psyche. Travers has praise for all the cast, saying each brings his or her "'A' game" to the film. He says Bale is "electrifying," evoking Al Pacino in *The Godfather Part II*, and that Eckhart's portrayal of Harvey Dent is "scarily moving." Travers says the actor moves the Joker away from Jack Nicholson's interpretation into darker territory, and expresses his support for any potential campaign to have Ledger nominated for an Academy Award, Travers says that the filmmakers move the film away from comic book cinema and closer to being a genuine work of art, citing Nolan's direction and the "gritty reality" of Wally Pfister's cinematography as helping to create a universe that has something "raw and elemental" at work within it. In particular, he cites Nolan's action choreography in the IMAX-tailored heist sequence as rivaling that of *Heat* (1995). *Entertainment Weekly* put it on its end-of-the-decade, "best-of" list, saying, "Every great hero needs a great villain. And in 2008, Christian Bale's Batman found his in Heath Ledger's demented dervish, the Joker."

Emanuel Levy wrote Ledger "throws himself completely" into the role, and that the film represents Nolan's "most accomplished and mature" work, and the most technically impressive and resonant of all the *Batman* films. Levy calls the action sequences some of the most impressive seen in an American film for years, and talks of the Hong Kong-set portion of the film as being particularly visually impressive. Levy and Peter Travers conclude that the film is "haunting and visionary," while Levy goes on to say that *The Dark Knight* is "nothing short of brilliant." On the other hand, David Denby of *The New Yorker* holds that the story is not coherent enough to properly flesh out the disparities. He says the film's mood is one of "constant climax," and that it feels rushed and far too long. Denby criticizes scenes which he argues are meaningless or are cut short just as they become interesting. Denby remarks that the central conflict is workable, but that "only half the team can act it," saying that Bale's "placid"

Bruce Wayne and "dogged but uninteresting" Batman is constantly upstaged by Ledger's "sinister and frightening" performance, which he says is the film's one element of success. Denby concludes that Ledger is "mesmerising" in every scene. While Denby has praise for Pfister's cinematography, he does not rate the film as a remarkable piece of craftmanship. He puts forward that while a lot happens in the film, it is often difficult to follow due to the close, dark photography and editing. Denby says the film is too grim and is seemingly "jammed together." He surmises that the "heavy-handed" score and "thunderous" violence only serve to coarsen the property from Tim Burton's vision of the franchise into a "hyperviolent summer action spectacle," and that the film embraces the themes of terror that it purports to scrutinize.

The Dark Knight was ranked the 15th greatest film in history on *Empire's* 2008 list of the "500 Greatest Movies of All Time," based upon the weighted votes of 10,000 readers, 150 film directors, and 50 key film critics. Heath Ledger's interpretation of the Joker was also ranked number three on *Empire's* 2008 list of the "100 Greatest Movie Characters of All Time."

Top ten lists

The film appeared on many critics' top ten lists of the best films of 2008.

- 1st – Elizabeth Weitzman, *New York Daily News*
- 1st – Frank Scheck, *The Hollywood Reporter*
- 1st – James Berardinelli, ReelViews
- 1st – Joe Neumaier, *New York Daily News*
- 1st – Mike Russell, *The Oregonian*
- 1st – Peter Hartlaub, *San Francisco Chronicle*
- 1st – *Premiere*
- 1st – *Empire*
- 2nd – Kirk Honeycutt, *The Hollywood Reporter*
- 2nd – Nathan Rabin, *The A.V. Club*
- 2nd – Richard Roeper, *Chicago Sun-Times*
- 2nd – Owen Gleiberman, *Entertainment Weekly*
- 3rd – Lawrence Toppman, *The Charlotte Observer*
- 3rd – Lisa Schwarzbaum, *Entertainment Weekly*
- 3rd – Marc Mohan, *The Oregonian*
- 3rd – Michael Rechtshaffen, *The Hollywood Reporter*
- 3rd – Peter Rainer, *The Christian Science Monitor*
- 3rd – Peter Travers, *Rolling Stone*
- 3rd – Sheri Linden, *The Hollywood Reporter*
- 4th – Kyle Smith, *New York Post*
- 5th – Keith Phipps, *The A.V. Club*
- 5th – Noel Murray, *The A.V. Club*
- 5th – Rene Rodriguez, *The Miami Herald* (tied with *Hellboy II*)
- 5th – Scott Foundas, *LA Weekly*
- 5th – Wesley Morris, *The Boston Globe*
- 6th – Philip Martin, *Arkansas Democrat-Gazette*
- 6th – Peter Vonder Haar, *Film Threat*
- 7th – Manohla Dargis, *The New York Times*
- 7th – Marc Doyle, Metacritic
- 7th – Sean Axmaker, *Seattle Post-Intelligencer*
- 9th – Robert Mondello, *NPR*
- 9th – Scott Tobias, *The A.V. Club*
- 10th – Michael Phillips, *Chicago Tribune*

Commentary

Mystery writer Andrew Klavan, writing in *The Wall Street Journal*, compared the extreme measures that Batman takes to fight crime with those U.S. President George W. Bush used in the War on Terror. Klavan claims that, "at some level" *The Dark Knight* is "a paean of praise to the fortitude and moral courage that has been shown by George W. Bush in this time of terror and war." Klavan supports this reading of the film by comparing Batman – like Bush, Klavan argues – "sometimes has to push the boundaries of civil rights to deal with an emergency, certain that he will re-establish those boundaries when the emergency is past." Klavan's article has received criticism on the Internet and in mainstream media outlets, such as in *The New Republic's* "The Plank." Reviewing the film in *The Sunday Times*, Cosmo Landesman reached the opposite conclusion to Klavan, arguing that *The Dark Knight* "offers up a lot of moralistic waffle about how we must hug a terrorist – okay, I exaggerate. At its heart, however, is a long and tedious discussion about how individuals and society must never abandon the rule of law in struggling against the forces of lawlessness. In fighting monsters, we must be careful not to become monsters – that sort of thing. The film champions the anti-war coalition's claim that, in having a war on terror, you create the conditions for more terror. We are shown that innocent people died because of Batman – and he falls for it." Benjamin Kerstein, writing in *Azure*, says that both Klavan and Landesman "have a point," because "*The Dark Knight* is a perfect mirror of the society which is watching it: a society so divided on the issues of terror and how to fight it that, for the first time in decades, an American mainstream no longer exists."

Themes and analysis

According to David S. Goyer, the primary theme of *The Dark Knight* is escalation. Gotham City is weak and the citizens blame Batman for the city's violence and corruption as well as the Joker's threats, and it pushes his limits, making him feel that taking the laws into his own hands is further downgrading the city. Roger Ebert noted, "Throughout the film, [the Joker] devises ingenious situations that force Batman, Commissioner Gordon and District Attorney Harvey Dent to make impossible ethical decisions. By the end, the whole moral foundation of the Batman legend is threatened."

Other critics have mentioned the theme of the triumph of evil over good. Harvey Dent is seen as Gotham's "White Knight" in the beginning of the film but ends up becoming seduced to evil. The Joker, on the other hand, is seen as the representation of anarchy and chaos. He has no motive, no orders, and no desires but to cause havoc and "watch the world burn." The terrible logic of human error is another theme as well. The ferry scene displays how humans can easily be enticed by iniquity.

Accolades

Main article: List of accolades received by The Dark Knight

The Tumbler in use at the film's European premiere

Most notable among the nominations were Heath Ledger's almost complete sweep of over twenty awards for acting, including the Academy Award for Best Supporting Actor, Screen Actors Guild Award for Best Supporting Actor, the Golden Globe Award for Best Supporting Actor – Motion Picture, and the BAFTA Award for Best Actor in a Supporting Role. *The Dark Knight* also received nominations from the Writers Guild of America (for Best Adapted Screenplay), the Producers Guild of America, and the Directors Guild of America, as well as a slew of other guild award nominations and wins. It was nominated for Best Film at the Critics Choice Awards and was named one of the top ten films of 2008 by the American Film Institute.

The Dark Knight was nominated for eight Academy Awards for the 81st Ceremony, breaking the previous record of seven held by *Dick Tracy* for the most nominations received by a film based on a comic book, comic strip, or graphic novel. *The Dark Knight* won two awards: Best Supporting Actor for Heath Ledger and Best Sound Editing. It was additionally nominated for six others, these being Best Art Direction, Best Cinematography, Best Sound Mixing, Best Visual Effects, Best Makeup, and Best Film Editing. Heath Ledger was the first posthumous winner of the Best Supporting Actor award, and only the second posthumous acting winner ever (Peter Finch posthumously won the Best Actor award for his performance in the 1976 film *Network*). In addition, Ledger's win marked the first win in any of the major Oscar categories (producing, directing, acting, or writing) for a superhero-based film. Notably, Richard King's win in the Sound Editing category blocked a complete awards sweep of the evening by the eventual Best Picture winner, *Slumdog Millionaire*. Although it did not receive a Best Picture nomination, the show's opening song paid homage to *The Dark Knight* along with the five Best Picture nominees, including host Hugh Jackman riding on a mockup of the Batpod made out of garbage.

Box office

The Dark Knight set a new midnight record on the opening day of July 18, 2008 with $18.5 million, beating the $16.9 million record set by *Star Wars Episode III: Revenge of the Sith* in 2005. $640,000 of the record gross came from IMAX screenings. However, this record was broken a year later by the film *Harry Potter and the Half-Blood Prince*, which grossed over $22 million.

The Dark Knight ultimately grossed $67,165,092 on its opening day in the domestic office, beating the previous record of $59.8 million held by *Spider-Man 3* in 2007. However, the record was broken by *The Twilight Saga: New Moon* a year later, which grossed close to $73 million.

For its opening weekend in the United States and Canada, *The Dark Knight* accumulated a total of $158,411,483 from 9,200 screens at a record 4,366 theaters, for an average of $36,283 per theater, or $17,219 per screen, beating out the original weekend estimate by more than $3 million, and topping the previous record of $151,116,516 held by *Spider-Man 3*, while playing in 114 more theaters but on 800 fewer screens. The following Monday, it grossed another $24,493,313, and the following Tuesday it grossed $20,868,722. *The Dark Knight* also set a new record for opening weekend gross in IMAX theaters, accumulating $6.2 million to beat *Spider-Man 3*'s previous record of $4.7 million.

Besides the United States and Canada, *The Dark Knight* premiered in 20 other territories on 4,520 screens, grossing $41.3 million in its first weekend. The film came in second to *Hancock*, which was in its third weekend, screening in 71 territories. *The Dark Knight*'s biggest territory for the weekend was Australia, grossing $13.7 million over the weekend, the third largest Warner Bros. opening and the largest superhero film opening to date. The film also grossed $7 million from 1,433 screens in Mexico, $4.45 million from 548 screens in Brazil, and $2.12 million from 37 screens in Hong Kong. Citing cultural sensitivities to some elements in the film, and a reluctance to adhere to pre-release conditions, Warner Bros. declined to release the film in mainland China.

A sign of the film's pre-release at the cinema *Colisevm* in Barcelona, Spain

The Dark Knight sold an estimated 22.37 million tickets with today's average admission of $7.08, meaning the film sold more tickets than *Spider-Man 3*, which sold 21.96 million with the average price of $6.88 in 2007. It also broke the record for the biggest opening week ever. As of December 23, 2008, *The Dark Knight* had grossed $530,833,780 in the North American box office, in the process becoming the second film to gross more than $500 million in the North American box office, after *Titanic*, and doing so in significantly less time. It had also grossed $465,993,073 in other countries. As of August 29, 2010, its total worldwide gross stands at $1,001,758,644, and is the seventh highest-grossing film of all time (unadjusted for inflation). *The Dark Knight* is the highest-grossing film of 2008 in North American box office and worldwide. Unadjusted for inflation, it is the third highest-grossing film of all time in North America with a total of $533,090,262, behind only *Avatar* and *Titanic*. *The Dark Knight*'s theatrical run was very different from that of *Avatar*, which broke some of its records, and *Titanic*, at the time the only movie to gross more in North America than it. While *The Dark Knight* broke records in its opening weekend, *Titanic* started out slowly (making $28.6 million in its opening weekend) and then increased ticket sales in the following weekends. *The Dark Knight* instead slowed down after the first few weekends; 50 other movies had better tenth weekends and 91 had better eleventh weekends. In its fifteenth weekend, *The Dark Knight* was at #26 at the box office.

Warner Bros. re-released the film in traditional theaters and IMAX theaters in the United States on January 23, 2009, at the height of the voting for the Academy Awards, to further the chances of the film winning Oscars, as well as attempt to cross $1 billion in worldwide gross, which it accomplished in February 2009.

Home media

The film was released on DVD and Blu-ray Disc in North America on December 9, 2008. Releases include a one-disc edition DVD; a two-disc Special Edition DVD; a two-disc edition BD; and a Special Edition BD package featuring a statuette of the Bat-pod. The BD version presents the film in a variable aspect ratio, with the IMAX sequences framed in 1.78:1, while scenes filmed in 35 mm are framed in 2.40:1. The DVD versions feature the entire film framed in a uniform 2.40:1 aspect ratio. Disc 2 of the two-disc Special Edition DVD features the six main IMAX sequences in the original 1.44:1 aspect ratio. Additional IMAX shots throughout the film that are presented in 1.78:1 on the Blu-Ray release are not, however, included in the DVD's special features. In addition to the standard DVD releases, some stores released their own exclusive editions of the film.

In the United Kingdom, the film had combined sales of 513,000 units on its first day of release, of which 107,730 (21%) were Blu-ray Discs, the highest number of first-day Blu-ray Discs sold. In the United States, *The Dark Knight* set a sales record for most DVDs sold in one day, selling 3 million units on its first day of release – 600,000 of which were Blu-ray Discs.

The DVD and Blu-ray Disc editions were released in Australia on December 10, 2008. Releases were in the form of a one-disc edition on DVD; a two-disc edition on DVD; a two-disc edition including a Batmask on DVD and BD; a two-disc Batpod statuette Limited BD Edition; a two-disc BD edition; and a four-disc *Batman Begins/The Dark Knight* pack on DVD and BD. As of December 19, 2008, the DVD release is the top selling film in the Australian DVD Charts and is expected to break the Australian sales record set by *Finding Nemo*.

Sequel

On March 10, 2010, Nolan confirmed his involvement with a sequel and gave some information regarding the story. The next Batman film will be Nolan's last and a conclusion to the story. Nolan says, "Without getting into specifics, the key thing that makes the third film a great possibility for us is that we want to finish our story. And in viewing it as the finishing of a story rather than infinitely blowing up the balloon and expanding the story . . . I'm very excited about the end of the film, the conclusion, and what we've done with the characters. My brother has come up with some pretty exciting stuff. Unlike the comics, these things don't go on forever in film and viewing it as a story with an end is useful. Viewing it as an ending, that sets you very much on the right track about the appropriate conclusion and the essence of what tale we're telling. And it hearkens back to that priority of trying to find the reality in these fantastic stories. That's what we do." Nolan has also confirmed that

Jonathan Nolan is writing the script and that the villain of the film "won't be Mr. Freeze." Nolan also confirmed that the Joker will not return.

In April 2010, Warner Bros. announced the as-yet-untitled sequel will be released on July 20, 2012. Nolan confirmed in an interview in July 2010 that his brother Jonathan has finished a screenplay that was based on a story by Nolan and David Goyer. Nolan is also still aiming for a 2012 release date. The film will begin shooting in April 2011. Christopher Nolan's long-time cinematographer Wally Pfister has expressed interest in shooting the entirety of the next Batman movie in the IMAX format, as both Pfister and Nolan have expressed distaste for shooting the film in 3-D. Nolan has confirmed that he will be directing the film and stated that he is currently polishing Jonathan Nolan's screenplay.

Further reading

- Byrne, Craig (2008) (Hardcover). *The Dark Knight: Featuring Production Art and Full Shooting Script*. Universe. ISBN 0789318121.
- Nolan, Christopher; David S. Goyer (2007). "Introduction" (Hardcover). *Absolute Batman: The Long Halloween*. New York: DC Comics. ISBN 1401212824.
- O'Neil, Dennis (2008) (Paperback). *The Dark Knight*. Novelization of the film. Berkley. ISBN 0425222861.

External links

- Official website [1]
- *The Dark Knight* [2] at the Internet Movie Database
- *The Dark Knight* [3] at Allmovie
- *The Dark Knight* [4] at Box Office Mojo
- *The Dark Knight* [5] at MySpace
- *The Dark Knight* [6] at Rotten Tomatoes
- *The Dark Knight* [7] at Metacritic
- *The Dark Knight: Blu-ray Disc Review"* [8] at HD Report
- Official site script [9]

Christian Bale

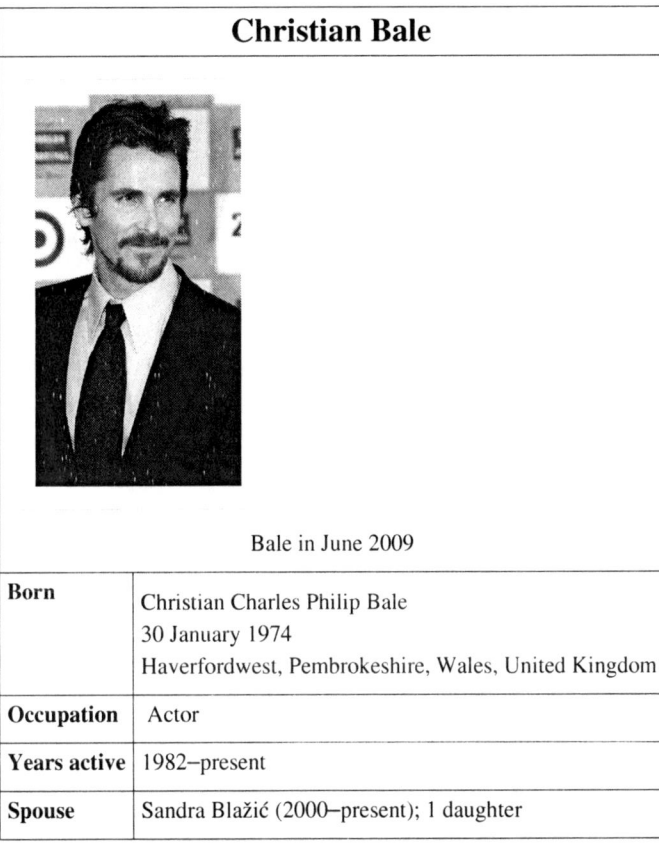

	Christian Bale
	Bale in June 2009
Born	Christian Charles Philip Bale 30 January 1974 Haverfordwest, Pembrokeshire, Wales, United Kingdom
Occupation	Actor
Years active	1982–present
Spouse	Sandra Blažić (2000–present); 1 daughter

Christian Charles Philip Bale (born 30 January 1974) is an English actor. In addition to starring roles in big budget Hollywood films, he has long been heavily involved in films produced by independent producers and art houses.

Bale first caught the public eye when he was cast in the starring role of Steven Spielberg's *Empire of the Sun* at the age of 13, playing an English boy who is separated from his parents and subsequently finds himself lost in a Japanese internment camp during World War II. Since then, he has portrayed a wide range of characters. Bale is especially noted for his cult following: the tenth anniversary issue of *Entertainment Weekly* hailed him as one of the "Top 8 Most Powerful Cult Figures of the Past Decade", citing his cult status on the Internet. *EW* called Bale one of the "Most Creative People in Entertainment" in anticipation of the release *American Psycho* (2000). *The Guardian* named Bale as one of the best actors never to have received an Academy Award nomination.

Early life

Bale was born in Wales to parents of English descent. His father, David Bale, was an entrepreneur, commercial pilot, and talent manager, and his mother, Jenny James, was a circus clown and performer. He is the youngest of four children. After leaving Britain in 1976, Bale spent his childhood in several countries, including Portugal and the United States.

Settling for four years in Bournemouth and Henley-on-Thames, Bale was educated at Shiplake Church of England Primary School; the independent Dolphin School, Berkshire; and at the Bournemouth School. He participated actively in rugby union. Bale has described his childhood, with respect to his mother being in the circus, as "interesting". He recalled his first kiss was with an acrobat named Barta.

As a child, he trained in ballet and guitar. His sister Louise's work in theatre also influenced his decision to become an actor. Bale's father was very supportive of his son's acting, resigning from his job as a commercial pilot to travel and manage Bale's burgeoning career. The elder Bale later married feminist icon Gloria Steinem, and died, aged 62, on 30 December 2003, from brain lymphoma.

Bale's first foray into acting was a commercial for the fabric softener Lenor in 1982, when he was eight years old. He appeared in a *Pac-Man* cereal commercial playing a child rock star a year later. In 1984 he made his stage debut in *The Nerd*, opposite Rowan Atkinson.

Career

1986–1998

Bale made his film debut as Tsarevich Alexei Nikolaevich of Russia in the made-for-television film *Anastasia: The Mystery of Anna* in 1986, which was followed by leading roles in the miniseries *Heart of the Country* and the fantasy adventure *Mio in the Land of Faraway*, in which he appeared for the first time with Christopher Lee and Nick Pickard.

A 14-year-old Bale in Stockholm, Sweden in February 1988 while promoting *Empire of the Sun*

In 1987, Amy Irving, his co-star in *Anastasia: The Mystery of Anna*, recommended Bale to her then-husband, Steven Spielberg, for a role in *Empire of the Sun*, adapted from the J.G. Ballard semi-autobiography. Bale's performance as Jim Graham earned him widespread critical praise and the first ever "Best Performance by a Juvenile Actor" award from the National Board of Review of Motion Pictures. The attention the press and his schoolmates lavished upon him after this took a toll on Bale, and he contemplated giving up acting until Kenneth Branagh approached him and persuaded him to appear in *Henry V* in 1989. In 1990 he played the role of Jim Hawkins opposite Charlton Heston (as Long John Silver) in *Treasure Island*, an adaptation of Robert Louis Stevenson's classic book.

In 1992, Bale starred as Jack Kelly in the Disney musical *Newsies*, and followed it up in 1993 with another release, *Swing Kids*, a movie about teenagers who secretly listened to forbidden jazz during the rise of Nazi Germany. Bale was recommended by actress Winona Ryder to star in Gillian Armstrong's 1994 film *Little Women*. Bale provided the voice for Thomas, a young compatriot of Captain John Smith, in Disney's *Pocahontas* (1995) and in 1997 played Arthur Stuart in *Velvet Goldmine*, Todd Haynes' tribute to glam rock. In 1999, Bale contributed to an all-star cast, including Kevin Kline, Michelle Pfeiffer, Stanley Tucci, and Rupert Everett, portraying Demetrius in an updated version of William Shakespeare's *A Midsummer Night's Dream*.

1999–2001

In 1999, Bale played serial killer Patrick Bateman in *American Psycho*, director Mary Harron's adaptation of Bret Easton Ellis' controversial novel. Bale was briefly dropped from the project in favor of Leonardo DiCaprio, but DiCaprio eventually dropped out to star in *The Beach*, and Bale was cast once again. He researched his character by studying the novel and prepared himself physically for the role by spending months tanning and exercising in order to achieve the "Olympian physique" of the character as described in the original novel. He went so far as to distance himself from the cast and crew to maintain the darker side of Bateman's character. *American Psycho* premiered at the 2000 Sundance Film Festival to much controversy. Roger Ebert condemned the film at first, calling it pornography and "the most loathed film at Sundance," but gave it a favourable review, writing that Harron "transformed a novel about bloodlust into a movie about men's vanity." Of Bale's performance, he wrote, "Christian Bale is heroic in the way he allows the character to leap joyfully into despicability; there is no instinct for self-preservation here, and that is one mark of a good actor."

On April 14, 2000, Lions Gate Films released *American Psycho* in theatres. Bale was later approached to make a cameo appearance in another Bret Easton Ellis adaptation, *The Rules of Attraction*, a film loosely connected to *American Psycho*, but he declined out of loyalty to Harron's vision of Bateman, which he felt could not be properly expressed by anyone else. In 2000, he again played a villain, this time in John Singleton's remake of the 1971 film, *Shaft*.

Bale has played an assortment of diverse characters since 2001. His first role after *American Psycho* was in the John Madden adaptation of the best-selling novel *Captain Corelli's Mandolin*. Bale played Mandras, a Greek fisherman who vied with Nicolas Cage's title character for the affections of the desirable Pelagia (Penelope Cruz). *Captain Corelli's Mandolin* was Bale's second time working with John Hurt, after *All the Little Animals*.

2002–2004

From 2002 to 2003, Bale starred in three feature films. *Laurel Canyon* (2002) was generally well received by critics. This film also marked the second time he worked with actress Kate Beckinsale, his costar in *Prince of Jutland* (1994). Critics generally focused on star Frances McDormand's performance over the rest of the cast.

Reign of Fire was Bale's first action vehicle and had, compared to all his previous work, an immense budget estimated at US$95,000,000. Bale entered into negotiations about starring in the film with reservations, but director Rob Bowman convinced him to take the lead role. Bale starred as Quinn Abercromby opposite Matthew McConaughey's Denton Van Zan. Bale and McConaughey trained for their respective roles by boxing and working out.

Equilibrium was Bale's third film of 2002, costing US$20 million to produce but earning just over US$5 million worldwide. In *Equilibrium*, Bale played John Preston, an elite law enforcer in a dystopian society. *Equilibrium* featured a fictional martial art called Gun Kata that combined gunfighting with hand-to-hand combat. According to moviebodycounts.com, the character of John Preston has the third most on-screen kills in a single movie ever with 118, exactly half of the movie's total of 236.

After a year's hiatus, Bale returned in 2004 to play Trevor Reznik, the title character in the psychological thriller *The Machinist*. Bale gained attention for his devotion to the role and for the lengths to which he went to achieve Reznik's emaciated, skeletal appearance. He went without proper rest for prolonged periods, and placed himself on a crash diet of generally coffee and apples, which reduced his weight by 63 pounds (4 st 4 lb/27 kg) in a matter of months. By the end of filming Bale weighed only 121 pounds (8 st 9 lb/55 kg), a transformation he described as "very calming mentally" and which drew comparisons to Robert De Niro's alternate weight-gaining regimen for his role as Jake LaMotta in the 1980 film *Raging Bull*. Bale claimed that he had not worked for a period of time before he was cast in the film. "...I just hadn't found scripts that I'd really been interested in. So I was really dying for something to arrive. Then when this one did, I just didn't want to put it down. I finished it and, upon the kind of revelation that you get at the end, I immediately wanted to go back and re-visit it, to take a look at what clues I could have gotten throughout". *The Machinist* was a low-budget production, costing roughly US$5 million to produce, and was given only a limited US release.

Bale, an admirer of Hayao Miyazaki's *Spirited Away*, was then cast as the voice of the title character, Howl, in the English language dub of the Japanese director's fantasy anime adventure *Howl's Moving Castle*, an adaptation of Diana Wynne Jones's children's novel. Its profits in the US were US$4,711,096, a fraction of its worldwide gross (US$235,184,110).

Batman: 2005–present

It was reported that Bale had previously auditioned for the role of Robin in *Batman Forever* (1995) and later *Batman and Robin* (1997), but lost out to Chris O'Donnell. However, this rumor was later dispelled by Bale himself in a magazine interview in 2008. In 2004, after completing filming for *The Machinist*, Bale won the coveted role of Batman and his alter ego Bruce Wayne in Christopher Nolan's *Batman Begins*, a reboot of the Batman film series. Bale beat out Jake Gyllenhaal, the closest competition for the role.

Still fresh off *The Machinist*, it became necessary for Bale to bulk up to match Batman's muscular physique. He was given a deadline of six months to do this. Bale recalled it as far from a simple accomplishment: "...when it actually came to building muscle, I was useless. I couldn't do one push up the first day. All of the muscles were gone, so I had a real tough time rebuilding all of that." With the help of a personal trainer, Bale succeeded in meeting the deadline, gaining a total of 100 lb (45 kg) in six months. He went from about 130 lbs to 230 lbs. He then discovered that he had actually gained more weight than the director desired, and dropped his weight to 190 lbs by the time filming began.

Bale had initial concerns about playing Batman, as he felt more ridiculous than intimidating in the Batsuit. He dealt with this by depicting Batman as a savage beast in his portrayal. To attain a deeper understanding of the character, Bale read various Batman comic books. He explained his interpretation of the young boy: "Batman is his hidden, demonic rage-filled side. The creature Batman creates is an absolutely sincere creature and one that he has to control but does so in a very haphazard way. He's capable of enacting violence — and to kill — so he's constantly having to rein himself in." For Bale, the most gruelling part about playing Batman was the suit. "You stick it on, you get hot, you sweat and you get a headache in the mask," he said. "But I'm not going to bitch about it because I get to play Batman." When promoting the film in interviews and public events, Bale retained an American accent to avoid confusion.

Batman Begins was released in the U.S. on June 15, 2005 and was a U.S. and international triumph for Warner Bros., costing approximately US$135 million to produce and taking in over US$370 million in returns worldwide. Bale earned the Best Hero award at the 2006 MTV Movie Awards for his performance.

Bale reprised his role as Batman in the *Batman Begins* sequel *The Dark Knight*. He trained in the Keysi Fighting Method, and performed many of his own stunts. *The Dark Knight* was released in the U.S. on July 18, 2008 and stormed through the box-office, with a record-breaking $158.4 million in the U.S. in its first weekend. It broke the $300 million barrier in 10 days, the $400 million mark in 16 days and the $500 million mark in 43 days, three new U.S. box office records set by the film. The film went on to gross over $1 billion at the box office worldwide, making it the fourth-highest grossing movie worldwide of all time, before adjusting for inflation.

It has been confirmed that Bale will star in the third projected movie in the rebooted franchise, that will be released on July 20, 2012, making Bale the actor who has played Batman more times than any other actor in feature film. Bale has given the same opinion as Nolan that, if the latter was forced to bring Robin into the films, he would never again play Batman; even though his favorite Batman story, *Batman: Dark Victory*, focuses on Robin's origin.

2006–2009

After *Batman Begins*, Bale returned to appearing in independent films. He was cast as one of the two leads in the South Central David Ayer-helmed crime drama *Harsh Times*, co-starring with Freddy Rodriguez and Eva Longoria. Bale played Jim Luther Davis, a grim Afghanistan War veteran afflicted with post-traumatic stress disorder, inexplicably approached by the Department of Homeland Security and hired as a federal agent. *Harsh Times* premiered at the 2005 Toronto International Film Festival and had a wide release on 10 November 2006.

Bale in 2008

Terrence Malick directed *The New World*, a period piece inspired by the stories of Pocahontas, and Bale was cast as John Rolfe. He shared the screen with Colin Farrell and Q'Orianka Kilcher, who played John Smith and Pocahontas. The majority of screen time was devoted to Farrell and Kilcher; Bale was a secondary character, and only appeared during the last third of the film. The film was a failure at the U.S. box office and its worldwide total (US$29,506,437) fell short of turning a profit (the production budget was placed at US$30 million).

In 2006, Bale took on four projects. *Rescue Dawn*, by German filmmaker Werner Herzog, had him playing U.S. Fighter pilot Dieter Dengler, who has to fight for his life after being shot down while on a mission during the Vietnam War. Bale left a strong impression on Herzog, with the director complimenting his acting abilities: "I find him one of the greatest talents of his generation. We made up our own minds long before he did *Batman*."

"I kind of like movies where I just get to just be dirty and crawling in the mud, "Rescue Dawn" it was all very primordial stuff, and with this one it was all about wearing the same clothes day after day and getting sweaty and dirty and sun exposure, and it's meant to be like that; Westerns are meant to be dirty, they shouldn't be all nice and clean. And I like getting my hand dirty."

Christian Bale on *3:10 to Yuma*

In *The Prestige*, an adaptation of the Christopher Priest novel about a rivalry between two Victorian stage magicians, Bale was reunited with *Batman Begins*' Michael Caine and director Christopher Nolan. The cast of *The Prestige* also included Hugh Jackman, Scarlett Johansson, Piper Perabo, and David Bowie. *I'm Not There*, a film in which Bale again worked alongside Todd Haynes and Heath Ledger (who would go on to play The Joker in *The Dark Knight*), is an artistic reflection of the life of

Bob Dylan. He starred opposite Russell Crowe in a commercially and critically successful remake of the Western film *3:10 to Yuma*.

Bale was originally cast to play George W. Bush in Oliver Stone's film *W.*, but dropped out due to the prosthetics involved. Bale played John Connor in *Terminator Salvation* and FBI agent Melvin Purvis in Michael Mann's *Public Enemies*.

Writer/director Joe Carnahan confirmed in November 2007 that Bale is also involved in the upcoming movie *Killing Pablo* in which he is to play Major Steve Jacoby.

According to a *Nuts* magazine interview, Bale stated that he will be in the running to play the role of Solid Snake in a film adaptation of *Metal Gear Solid*. He has been cast alongside Mark Wahlberg in David O. Russell directed drama *The Fighter*.

Terminator Salvation incident

In July 2008, Bale had an angry tirade on the sets of *Terminator Salvation*, while filming in New Mexico. In February 2009, the audio recording of the incident was released. The tirade was directed at Shane Hurlbut, director of photography for the film. According to Bale, Hurlbut had, for the second time, ruined his concentration by walking into his line of sight during a scene. The recording is of a highly agitated Bale directing profanities at Hurlbut, threatening and belittling him, and finally threatening to quit the film if Hurlbut repeated his offence without being fired for it. It was reported that Warner film executives sent the tape to the insurer of the film in case Bale decided to quit the movie. In an interview with *E! Online*, assistant director and producer of *Terminator Salvation*, Bruce Franklin, said it was an isolated incident. *"If you are working in a very intense scene and someone takes you out of your groove ... It was the most emotional scene in the movie ... [A]nd for him to get stopped in the middle of it. He is very intensely involved in his character. He didn't walk around like that all day long. It was just a moment and it passed"*, Franklin said.

Actors Whoopi Goldberg and Terry Crews, directors Darren Aronofsky and Ron Howard, as well as *Ain't It Cool News* website creator Harry Knowles have also publicly defended Bale's actions, some of them citing the practice that crew members are to remain still while the camera is rolling. The incident also inspired experimental band The Mae Shi to write the song, "R U Professional", which features samples from the recording. Stephen Colbert parodied the incident on the 4 February 2009 episode of *The Colbert Report*, in which guest Steve Martin repeatedly walked in front of the camera and was berated by Colbert. The incident was re-enacted on *Late Night with Conan O'Brien*, with *Inside the Actor's Studio* host James Lipton giving performances of both Bale and the crewmember. An episode of the animated comedy series *Family Guy* also mixed in the voice of Peter Griffin interacting with Bale and reacting to Bale's comments as if they were directed at him to comedic effect.

After remaining silent for most of the week, Bale gave a public apology on 6 February 2009, to a Los Angeles radio station, KROQ. He stated that the outburst was "inexcusable" and that it was motivated by the day's shooting intensity. Bale said he "acted like a punk", and that he and Hurlbut talked after the incident and "resolved this completely". Bale acknowledged that the two worked together for several hours after the incident, and *"at least a month after that... I've seen a rough cut of the movie and he has done a wonderful job. It looks fantastic"*.

2010–present

In early 2010, Bale was confirmed to be starring in a romantic love story that will be directed by Terrence Malick and will also star Javier Bardem, Rachel McAdams and Olga Kurylenko.

Personal life

On 29 January 2000, Bale married Sandra "Sibi" Blažić (born 1970), a former model, make-up artist and personal assistant to Winona Ryder; the couple have a daughter, Emmeline, who was born on 27 March 2005 in Santa Monica, California. Since 1992, Bale has resided in Los Angeles.

Bale has three elder sisters – Erin Bale, a musician; Sharon Bale, a computer professional; and Louise Bale, a theatre actress and director. The Bale family is deeply rooted in show business, especially theatre. Bale is a distant relative of British actress Lillie Langtry, while his uncle, Rex Bale and maternal grandfather were actors as well.

Like his late father, businessman David (1941–2003), Christian Bale actively supports environmental groups such as Greenpeace and the World Wildlife Fund. Feminist activist Gloria Steinem became Christian Bale's stepmother when she married David Bale on 3 September 2000.; it was Steinem's first marriage (at the age of 66), and the couple were together until David Bale's death in 2003, aged 62.

During an interview promoting his 2009 film *Public Enemies* Bale said he is a video game fan, specifically of the *Metal Gear Solid* series. When questioned if he was in the running to play *Solid Snake*, Bale stated that he prefers to devote his spare time to constructive things and dislikes discussing his personal life.

Film and television credits

List of film and television credits

Year	Title	Role	Notes
1986	*Anastasia: The Mystery of Anna*	Alexei	television film
1987	*Heart of the Country*	Ben Harris	miniseries
1987	*Empire of the Sun*	Jamie "Jim" Graham	
1987	*Mio min Mio*	Benke Jum-Jum	
1989	*Henry V*	Falstaff's Boy	

Year	Title	Role	Notes
1990	Treasure Island	Jim Hawkins	
1991	A Murder of Quality	Tim Perkins	television film
1992	Newsies	Jack "Cowboy" Kelly Francis Sullivan	
1993	Swing Kids	Thomas Berger	
1994	Little Women	Theodore "Laurie" Lawrence	
1994	Prince of Jutland	Amled	
1995	Pocahontas	Thomas	animated film voice only
1996	The Portrait of a Lady	Edward Rosier	
1996	The Secret Agent	Stevie	
1997	Metroland	Chris Lloyd	
1998	Velvet Goldmine	Arthur Stuart	
1999	All the Little Animals	Bobby Platt	
1999	Mary, Mother of Jesus	Jesus of Nazareth	television film
1999	A Midsummer Night's Dream	Demetrius	
2000	Shaft	Walter Wade, Jr.	
2000	American Psycho	Patrick Bateman	
2001	Captain Corelli's Mandolin	Mandras	
2002	Equilibrium	Cleric John Preston	
2002	Reign of Fire	Quinn Abercromby	
2002	Laurel Canyon	Sam Bentley	
2004	Howl's Moving Castle	Howl	English dub voice only
2004	The Machinist	Trevor Reznik	
2005	Batman Begins	Bruce Wayne/Batman	
2005	The New World	John Rolfe	
2006	The Prestige	Alfred Borden	
2006	Harsh Times	Jim Luther Davis	
2007	Rescue Dawn	Dieter Dengler	
2007	I'm Not There	Jack Rollins/Pastor John	
2007	3:10 to Yuma	Dan Evans	
2008	The Dark Knight	Bruce Wayne/Batman	

2009	Terminator Salvation	John Connor	
2009	Public Enemies	Melvin Purvis	
2010	The Fighter	Dick Eklund	*post-production*
2012	Untitled Batman Project	Bruce Wayne/Batman	*announced*

Awards and nominations

List of awards and award nominations

Year	Award	Award category	Title of work	Result
1987	NBR Award	Best Juvenile Performance	*Empire of the Sun*	Won
1989	Young Artist Awards	Best Young Actor in a Motion Picture–Drama	*Empire of the Sun*	Won
2001	Chlotrudis Awards	Best Actor	*American Psycho*	Won
2001	Empire Award	Best Actor	*American Psycho*	Nominated
2001	London Film Critics' Circle Awards	British Actor of the Year	*American Psycho*	Nominated
2001	OFCS Award	Best Actor	*American Psycho*	Nominated
2004	CIFF	Best Actor	*The Machinist*	Won
2005	Irish Film and Television Award	Best International Actor	*Batman Begins*	Nominated
2005	European Film Awards	Best Actor	*The Machinist*	Nominated
2005	Saturn Awards	Best Actor	*The Machinist*	Nominated
2006	London Film Critics' Circle Awards	British Actor of the Year	*The Machinist*	Nominated
2006	MTV Movie Awards	Best Hero	*Batman Begins*	Won
2006	Empire Awards	Best Actor	*Batman Begins*	Nominated
2006	Saturn Awards	Best Actor	*Batman Begins*	Won
2006	Scream Awards	Best Superhero	*Batman Begins*	Nominated
2006	Scream Awards	Most Heroic Performance	*Batman Begins*	Nominated
2007	Empire Award	Best Actor	*The Prestige*	Nominated

2007	San Diego Film Critics Society Awards	Special Award	*3:10 to Yuma*, *I'm Not There*, *Rescue Dawn*	Won
2007	Satellite Award	Best Actor in a Motion Picture, Drama	*Rescue Dawn*	Nominated
2008	London Film Critics' Circle Awards	British Actor of the Year	*3:10 to Yuma*	Nominated
2008	Independent Spirit Award	Robert Altman Award (with Todd Haynes, Laura Rosenthal, Cate Blanchett, Richard Gere, Heath Ledger, Ben Whishaw, Marcus Carl Franklin, Bruce Greenwood, Charlotte Gainsbourg)	*I'm Not There*	Won
2008	Scream Awards	Best Fantasy Actor	*The Dark Knight*	Nominated
2008	Scream Awards	Best Superhero	*The Dark Knight*	Won
2009	Empire Awards	Best Actor	*The Dark Knight*	Won
2009	People's Choice Awards	Favorite Male Action Star	*The Dark Knight*	Nominated
2009	People's Choice Awards	Favorite Leading Man	*The Dark Knight*	Nominated
2009	People's Choice Awards	Favorite Superhero	*The Dark Knight*	Won
2009	People's Choice Awards	Favorite On Screen Match Up (with Heath Ledger)	*The Dark Knight*	Won
2009	People's Choice Awards	Favorite Cast (with Heath Ledger, Gary Oldman, Michael Caine, Morgan Freeman, Aaron Eckhart, Maggie Gyllenhaal)	*The Dark Knight*	Won
2009	West Point Cadet Choice Awards	Best Exemplification of Leadership		Won

External links

- Christian Bale [1] at the Internet Movie Database
- Christian Bale [2] at Allmovie
- Christian Bale [3] at Yahoo! Movies
- Christian Bale [4] at TV.com
- Christian Bale [5] at the Open Directory Project

Article Sources and Contributors

Batman *Source*: http://en.wikipedia.org/?oldid=390579263 *Contributors*: JGossard

Bruce Wayne *Source*: http://en.wikipedia.org/?oldid=390592553 *Contributors*: -5-

Batman franchise media *Source*: http://en.wikipedia.org/?oldid=387017401 *Contributors*: J Greb

Batman in film *Source*: http://en.wikipedia.org/?oldid=390651185 *Contributors*: -5-

Batman (serial) *Source*: http://en.wikipedia.org/?oldid=389935114 *Contributors*: -5-

Lewis Wilson *Source*: http://en.wikipedia.org/?oldid=389920152 *Contributors*:

Batman and Robin (serial) *Source*: http://en.wikipedia.org/?oldid=389935197 *Contributors*: -5-

Robert Lowery (actor) *Source*: http://en.wikipedia.org/?oldid=388916407 *Contributors*:

Batman (1966 film) *Source*: http://en.wikipedia.org/?oldid=389935294 *Contributors*: -5-

Adam West *Source*: http://en.wikipedia.org/?oldid=390517689 *Contributors*:

Batman (1989 film) *Source*: http://en.wikipedia.org/?oldid=390664724 *Contributors*: Martarius

Batman Returns *Source*: http://en.wikipedia.org/?oldid=389927175 *Contributors*: -5-

Michael Keaton *Source*: http://en.wikipedia.org/?oldid=389454138 *Contributors*: Cresix

Batman Forever *Source*: http://en.wikipedia.org/?oldid=389646785 *Contributors*: -5-

Val Kilmer *Source*: http://en.wikipedia.org/?oldid=389192503 *Contributors*: Donmike10

Batman & Robin (film) *Source*: http://en.wikipedia.org/?oldid=389646046 *Contributors*: -5-

George Clooney *Source*: http://en.wikipedia.org/?oldid=388202720 *Contributors*: All Hallow's Wraith

Batman Begins *Source*: http://en.wikipedia.org/?oldid=390526899 *Contributors*: Allmightyduck

The Dark Knight (film) *Source*: http://en.wikipedia.org/?oldid=390429611 *Contributors*: FrankRizzo2006

Christian Bale *Source*: http://en.wikipedia.org/?oldid=390642247 *Contributors*: Jack Merridew

Image Sources, Licenses and Contributors

File:USD205998.png *Source*: http://bibliocm.bibliolabs.com/mwAnon/index.php?title=File:USD205998.png *License*: unknown *Contributors*: -

Image:Comic image missing.svg *Source*: http://bibliocm.bibliolabs.com/mwAnon/index.php?title=File:Comic_image_missing.svg *License*: unknown *Contributors*: -

Image:1960s Batmobile (FMC).jpg *Source*: http://bibliocm.bibliolabs.com/mwAnon/index.php?title=File:1960s_Batmobile_(FMC).jpg *License*: unknown *Contributors*: -

File:Adam West at WonderCon 2009 1.JPG *Source*: http://bibliocm.bibliolabs.com/mwAnon/index.php?title=File:Adam_West_at_WonderCon_2009_1.JPG *License*: unknown *Contributors*: -

File:Adam West 1989 crop 2.jpg *Source*: http://bibliocm.bibliolabs.com/mwAnon/index.php?title=File:Adam_West_1989_crop_2.jpg *License*: unknown *Contributors*: -

File:Michael-Keaton.jpg *Source*: http://bibliocm.bibliolabs.com/mwAnon/index.php?title=File:Michael-Keaton.jpg *License*: Creative Commons Attribution 2.0 *Contributors*: Alex Archambault

File:Val-Kilmer.jpg *Source*: http://bibliocm.bibliolabs.com/mwAnon/index.php?title=File:Val-Kilmer.jpg *License*: Creative Commons Attribution-Sharealike 2.0 *Contributors*: John Griffiths from London, United Kingdom

File:George Clooney Walk of Fame.JPG *Source*: http://bibliocm.bibliolabs.com/mwAnon/index.php?title=File:George_Clooney_Walk_of_Fame.JPG *License*: Creative Commons Attribution-Sharealike 3.0 *Contributors*: User:Superchilum

File:George Clooney-4 The Men Who Stare at Goats TIFF09.jpg *Source*: http://bibliocm.bibliolabs.com/mwAnon/index.php?title=File:George_Clooney-4_The_Men_Who_Stare_at_Goats_TIFF09.jpg *License*: Creative Commons Attribution 2.0 *Contributors*: Michael Vlasaty

Image:George Clooney with Samoura and Reck.JPG *Source*: http://bibliocm.bibliolabs.com/mwAnon/index.php?title=File:George_Clooney_with_Samoura_and_Reck.JPG *License*: Public Domain *Contributors*: User:Nando65

File:Batman Begins Batmobile1.jpg *Source*: http://bibliocm.bibliolabs.com/mwAnon/index.php?title=File:Batman_Begins_Batmobile1.jpg *License*: Creative Commons Attribution-Sharealike 3.0 *Contributors*: Alexander Horn, Dédélembrouille, Jarekt, Morio, TwoWings, 4 anonymous edits

File:Batman Begins Batmobile2.jpg *Source*: http://bibliocm.bibliolabs.com/mwAnon/index.php?title=File:Batman_Begins_Batmobile2.jpg *License*: unknown *Contributors*: -

File:The Dark Knight European Premier - Leicester square.jpg *Source*: http://bibliocm.bibliolabs.com/mwAnon/index.php?title=File:The_Dark_Knight_European_Premier_-_Leicester_square.jpg *License*: unknown *Contributors*: -

Image:Batpod.jpg *Source*: http://bibliocm.bibliolabs.com/mwAnon/index.php?title=File:Batpod.jpg *License*: unknown *Contributors*: -

Image:Jarno Trulli 2008 Britain.jpg *Source*: http://bibliocm.bibliolabs.com/mwAnon/index.php?title=File:Jarno_Trulli_2008_Britain.jpg *License*: unknown *Contributors*: -

File:The Dark Knight Tumbler at European Premiere.jpg *Source*: http://bibliocm.bibliolabs.com/mwAnon/index.php?title=File:The_Dark_Knight_Tumbler_at_European_Premiere.jpg *License*: unknown *Contributors*: -

File:The Dark Knight - PR - Barcelona.jpg *Source*: http://bibliocm.bibliolabs.com/mwAnon/index.php?title=File:The_Dark_Knight_-_PR_-_Barcelona.jpg *License*: Public Domain *Contributors*: user:Mutari

File:ChristianBaleJun09.jpg *Source*: http://bibliocm.bibliolabs.com/mwAnon/index.php?title=File:ChristianBaleJun09.jpg *License*: Creative Commons Attribution 2.0 *Contributors*: Asim Bharwani at http://www.flickr.com/photos/modenadude/

File:Ch Bale 02.jpg *Source*: http://bibliocm.bibliolabs.com/mwAnon/index.php?title=File:Ch_Bale_02.jpg *License*: GNU Free Documentation License *Contributors*: Towpilot

Image:Christian Bale - 002.jpg *Source*: http://bibliocm.bibliolabs.com/mwAnon/index.php?title=File:Christian_Bale_-_002.jpg *License*: Public Domain *Contributors*: User:Mutari

The cover image herein is used under a Creative Commons License and may be reused or reproduced under that same license.

http://images.cdn.fotopedia.com/flickr-564402795-hd.jpg